Love
DOES NOT KEEP SCORE:
LET LOVE ABIDE

MARIAN OLIVIA HEATH GRIFFIN

ISBN: 979-8-89419-256-7 (sc)
ISBN: 979-8-89419-257-4 (hc)
ISBN: 979-8-89419-258-1 (e)

THE EWINGS
PUBLISHING

One Galleria Blvd., Suite 1900, Metairie, LA 70001
(504) 702-6708

OTHER BOOKS BY
MARIAN OLIVIA HEATH GRIFFIN

A BLIND HEART AS I SEE IT

THE DAY I MET NANO

*A VOICE CALLS IN THE NIGHT, FIND MY PEOPLE,
SAVE MY PEOPLE*

*ACHIEVEMENTS AND ACCOMPLISHMENTS OF
AFRICAN AMERICANS, BEFORE AND AFTER
THE CIVIL RIGHTS MOVEMENT*

LOOK TO THE LIGHT, SISTERS

TALK TO MY HANDS

I KNOW ME

*MEETING AT THE FIRES: MYSTERIES AND MIRACLES
OF RELATIONSHIPS*

SUFFER THE INNOCENT CHILDREN

IN HIS OWN IMAGE, HOW I GOT OVER

STRAIGHTEN UP, AMERICA

NEVER SETTLE FOR LESS, ALWAYS THE BEST

IF BLACK IS A COLOR, WHAT IS MELANIN?

NEVER ALONE: LIVING IN THE REAL WORLD

MORE WATER FOR MY CONCRETE

THE CULTURE IN OUR NATION

WHEN THE OLD PREACHER SPEAKS, FOLK LISTEN

WHEN THE OLD PREACHER SPEAKS, PRISONERS LISTEN

PHOTOGRAPH BOOKS

THE FAMILY OF HATTIE WISE HEATH

THE FAMILY OF MARIAN HEATH GRIFFIN

FIFTIETH WEDDING ANNIVERSARY

CONTENTS

PART I: KNOW THYSELF

PART IV: NEW GENERATIONS

DEDICATION

THIS BOOK IS DEDICATED TO ALL OF HUMANITY
WHO HAS EVER LOVED ANOTHER PERSON
AND OUR CREATOR

FOREWORD

Historians or ordinary citizens are probably as qualified to write as an act of faith as others who have accepted this task as a career. Marian Heath Griffin wrote this book, LOVE DOES NOT KEEP SCORE, as well as her first well written book, CULTURAL GUMBO: OUR ROOTS, OUR STORIES; she subsequently wrote thirty other books after she retired from working at a Historically Black College and University as a Psychological Counselor and Administrator for thirty-six years. She had a remarkable career.

I joyfully celebrate the completion and publication of her many books as they are genealogical and historical masterpieces and templates. Her books contain a wealth of information about life, past and present. She writes so graphically and compellingly that she brings history back to life. She pulls no punches and tells it like it is. She straightforwardly speaks of the good and the beautiful, the bad and ugly of human conditions in general and situations in her family in particular. In this she does a stupendous, masterful job.

Marian is incredibly multitalented and has a special way with words. Verbalization is among her many comfort zones. Her writings are a beacon for the new revolutionary age and a treasure for the new generations.

She is a gifted, committed Christian, wife, sister, mother, grandmother, musician, social worker, missionary in Africa and China, organizer, researcher and storyteller.

We were classmates together in seminary along with her husband, Chaplain Bertrand Griffin, who is an Ordained Minister; we attended Gammon Theological Seminary of the Interdenominational Theological Center in Atlanta, Georgia.

After her husband and I graduated from seminary in Atlanta, Georgia and returned to Louisiana to be ordained and receive employment at a church, Marian enrolled in the New Orleans Baptist Theological Seminary in New Orleans, Louisiana as the first and only Black person in 1964 and 1965 as she desired to complete her seminary degree. She did this with doubts and fears, yet perseverance and dedication. In the moments her doubts faded, she persisted with faith; she completed her degree and received her diploma. There were many miraculous signs in Marian Griffin's life and God prevailed and kept His promise.

Dr. Leslie Peter Norris, Ordained Minister, College Chaplain, District Superintendent of the United Methodist Church, Author, Missionary (LAVIM).

PREFACE

The love of God is unconditional love; it has no bounds. Love is a powerful and meaningful word. It is a noun, involving every creature in the universe. It is a verb, called to action. Every one and everything needs and wants love from its creator, no less humans. We can feel most at home in God's presence and know that Jesus is our constant companion. He shoulders our burdens, celebrates our joys and constantly reminds us of His unconditional love. We can feel His presence and know that He is our hope and refuge; our source of courage and love.

David Cooks, in his book, JOURNEY THROUGH ROMANS said, "The world needs to hear how people can be in the right with God through love, and we need to see how righteousness is loved out in practice. God's perfect plan is bringing us to himself through his son Jesus Christ. ROMANS shows us that there is a world of difference between trying to do what religion requires of us to satisfy God's righteous requirements and trusting in what He has done to bridge the gap between Himself and us." (Forward, para.)

Let us love you more than ourself and be the living embodiment of your will in all things. Let us do our best to move out of darkness and serve all who need help as we reach out with God's unconditional love.

PRAYER OF ST. FRANCIS Of ASSISI

Lord, make me an instrument of your peace.
Where there is hatred, let me sow love;
Where there is injury, pardon;
Where there is doubt, faith;
Where there is despair, hope;
Where there is darkness, light;
Where there is sadness, joy.

Grant that I may seek, not to be consoled;
But to console;
Not to be understood, but to understand;
Not to be loved, but to love.
For it is in giving that we receive;
It is in pardoning that we are pardoned;
And it is in dying, that we are born to eternal life.

In Christ name,

AMEN

PROLOGUE

Paul wrote a letter around AD 57, towards the end of his third missionary journey. Perhaps he was in Corinth at the time. As an overview, this letter written by Paul has been called the greatest theological document ever written. In it, Paul outlines what Christians believe and explains God's perfect plan in bringing us back to Him. It explains how a person can be in the right standing with God, how man can live a God-honoring righteous life. (para).

Let us do the best we can with our abundant blessings, to reach out with God's unconditional love to serve all who need help. God protects us against the forces of evil. On one occasion while Paul was asleep, the Lord spoke to him in a vision: "Do not be afraid, keep on speaking, do not be silent. For I am with you, and no one is going to attack you, because I have many people in this city (Corinth)."

You can read from Philippians 4: 12-13, "I have learned the secret of being content in any and every situation, whether well fed or hungry, whether living in plenty or in want. I can do all this through Him who gives me strength." (NIV).

A NEWLY APPOINTED DISCIPLE

At the beginning of the book of ACTS, Luke states in his second volume of his history of Christianity, telling how Jesus pours out the Holy Spirit on the apostles. The Spirit inspires them to spread the message of salvation from Jerusalem to Rome. In his message Luke stresses how unity and love prevail in the church and the world and how God protects his missionaries from their enemies. When we read this chapter, we must think about how powerful the Holy Spirit is in our lives, in other's lives and in the church. (ACTS 1: 1-3, para, NIV).

Therefore, after Jesus' death, it was necessary to choose one of the men who had been with them the whole time to replace Judas that the Lord Jesus recognized that went in and out among them.

So, they proposed two men: Joseph called Barsabbas (also known as Justus) and Mattias.

They prayed, "Lord, you know everyone's heart. Show us one of these two you have chosen to take over this apostolic ministry, which Judas left to go where he belongs."

Then they cast lots, and the lot fell to Mattias, so he was added to the eleven apostles. (ACTS 1: 21-26, NIV).

God is always with you regardless of where you are and what your circumstances are. Moreover, love involves the creation of everything; it involves forgiveness and grace. Only God is our judge. We have no right to judge others. Therefore, the love of God does not keep score.

After his suffering, Jesus showed himself to these men and gave many convincing proofs that he was alive. Then he gave instructions through the Holy Spirit to the apostles he had chosen. He appeared to them over a period of forty days and spoke about the kingdom of God. He said to them, "It is not for you to know the times or dates the Father has set by His own authority. But you will receive power when the Holy Spirit comes on you and you will be my witnesses in Jerusalem and all of Judea and Samaria, and to the ends of the earth." (ACTS 1: 3-6, para, NIV).

C. S. Lewis, in his several well written books, speaks of love:

God created Needs-love and Wants-love. There are several types of love: God's love and mercy (benevolence) for humankind, mankind's devotion toward or adoration for God. Further, EROS is an enamored, deep, tender, affection for another person and AGAPE – is brotherly love toward another person - PHILLI.

"Affection, we have seen, includes both Need-Love and Gift-Love. Affection will arise and grow strong without demanding any shining qualities in its object. If it is given us, it will not necessarily be given us on our own merits: we may get it (love) with very little trouble. From a dim perception of the truth, many are loved with affection far beyond their deserts. Mr. Pontifex draws the ludicrous conclusion, "Therefore, I, without desert, have a right to it." (Lewis, THE FOUR LOVES, p. 64).

We may not have people hungry for a plate of rice or for a piece of bread in New York City, but there is a tremendous hunger and a tremendous feeling of unwantedness everywhere. And that is really a very great poverty. It is easy to think of the poverty far away and forget about it quickly. But there is a terrible loneliness and feeling of not being loved right here. It is found in families and everywhere. (Source: Mother Teresa, para).

GOD IS LOVE

"For God so loved the world that He gave his one and only son, that who ever believed in him shall not perish but have eternal life. God did not send his son into the world to condemn the world, but to save the world through him." (JOHN 3: 16, NIV).

God works in mysterious ways that we cannot understand. He can calm oceans and waters with the wave of his hand. Early in our Christian journey, we pray with high expectations, and assume that God will give us the deepest desires of our heart. Through prayer we intend to experience the closeness, joy and happiness we long for. With our confidence in God, we believe that we will rise above any problem.

Those who come nearest to a Gift-love for God will the next moment, be beating their breasts with the publican and laying their indigence before the only real Giver. And God will have it so. He addresses our Need-love: "Come unto me all ye that travail and are heavy-laden."

"Thus, one Need-love, the greatest of all, either coincides with or at least makes a main ingredient in man's highest, healthiest, and most realistic spiritual condition. Man approaches God most nearly when he is in one sense least like God. For what can be more unlike Him than fullness and need, sovereignty and humility, righteousness and penitence, limitless power and a cry for help?" (Lewis, p 14).

Since God is blessed, omnipotent, sovereign and creative, there is obviously a sense in which happiness, strength, freedom and fertility, whether of mind or body, wherever they appear in human life constitutes likenesses and in that way proximities to God. (Lewis, p. 14-16, para).

Rightly understood, we do not just have emotions expressed to God. Jesus' willingness to share in our deepest thoughts and moments of struggles secures our right relationship with God but enables us to trust Him, to lean on him for strength and support because He is able!

There is death and destruction all over the news and we ask, "Where is God?"

"This is the whole of Christianity," said Lewis as he stated in another one of his books, MERE CHRISTIANITY. "There is nothing else. It is so easy to get muddled about that. It is easy to think the church has a lot of different objects – education, buildings, missions, holding services."

It is just as easy to think the State has a lot of different objects – military, political, economic and what not. The state exists simply to promote and protect the ordinary happiness of human beings. Unless they are helping to increase and prolong and protect such times, all the laws, parliaments, armies, courts, police, economics are simply a waste of time.

In the same way, the church exists for nothing but to draw men unto Christ, to make them the little "Christs." If they are not doing that, all the cathedrals, clergy, missions, sermons, and even the Bible itself are simply a waste of time. God became man for no other purpose. (p.199, para).

As we search for clues, we are amazed by the evils that mankind can do.

In the Scriptures, "When Joshua was near Jericho, he looked up and saw a man standing in front of him with a drawn sword in his hand. Joshua approached him and asked, "Are you for us or for our enemies?"

"Neither," he replied. "I have now come as the Lord's army." (JOSHUA 5: 13-14, HBCS).

Gwen Ford Faulkenberry denotes that Joshua's meeting with this man, we understand, was Jesus. Joshua's first question when he met Him was, "Whose side are you on?" And, essentially, Jesus answered him, "I am on my side." (MORNING WITH JESUS, NOV-DEC, 2019, p. 13).

There is great freedom in this, because it takes the focus off ourselves and turns it to Jesus. He is on the side of love every time. It makes sense if you think about it. God is love!

Is it more important to be right or to love?

"When you search for me, you will find me; if you seek me with all your heart, I will let you find me," says the Lord. (JEREMIAH 29: 13-14, NRSV).

We often forget there are miracles, too. We must reflect on how much we take for granted.

Now then, let the power of my Lord be displayed in its greatness; the Lord is slow to anger, abounding in love and forgiving sin and rebellion. (NUMBERS 14: 17-18, NIV).

"But how can they call on Him to save them unless they believe in Him?"

"And how can they believe in Him if they have never heard about Him?"

"And how can they hear about Him unless someone tells them?" (ROMANS 10: 14, NLT).

Someone once said his faith would be much stronger if he had lived during the time Jesus walked the earth and he had seen him in the flesh. The Scripture informs us that many people's lives were transformed after seeing Jesus face-to-face.

According to the Scriptures, Jesus is and always will be our Savior. He is the reason our lives can be transformed from hopelessness to joy and love. He can show us courage, determination and faith.

Paul who wrote the epistle of ROMANS and was an apostle, called himself a servant of Jesus Christ.

Paul, a servant of Jesus Christ, called to be an apostle, separated unto the gospel of God, (which he had promised afore by his prophets in the Holy Scriptures) concerning his Son Jesus Christ our Lord, which was made of the seed of David according to the flesh.

There was a short man who was a tax collector; he climbed a sycamore tree just to get a glimpse of Jesus. His name was Zacchaeus. Jesus called his name and Zacchaeus was a changed man.

Thomas, one of the disciples, saw the resurrected Christ and became a changed person. He was awestruck with the knowledge that Jesus was his Lord and Savior.

Moreover, most of the people who were acquainted with Jesus while He was on earth did not understand him because he was just another human being to them. Even the religious leaders – the Pharisees failed to see who Jesus was because they were looking at him from a human perspective. Jesus stood in front of them many times, trying to help them understand who he was.

Let us acknowledge the Lord; let us press on to acknowledge him. As surely as the sun rises, he will appear; he will come to us like the Winter rains, like the Spring rains that water the earth. (HOSEA 6:3, NIV).

Hosea prophesies during the last days of Israel (2 Kings 14: 23; and 17: 41), focusing on her sin of spiritual adultery (actually, idolatry). He warns them that God will punish them unless they change their ways. But Hosea also reminds them of God's incredible love, pleading with them to repent. Reading this book, you must think of God's love in sending His son Jesus to die for us in spite of our sins. Repent of your unfaithfulness to the Lord and turn to Him.

With the Bible, we have an advantage because we have the Old Testament and the New Testament.

President Lyndon Baines Johnson said, "We hope the world will not narrow into a neighborhood until it has broadened into a brotherhood."

From suffering and sorrow, new heroes are born. Sometimes we just have to keep swimming with the current, trying not to drown. There is luck and there are exceptions. The boundaries of one's world are four walls and a few blocks.

Those who grow up in the right household with the right role models, find access to resources and beat the odds. They develop the engine to get out and find the tracks to lead the way. Others do not have such help to navigate their future with what is available to them. (St. Germain, pp. 22-23, para).

Our faith can be tested as we are tattered and torn. There are divine interventions that shape who we are when God's guardian angels keep watch from afar.

"America is our country. Here is freedom. This is the land of opportunity – the PROMISED LAND," says President Barack Obama, 44th president of the United States of America.

"The dreams of our ancestors are the dreams of everyone here. Some say this is the land of milk and honey."

Mary Pipher, in THE MIDDLE OF EVERYWHERE, said, "America is where the streets are lined with compact discs and SUVS. We have free schools and free people. EVERYBODY has a dream in America." (p. xxv). "Many of us," she said, "had no contact with people who were different from us." (para).

Therefore, she knew nothing of them, had never seen a black person or a Latino. She had never heard of Jewish people.

"America keeps taking people in. By 2050, whites of European origin will no longer be the majority race in our country. We are becoming a richer curry of people. Before 1990, most people (Refugees) settled in the six big states: California, New York, Texas, Florida, Illinois and New Jersey. But during the 1990's, refugees moved into the Midwest and elsewhere. Most of us are humble people and came from farms where grandparents barely survived the Great Depression." (p.10).

No wonder there is so much hatred in our land. We are becoming a much more diverse nation who do not always understand each other. God is nowhere in the picture.

However, "God still rules the world with His Omnipotent hand. He works in mysterious ways that we do not understand." (Source: Clay Harrison, SALESIAN INSPIRATIONAL BOOKS, para).

AUTHOR'S NOTES

I know many stories told to me by my mother and grandmothers; these are just a few of them.

My mother, Lettie Harper Heath, told me that around the time of the Great Depression before and during the early 1930's, she was in college. She attended two colleges during that time – Cheyney State College and Delaware State College. Times were tight but her family was willfully ready to see her finish her schooling at Cheyney State College in Pennsylvania in the field of music and then attend Delaware State College in the field of elementary education.

Back home, in Delaware, Mother's grandparents, Amanda and John Henry Fountain, parents, Sadie Fountain Harper and Herbert Harper, Uncle Sylvester Fountain and young brother, Clarence Harper were squeezing money tight and held close to see my mother through college; there was not always enough food for the rest of the family in their small town of Middleford, Delaware. Others in this rural town were suffering too. When it comes to battling crisis and suffering, sometimes we may be the one in need of care as well as our neighbors.

It appears that my grandmother was most concerned about my mother's future as she was a diabetic at birth. She wanted Mother to get a good education so she could take care of herself and survive all the ills that would face her. They were living in a small rural town and schooling was frowned upon for Black children. My grandmother was fearful of the impoverished school; afraid that it would hinder her children in their future endeavors.

Myles Munroe, in his book, OVERCOMING CRISIS said, "Where do you go when the ones you go to for help are in need of help themselves?"

Each one of us will face some type of crisis. We all have situations over which we have no personal control, or could not prevent or did not expect. Living on earth requires that we must expect the unexpected and prepare for the unforeseen. Many of us do not possess the emotional, mental, psychological and spiritual tools necessary to successfully and effectively weather these seasons of turmoil and crisis.

We are all vulnerable and fragile in this world. There is fear of the unknown. Completely beyond our control, many forces threaten human welfare. Somewhere there are answers to every question. There is a way to overcome every catastrophe.

During the time of the Depression, it was a mutual blessing to help someone as well as be helped.

Jesus taught very clearly that giving to the needy must not be done for praise. When you give to the needy, he said, "give in secret and your father will reward you." (MATTHEW 6: 1-4, para, NIV).

GOD HAS NEVER FAILED HIS PEOPLE YET.

Someone said, "Do what you can for others, not what you cannot. In this context, neighbors were battling chronic illnesses, aging and hunger.

Mother's family was saying a little prayer for other family members and friends as well as the only teenager who was going to boarding school and college (my mother, Lettie). Only later did my mother realize that her life had added a new dimension to her family's life and her understanding increased and gave rise to her ability to strengthen and form better relationships and make life more meaningful.

Life's meaning, its virtue had much to do with the depth of the relationships we form.

"Their spirits were willing but the flesh was sometimes weak." (MATTHEW 26: 41, NIV).

"Watch and pray so that you will not fall into temptation."

Make sure that you are walking according to His principles as a citizen of His Kingdom; it will help you hold up a measuring rod to your current situation. Then you can turn to your neighbor in their time of need.

Paul Kalanithi denotes in his book, WHEN BREATH BECOMES AIR, "There must be a way that the language of life as experienced – passion, hunger, love – would bear a relationship, however convoluted to the language of digestive tracts and heartbeats. It was the relational aspect of humans, i.e. "human relationality" that undergirded meaning, yet existed in the brains and bodies, and are prone to breaking and failing. (p. 39, para).

Jesus said, "In this world you will have trouble. But take heart! I have overcome the world. (JOHN 16: 33, NIV.)

Sadie and Herbert Harper, had planted a garden to feed themselves and help and encourage someone else, but there was not always a variety of food, meat or bread for their family or others.

My mother finished college, secured a job playing the piano for several venues, got married and had several children. When my parents moved to their own home, my parents and grandparents exchanged visiting in each others' homes regularly, which was very pleasant for my siblings and me.

My grandfather, Herbert did much of the cooking in the Fountain household as my grandmother was often, as a Mid-wife, delivering babies. Grandpop use to say to us when we were small children visiting him, "I used what I had."

He made citrus bread with watermelon rind, flour, lard and sugar. We did not like it at all, but we ate it because we were hungry.

My grandparents realized that they could never have the option of not loving their children, grandchildren, neighbors, or stop giving to the community. They would not even tell their loved ones or friends any of their negative feelings. They thought it would be a lack of faith to challenge God.

God understands our feelings. He has made a way for us to come with confidence to his throne of grace. Sadie and Herbert were so proud of their daughter Lettie; she gave them hope and opportunities to foresee a better life. Moreover, from the beginning of time, there were always times "already tough for young adults looking for ways to start living independent lives after high school and college." (Source: B. Janet Hibbs and Rostain, YOU'RE NOT DONE YET: PARENTING YOUNG ADULTS IN AN AGE OF UNCERTAINTY, p.1, para).

My mother, like so many other young adults, had more growing up to do after college and even after marriage and having children. She, like her parents, prayed a lot and asked God to hold them in His right hand.

Oswald Chambers said, "The point of prayer is not to get answers from God; the goal of prayer is perfect and complete oneness with God." (Chambers, PRAYING WITH CONFIDENCE, p. 16, para).

Many of us have accepted society's idea that struggle and love do not go together. We assume that a good relationship is good only as long as there is peace and harmony. The fact remains that we struggle in relationships because we really do care. Finding the courage to struggle and take risks is what strengthens and deepens our relationships with God and each other.

> *"Like Jacob at Bethel, we do well to wrestle with God once in a while. It can bring us the blessings we need." (GENESES 32: 24-32, para, NIV).*

GOD BLESS YOU IS MY PRAYER!

INTRODUCTION –
HISTORICAL PERSPECTIVE

C. S. Lewis said, "Need-love cries to God from our poverty; Gift – love longs to serve, or even to suffer for God.

Appreciative - love says "We give thanks to thee for thy great glory." Appreciative - love gazes and holds its breath and is silent, rejoices that such a wonder should exist even if not for him. Perhaps none exists except Need-love, and in this life, nothing except our neediness is permanent." (p. 33, para).

Every problem with our children and their children or disagreement with others provides an opportunity to call on God to strengthen our faith and their faith, to develop perseverance, to build our character and their character and to ground our hope deeper in Christ. Because we all have access to God, we become Christians with enormous consequences. Our relationships change; once we were given privileges and we looked at life differently. Our resources are inexhaustible; and we look at life with hope. We are joyful even when we are facing hard things and hard times that enter our lives. We are invited into God's presence.

THE OPEN VIEW OF GOD

According to Gregory A. Boyd, in GOD OF THE POSSIBLE, there is a statement generally called the "open view" of God. Boyd discovered a new appreciation and excitement regarding one's own responsibility in bringing about the future. We must find confidence in what God wants for us. When we come to Him in prayer, we need to be honest with ourselves about whether our desires are His desires, whether our will is His will, and whether our requests are in sync with His requests.

The passion and urgency with which one prayed increased immensely. He no longer struggled with the problem of evil the way he used to. He came to believe that the future is open – ended and that God knows it as such.

Boyd realizes that a Bible-Believing-Christian could come to believe, on the authority of God's Word, that the future is not exhaustively settled. He wants to explain the philosophical basis and defense of this "open view" and point out how this view could have positive ramifications in a person's life. (para).

I was reading in DISCOVERY SERIES, a pamphlet by Dennis Moles, IS THE BIBLE RELIABLE?

JESUS ENDORSED THE BIBLE

Moles states, "Jesus made it clear that he believed the Old Testament was more than just national history or religious fable." (MATTHEW 4: 1-11, 5: 1-19, para, NIV).

He believed that the Scriptures were about him; they told the story of God's love and promise of a coming Messiah. (JOHN 5:39-40, para, NIV).

Those who accept that the Bible is grounded not merely in the opinion of its readers, and accept that the Bible is true and trustworthy, often find these features of Scripture to be compelling proofs for the veracity of those Scriptures. "Internal evidences" often reassure the faith of the believer.

It will open your mind to an intriguing way of thinking about God and the future.

Boyd ruminates, "Moreover, if God is eternally certain that various individuals will end up being eternally damned, why does He go ahead and create them?"

"If hell is worse than never being born," as Jesus suggest, (MATTHEW 26: 24,NIV), wouldn't an all-loving God refrain from creating people he is certain will end up there?"

"If God truly does not want "any to perish" (2 PETER 3: 9, NIV), why does He create people he is certain will do just that?"

Why does the Bible say that God frequently alters His plans, cancels prophecies in the light of "maybe" or a possibility? Why does it describe God as expressing uncertainty about the future, being disappointed in the way things turn out and even occasionally regretting the outcome of His own decisions?

"Far from being beneath God, Scripture describes the openness of God to the future as one of His attributes of greatness. God who knows all possibilities, experiences novelty and is willing to engage in an appropriate element of risk, is more exalted than God who faces an eternally settled future. The "open view of the future" does not hold the future as wide open; or most of it as settled ahead of time, either by God's predestining will or by existing earthly causes, but the future is not exhaustively settled ahead of time." (Para). This is why God or LOVE does not keep score.

"To whatever degree the future is yet open to be decided by free agents, it is unsettled. To this extent, God knows it as a realm of possibilities, not certainties. The issue is not whether God's knowledge is perfect, because it is. The issue is the nature of the reality that God perfectly knows. More specifically, what is the content of the reality of the future? Whatever it is, we all agree that God perfectly knows it." (Boyd, p. 15-17, para).

"For God, reality is eternally definite, settled, fixed and certain. Since God knows reality perfectly, it followed for classical theology that reality must be eternally and exhaustively settled. Moreover, humans experience the future as possibly one way or the other only because we are imperfect." (p. 18, papa).

JOY IN OUR LIVES

We rejoice in the hope of the glory of God. Not only so, but we also pray in our suffering, because we know that suffering produces perseverance; perseverance, character, and character, hope. And hope does not disappoint us, because God has poured out his love into our hearts by the Holy Spirit whom He has given us. (ROMANS 5: 3-5, NIV).

God is taking the stuff of our lives and making something good out of it. He keeps pouring His love into our hearts; He not only makes us feel loved but He is so generous in his supply that we have an overflow of love for other people. He transforms our thinking, gives us the Holy Spirit and makes His love real to us. (para).

Blessed are they whose transgressions are forgiven, whose sins are covered. Blessed is the man whose sin the Lord will never count against him. (ROMANS 4: 7-8, NIV).

No one is good enough for God. "You cannot pile up Brownie points and hope they make you acceptable in His sight. The only people who think they can make it on their own (like Donald J. Trump) are people who have "cut" God down to their size. The problem is that God is who He is and He is perfect holiness. That is the bad news and the good news. How can people like you and me be made right with God? Where do we get the righteousness we need? The good news is that God's kind of righteousness has been made available to us as a free - gift; it is for anyone who has faith in Jesus Christ, which means you do not get the gift unless you accept it. God cannot pretend that sin does not exist. He cannot look at us and make excuses for us. He had to do something about sin to break its power over us.

So, He sent Jesus and we have been rescued -redeemed -by him. Christ died as a price, a sacrifice to pay sin's penalty and to those who believe and receive his offer, He does a wonderful thing; He justifies us. (ROMANS 3: 21-24, para, NIV.)

Suffice it to say, if we need to be justified, that means something is wrong. We do not match the standard. In justifying us, he does something even greater. He gives us the righteousness of Jesus. What does Jesus give us? His righteousness!

He does not change his standards to include us. He changes us to fit his standard. Do we deserve it? No! It is God's grace that brings about this change in our lives. How should a person respond to such a gift? Receive it thankfully. (para.)

President Jimmy Carter who is ninety-nine years old, once said, "Whether the boundaries that divide us are picket fences or national borders, we are all neighbors in a global community. Together we can improve and save millions of lives."

After leaving the White House, former United States President Jimmy Carter and former First Lady Rosalynn Carter searched for ways to use their unique position to help those less fortunate around the world. Two main issues were of paramount importance: preventing human suffering and advancing peace in the world. These concerns are equally urgently important today. They share with others a deep concern for the current conditions of this world and its future. President Carter has the understanding that resolving conflict and hatred are the first steps toward improving any society's ills. It is equally important to seek new human rights laws and teach our citizens how to keep their government accountable and rise out of poverty.

JESUS' ISSUES

Jesus' final prayer to the Father for his people was "that they may be one, as we are one." (JOHN 17: 22, NIV).

He said, "Sanctify them by the truth; Your Word is truth."

Believers are called to exhibit a loving unity among each other that reflects nothing less than the eternal, perfect love of the Trinity. When our hearts and minds are focused properly, our dialogue becomes the means by which we lovingly help each other appreciate aspects of God's Word, thus, we might otherwise overlook or fail to understand. For lovers of truth, all issues are important, especially the nature of the future. This does not mean that we should pretend that our differences do not exist. It means that we must face our differences and discuss them openly in love.

> *Resist the devil and he will flee from you. Draw nigh to God, and He will draw nigh to you. (JAMES 4: 7-8, NIV).*

> *Instead, as we speak the truth in love, we will in all things grow up into him who is the Head, that is Christ. From him, the whole body, joined and held together by every supporting ligament, grows and builds itself up in love, as each part does its work. (EPHESIANS 4: 15-16, NIV).*

REMEMBER WE CAME TO BELONG TO HIM.

PART I

KNOW THYSELF

CHAPTER I

ABUNDENT GRACE

J esus' obedience was not for himself but for us. "We were obliged to obey but could not. He was not obliged to obey but by his free will, did. God gave him this honor; that he should obey for the whole church, the whole world."

Christ was the Son and though he was a son, yet he learned obedience by the things which He suffered. (HEBREW 5: 8, NIV).

"The glory of His obedience becomes more wonderful when we realize who he is and who thus obeyed God. He was none other than the Son of God made man. God was in heaven, above all, Lord of all, lived in the world, having no earthly glory or reputation, obliged to obey the whole world perfectly.(John Owen, and Elizabeth Kea, ed, AMAZED BY GRACE, p. 60).

Dale Evans Rogers (Roy Roger's wife) wrote this statement:

"God is a good God. The indescribable joy He has let me experience is the Spirit that transcends any trials He has let me experience. The fact that He has permitted me to see each one of my children and Roy come to Christ means that He has been far more than fair to me. The

tears he has allowed to dim the eyes of my flesh have cleared the eyes of my soul; bringing each time a new dept of spiritual understanding and vision to me. I trust Him."

Chris Tomlin wrote the lyrics:

You are a good Father – it is who you are.
And I am loved by You, it is who I am.

There was a young man named Gregory who first heard about Jesus and his love for us In his twenties. He walked into a down-town church one day and sat down. He started attending this church where he met someone who helped him grow in Christ. Gregory's mentor, seeing the great need in him, assigned Gregory to teach a small Sunday school class of pre-teen boys, thus helping him to learn and grow in his faith. He was helped to get a full scholarship to attend college in that city. Upon completing his college degree, he began an at-risk organization in the city and through the years, Gregory became a minister – all for the honor of God.

According to the Scriptures, Timothy was a child when his mother Eunice and grandmother Lois taught him how to pray and learn about Jesus. He was taught to be faithful and joyful.

Just before he died, Paul wrote in his second letter to Timothy:

"I am reminded that sincere faith lives in you, which first lived in your parents." (para).

"For this reason, I remind you to fan into flame the gift of God, which is in you, also through the laying on of my hands. For God did not give us a spirit of timidity, but a spirit of power, of love and of self-discipline.

And we know that in all things, God works for the good of those who love Him, who have been called according to his purpose." (ROMANS 8: 28, NIV).

HOW OUR NEEDS ARE MET

Many stories are told about the chicken and the egg. The basic argument is which came first, the chicken or the egg?

One day my grandmother Sadie Fountain Harper noticed that a chicken wandered into their back yard and laid an egg. The family's chickens had long since been eaten by the family. This was at the height of her family's poverty and the Depression was full blown. Therefore, when the hen began coming into their yard every morning to lay an egg, this upped their spirits.

Afterward the chicken would leave their yard, only to return the next morning to lay another egg. Grandmom would save one or two of the eggs to help the neighbors out or to make cornbread or delightful sweet treats as well as mix the eggs with vegetables for breakfast, lunch and supper.

As a praying family, they looked to the life of Jesus to learn how to live right and help others.

The family got by, the neighbors were helped and my mother, Lettie Harper, graduated from the Harper Boarding School in North Carolina, and received her Bachelor of Art's degree in music from Cheyney State College in Cheyney, Pennsylvania and Bachelor of Science's degree in education from Delaware State college (University) in Dover, Delaware. She was in school attending a boarding school in high school and two colleges studying classical music in Cheyney State and elementary education at Delaware State. This was around the mid-1920's. She graduated in 1930 and the Great Depression was winding down in our country. Her family had lived through it with hope and blessings from God.

Her uncle, Sylvester Fountain, who had been raised by his older sister, Sadie, and was only about eight years older than Lettie, gave Lettie a gold bracelet for a graduation gift. He had been working and saving his money for such an occasion as this. The love of God was sacred in this family. Love abided and never kept score.

Years later, when I was at Delaware State University, my senior year, my mother gave me her bracelet in November, 1960 for a Thanksgiving gift, and as a keepsake for her. The next time I saw my mother was in

December that year. She was in a hospital bed in a coma. She never woke up but rather died on January 30, 1961. I graduated in May, 1961 and went to Atlanta, Georgia to attend the School of Social Work there. I wore my mother's gold bracelet every day.

Most of us possess the ability to achieve, develop, accomplish, produce, create and perform anything our minds can conceive. God created us with all the potential we need to fulfill our purpose in this life.

Are we using our gifts to serve others? It is so easy to enter the trap of wanting to please ourselves and wanting praise from others instead of focusing on the God who truly matters.

Let us be determined to take advantage of the limited knowledge we have and expand upon it. There are so many questions to be answered about life and we must be a leverage for the present time.

We must make a personal effort to build understanding and acceptance, forging from natural pursuits and interests. We must search our hearts and align our thoughts and actions with His will and gifts to us.

Christopher Robin pronounced in WINNIE THE POOH, "Promise me you'll always remember -you're braver than you believe, and stronger than you seem, and smarter than you think."

Benjamin Watson said in his book, UNDER OUR SKIN: GETTING FREE FROM THE FEARS AND FRUSTATIONS THAT DIVIDE US, "I pray that we will move away from the fear and frustration that divide us."

God granted us an increase in our needs and strengthened our faith in Him. When He sent Jesus Christ to us to do a ministry and to teach the people, we did not know who Jesus was and did not understand him or his mission. We only had a human perspective of Jesus and would not know his divine side until later. We saw only unexpected and challenging changes come about in the world. We saw a man with wisdom and compassion despite our fears of living. Our faith grew in spite of our fears. It is the same today. We make mistakes which is a part of living. We are reminded that mistakes pave the way to our success and accomplishments. We are slowly learning how to pray and accept His grace despite our fears and resistance.

STRONGHOLD OF FAITH

God is an essential part of our lives. In Matthew 5, Jesus called believers the light of the world. "You are the light of the world; just like him."

Jesus said, "We are a city on the hilltop that cannot be hidden. No one lights a lamp and then puts it under a basket. Instead, he places a lamp on a stand where it gives light to everyone in the house. (MATTHEW 5: 14-15, NLT).

Now we know more about Jesus and can defy the odds with mental toughness. The light of Jesus shining through us lets people know just how much God cares for all of us. I am reminded that "the Lord tends his flock like a shepherd. He gathers the lambs in His arms and carries them close to His heart. He gently leads those that have young." (ISAIAH 40: 11, NIV).

Paul said, "We do not have any room for misunderstanding. We must understand the challenges others face."

The Lord promises His people through the prophet Isaiah that He is our Shepherd, guiding us in our daily lives and giving us comfort; He is tending to us through our anxieties and carrying us in His everlasting arms.

Is it more important for us to be right or to love? There is great freedom in love. There is great freedom in not counting the cost or not keeping score of how much love we give. Does it not make sense to be on the side of love.

GOD IS LOVE!

CHAPTER 2

THE CHICKEN OR THE EGG?

What is first; the chicken or the egg? There have been great arguments about what comes first. Classical theologians, such as Augustine and Calvin, maintain "that the future will be a certain way because God foreknows it this way.

Others follow the great Arminius and argue that the future simply will be that way. Does God's foreknowledge determine the future, or does the future determine God's foreknowledge? Arminius denotes that the cause of God's eternal foreknowledge is a mystery and we cannot avoid the dreadful conclusion that God is ultimately responsible for everything that transpires in history, including evil.

Augustine and Calvin maintain that since God alone exists eternally, the eternal settled-ness of the future can only come from Him.

The strongest statements in all of Scripture regarding the foreknowledge of God come from Isaiah. The Lord repeatedly demonstrates that He is Lord of history and very distinct from the idols many Jews attempted to follow.

In Isaiah 40: 9-10, the Lord declares:

I am God and there is no other;
I am God, and there is no one like me,
declaring the end from the beginning;
and from ancient times, things not yet done.

More emphatically, God said:

"The former things I declared long ago,
They went out from my mouth and I made them known,
Then suddenly I did them and they came to pass.
Because I know that you are obstinate,
And your neck is an iron sinew and your forehead brass,
I declared them to you from long ago.
Before they came to pass, I announced them to you,
So that you would not say, "My idol did them;
my carved image and my cast image commanded them."

(ISAIAH 48: 3-5, NIV).

Gregory Boyd, in his book, GOD OF THE POSSIBLE, said, "Examples of God predicting future events throughout Scripture are interpreted as confirmations of the classical view of God's foreknowledge. God is so confident in his sovereignty; he does not need to micromanage everything. He could if He wanted to, but this would demean His sovereignty. So, he chooses to leave some of the future open to possibilities, allowing them to be the decisions of free agents. It takes a greater God to steer a world populated with free agents than it does to steer a world of preprogrammed automatons." (para).

There are so many incidents of what comes first and what comes last. My grandparents always practiced putting things into perspective as they attempted optimistic and positive thinking. They attempted to control their feelings and consciousness in the face of great sadness and trauma. They did not want to wallow in the dirt and have one great long "pity party."

This story about the chicken and the egg, told by my mother, serves to feed the soul as well as the body. The daily egg (nucleus) not only served to meet the physical needs of my mother's family, but served as a symbol of God's love and caring for them.

My mother was right when she told this story to us. There was not as much anxiety in our family after the chicken found them and serviced them; as they trusted in God and displaced their feelings of poverty and other unknown events of the future during the Great Depression era. As they ate their daily bread, they were reminded of God's loving provisions. They were given the wisdom to know that God did not keep score but instead provided for their needs every day and greatly guided them in His way of life for them.

SURROUNDED BY LOVE

They chose to let the struggles of life make them better, not bitter. One of the most important skills in life is knowing the difference between what one wants and what one needs. It is also important to know how to pick persons who will help us make adjustments and good choices.

Suffice it to say, my ancestors were given strength and courage to face another day and be of service to others. Therefore, the chicken gave service to this family and the whole community. When they were at their lowest, that is when lovability, a complex attribute came around the corner and surrounded them.

Love has a certain energy, verbal expression, empathy, and good character that helps others feel good. Even more important than being loved is being able to love. Love gives our lives purpose and meaning. Therefore, caring for others is what motivates humans to get out of bed every morning.

Paul said, "For God is my witness, whom I serve with my spirit in the gospel of His Son." (v. 9).

FOR THE BELIEVER, THERE ARE STILL QUESTIONS:

He gives strength to the weary and increases the power of the weak. (ISAIAH 40: 28-31, NIV).
There are still so many more questions to be answered:

Who is our God?

To whom will you compare me? (ISAIAH 40: 25, NIV).

Or who is my equal? says the Holy One.

Who has measured the water in His hand, or with the breath of His hand marked off the heaven?

Who has held the dust of the earth in a basket, or weighted the mountain on the scales and the hills in a balance?

Who did the Lord consult to enlighten Him and who taught Him the right way?

Who was it that taught Him knowledge?

Who taught Him the path of understanding? (ISAIAH 40: 12-14, NIV).

Who has understood the mind of the Lord, or instructed Him as our Counselor?

WHERE IS OUR FOCUS?

Where is our focus?
Life for God's people is not a steady paced -stroll in the park or through time. We do not just have a beginning, a middle or ending. Life is filled with change. Life is Holy and every moment is precious. We change schools, careers, relationships, homes and images as often and as casually as our grand parents changed horses.

Maya Angelou, a great poet and author said, "All great moments take time." (para).

Instead of feeling upset and anxious, God's people fixed their mind on Jesus instead of their problems. Despite disasters and upsetting news, they remained calm and kept their eyes on God and His love for them. They kept body and soul together knowing that God was walking and talking with them.

They kept their lives together through prayer and positive thinking. Those were God-given days.

In praying for strength, Pamela Hirson said, "Lord, strengthen us with your word so we can bring patience and loving care to those who need us."

Through the years, my mother felt the love of her family as they suffered hardships. She learned that relationships of caring and supporting others are so much of what life is all about.

In the face of deaths of her grandparents, and during the Great Depression years, as they struggled to send her to college, Mother knew that her father, Herbert and two uncles, Robert and Burton – all Harpers, had attended Bible College in the late 1890's, and felt it was only befitting that their children and grandchildren also get a good education and learn of God's love and purpose.

Cultivating love and relationships with family and communities are essential for our personal as well as community resilience.

In a threatened world, in the kaleidoscopic whirl of our lives, it is reassuring to remember that God is unchanging. God is unconditional Love.

He said, "I the Lord do not change." (MALACHI 3: 6, para, NIV).

Paul wrote in exaggerated language to emphasize his point, "If my readers have all knowledge, if they give away every single thing they owned, and even if they willingly suffer hardships, without the essential foundation of love, their actions will amount to nothing." (I CORINTHIANS 13: 1-3, para, NIV).

Paul therefore, encouraged his followers to always infuse their actions with love, movingly describing the beauty of a love that always protects, trusts, hopes, and perseveres.

One of the most thrilling and fulfilling experiences can be to share Jesus Christ beyond the baby in the manger with others. The most important issue to live by is to know what our Creator has for us. Love is what motivates us to move forward every day and accomplish success in our endeavors.

When we use our spiritual gifts to teach, encourage, or serve in our faith communities, we must remember that God's design always calls for love. Otherwise, it is like a table or chair missing a leg. It cannot achieve the true purpose for which it is designed.

Humans must experience love, not be hostile towards the Gospel or there will be a missing link or ingredient. We must learn to love like God and learn not to keep score but always practice an act of forgiveness.

THE GREAT COMMISSION

According to the Book of Matthew, we have a mission to carry out and there are plenty of souls ripe for the harvest. God has many beautiful children, and He wants them all to know how much He loves them. So, He is counting on us to fulfill the Great Commission.

After breathing life into His most precious and important creation, humans, God placed them into His garden and gave them the responsibility to work and take care of it. (GENESIS 2:15, NIV).

It is much more difficult now to carry out God's commission, especially after Adam and Eve were expelled from the garden for not carrying out God's plan.

To this day, God Himself cares for His people and His planet, (PSALM 65:9 -13, NIV).

He asks us to do the same. (PROVERBS 12: 10, NIV).

Then Jesus came to them and said, "Therefore, go and make disciples of all nations, baptizing them in the name of the Father and of the Son and of the Holy Spirit and teaching them to obey everything I have commanded you. And surely, I am with you always, to the very end of the age." (MATTHEW 28: 19-20, NIV).

THE DAUGHTER WITH ONE DOLLAR

Kathryn Hillen told a story about a little five-year-old girl "who spent all that she had, one dollar, for a gift of an inexpensive dish for her Mother's Day present," just as Jesus came to the dime store of earth and chose to sacrifice his all for us.

"As God the Father watched his son sacrifice himself, his love for his son must have deepened. How does God feel about those he purchased through death on the cross? Does God love us even more because of what his son did for us? After all, that is what gives us worth."

But love does not keep score. The power of Jesus is always at work in us, energizing and enlightening us from day-to-day.

I pray that the eyes of your heart may be enlightened in order that you may know the hope to which He has called you. (EPHESIANS 1:18, NIV).

Even as a small child, we can experience and feel love.

Bell Hooks expressed in her book, ALL ABOUT LOVE, "When I was a child it was clear to me that life was not worth living if we did not know love. I wish I could testify that I came to this awareness because of the love I felt in my life. But it was love's absence that let me know how much love mattered. I was my father's first daughter. At the moment of my birth, I was looked upon with loving kindness, cherished and made to feel wanted on this earth and in my home." (p. ix-x).

Hooks does not remember the day she had the feeling that love had left her. She just knew that one day she was no longer precious. Persons who initially loved her turned away from her. The absence of their regard and recognition pierced her heart and left her devastated and brokenhearted. An individual, even a baby, can feel abandonment and hurt. Not feeling love is like mourning for something that is lost.

We can find the love we lost long ago, when we were little, but not until we let go of the grief of the moment love left us when we had no voice to speak the heart's longing.

When an individual awakens from the trance he or she is in, it is stunning to find the world we live in as a loveless future which was the order of the day. When we love, we can let our hearts speak.

Hooks states, "I am afraid that we may be raising a generation of young people who will grow up afraid to love, afraid to give themselves completely to another person. They will have seen how much it hurts to take the risk of loving and have it not work out for them." (p. xviii, para).

GOD-LOVE

Earlier, I discussed C. S. Lewis' concept describing two types of love as Gift-love and Need -love. A Gift-love, as a typical example would be the love which moves a man to work and plan and save for the future well-being of his family; whereas the second type, the Need-love would send a lonely or frightened child to its mother's arms.

Sometimes this is exactly what the journey of life feels like. We can identify with the Israelites' tough life in the wilderness.

Because we have been given the capacity to love and enjoy life with another person or with others, we can be happier, heathier, more self-sufficient and secure in life. We liken to our Creator who loved all his creation and in turn wanted love returned.

We are born helpless. As soon as we are fully conscious, we discover loneliness. We need others physically, emotionally, spiritually and intellectually.

It appears that man can only bring to man nothing at all but sheer Need-love. None of us are getting better at loving. It seems we are getting more frightened of it. It appears that we do not accept the given skills of love to begin with, and the choices we make tend to only emphasize how much it hurts to take the risk of loving and have it not be sufficient or enough.

Young people are cynical about love; so, they are afraid that they will grow up looking for intimacy without risk, for pleasure without significant emotional investment. They will be so fearful of the pain of disappointment that they will forgo the possibilities of love and joy. This reinforces the thought that it is hopeless and useless.

Elizabeth Wurtzel, as a spokesperson for this disillusioned generation states, "Young people feel that love is for the naïve, the weak, the hopelessly romantic. Their attitude is mirrored in the grown-ups they turn to for explanations."

"Every human love, at its height, has a tendency to claim for itself a divine authority. Its vice tends to sound as if it were the will of God Himself. It tells us not to count the cost, it demands of us a total commitment, it attempts to over-ride all other claims and insinuates that any action which is sincerely done "for love's sake" is thereby lawful and even meritorious."

Make no mistake, our God-loves are really God-like which are most boundless and unwearied in giving.

"Truly the poets observe that joy, energy, patience, and readiness to forgive, a desire for the good of the beloved is a real and adorable image of the Divine life. In its presence we are right to thank God who has given such power to man." (Source: Lewis, p. 20, para).

Suffice it to say, we may give our human love the unconditional allegiance, which we owe only to God.

OUR NEED-LOVE

Our Need-love may be greedy and exacting. Plato saw Need-Love as "the son of poverty." It is the accurate reflection in consciousness of our actual nature. As we are born weak and incapable of doing anything, yet we still crave to be loved. Therefore, our lives are more complicated than we know. We are not near enough by likeness of God to be gods. We must listen neither to "the over-wise or the over-foolish giant." (p.20, para).

The highest does not stand without the lowest. A plant must have roots below as well as sunlight above and roots must be grubby. Much of the grubbiness is clean dirt if only you leave it in the garden. The human love can be glorious images of divine love; no less and no more- just proximities of likeness which in some instances may help.

Every human being would agree that a man's spiritual health is exactly proportional to his love for God. But it is more apparent in our growing awareness that our whole being by its very nature is one vast need: incomplete, preparatory, empty, yet cluttered, crying out for Him who can untie things that are now knotted together and tie up things that are still dangling loose. Man approaches God most nearly when he is in a sense least like God. (Source: Lewis, p. 12, para).

What can be more unlike than fullness and need, sovereignly and humility, righteousness and penitence, limitless power and a cry out for help?

"Here is what one great saint and great thinker, St. Augustine describes as the desolation in which the death of his friend, Nebridius plunged him."

"This is what comes," he says, "of giving one's heart to anything but God. All human beings pass away. Do not let your happiness depend on something you may lose. To love at all is to be vulnerable."

"If love is to be a blessing, not a misery, it must be for the only Beloved who will never pass away." (CONFESSIONS IV, 10).

ALL THAT IS MADE

God carried in His hand a little object like a nut, and that nut was "all that is made."

God needs nothing! But He loves into existence holly superfluous creatures in order that He may love and perfect them.

"He creates the universe and is a "host" to the "buzzing cloud of flies about the cross, the flayed back pressed against the uneven stake, the repeated incipient suffocation as the body droops, the nails driven through the mesial nerves, the repeated torture of back and arms as it is time after time, hitched up for breath's sake." (Lewis, p. 176).

Our Creator addresses our Need-love: "Come unto me all ye that travail and are leavy laden."

He creates in us both Gift-loves and Need-loves. The Gift-loves are natural images of Himself. This is the diagram of Love Himself, the inventor of Love itself. Therefore, love does not keep score.

Need-loves have no resemblance to the Love which God is. They rather are correlatives, opposites, as the form of the blancmange is an opposite to the form of the mold.

God, however bestows two other gifts, a supernatural Need-love of Himself and a supernatural Need-love of one another. Our Creator pours our need of himself into a need of Him. First this supernatural Need-love of Himself is bestowed by grace. Grace, moreover, does not create the need. It is already there by the mere fact of our being fallen creatures.

What grace gives is the full recognition, the sensible awareness, the complete acceptance of need. Without grace, our wishes and our necessities are in conflict. A good person is sorry for the sins which have increased his needs. Our Creator transforms our Need-love for one another which requires equal transformation.

We all need charity at times, which means love the unlovable. But this is not the sort of love we want. We want to be loved for our cleverness, beauty, generosity, fairness and usefulness.

We are all receiving charity. There is something in all of us that cannot be naturally loved.

Thus God, committed to the human heart, transforms not only Gift-love but Need-love to one another.

As C.S. Lewis continues to write: another book, MERE CHRISTIANITY, he states: "We have cause to be uneasy." (p. 28).

"We all want progress. But progress means getting nearer to the place where we want to be."

"If we have taken the wrong turn, then to go forward does not get you any nearer. If you are on the wrong road, progress means doing an about-turn and walking back to the right road; and in that case the man who turns back soonest is the most progressive man. The sooner we admit this and go back to start again, the faster we shall get on. There is nothing progressive about being pig-headed and refusing to admit a mistake." If you look at the present state of the world, it is pretty plain that humanity has been making some big mistakes. We are on the wrong road. And if that is so, we must go back. Going back is the quickest way on."

LOVE AND UNDERSTANDING

A story is told by Rebecca Manley Pippert about a young college student who attended one of the colleges in Portland, Oregon. A young freshman student wandered into a well-dressed middle-class church which stood near the college campus. He slowly walked down the center aisle. He was dressed like any regular college student, blue jeans, tee shirt and of course, no shoes. People looked a bit uncomfortable, but no one said anything.

So, the young man was looking for a seat but the church was quite crowded that Sunday. He got to the front pew and there were no seats. He squatted on the carpet-perfectly acceptable behavior for a college fellow, but perhaps unnerving for a church.

Suddenly an elderly well-dressed, well-respected man started walking down the aisle toward the young man. The whole church held its breath. Was the elderly man going to scold the youngster? You could not blame the man for what he was about to do. The church became utterly silent, all eyes were focused on the elderly man; when he reached the man-child seated on the floor, with some difficultly, he sat down next to him on the carpet. He and the student worshiped together on the floor that day.

Perhaps the only persons who failed to see how great the giving had been that Sunday were the two seating on the floor. But grace is always that way. It gives without the receiver realizing how great the gift really is. This was the essence of brotherly love received from Christ's love. Love does not keep score.

"When I came to you, Brother, I did not come with eloquence or superior wisdom as I proclaimed to you the testimony about God. For I resolve to know nothing while I was with you except Jesus Christ. I came to you in weakness and fear, and with much trembling. My message was not with wise and persuasive words, but with a demonstration of the

Spirit's power, so that your faith might not rest on men's wisdom, but on God's power." (1 CORINTHIANS 2: 1-5, NIV).

A GREAT NEED

"Care to go for a walk?" he asked in his quiet voice. His granddaughter's mind went to all the forty things she had to do that day: do the laundry, scrub the kitchen floor, make a batch of cookies for the PTA luncheon tomorrow and open the mail from several days ago. She was way behind on everything.

But then she realized how important and great it was for Papa to come up with something he wanted to do instead of always napping. He needed the exercise and so did she. Besides this was her ailing grandfather, who had been diagnosed with Alzheimer, asking her to spent time with him. Were the things she had to do more important? How many more times would she have to walk and talk with her grandfather?

An elderly lady that I worked with on the university campus told me that her grandmother planted several types of beans in her tiny yard. She had eleven children and her husband had died several years ago.

Instead of wondering what to do next, she hopped to and immediately planted her beans. She made certain that each child went to school when it was time for him or her to go. She had no education herself but had "good old horse sense." She wanted all her children to be self-sufficient and be able to take care of themselves.

Every morning after all the older children were sent off to school and the small ones settled down foe the morning, she picked a large pail of beans and put them on her wood stove to cook until all the children were gathered home for the evening. She fed them each a bowl of hot beans every day. No one complained; they ate until they were satisfied and went to bed.

If the universe is not governed by an absolute goodness, then all our efforts are hopeless.

"We cannot do with it and we cannot do without it. God is the only comfort; He also is the supreme terror: the thing we most need and the thing we most hide from. He is our only ally and we have made ourselves His enemies. Goodness is either the great safety or the great danger – according to the way we act to it."

THE LOVE OF ANIMALS

Even lower animals – dogs and cats, birds and sea animals – want and need unconditional love and will return it. We have attached emotional feelings of love, as for a pet or treasured object.

A single lonely bird hovered over a submerged world. Below her were the results of the catastrophic flood. There was nothing to be seen but water. The world below her was desolate and seemingly without a future. Nowhere could she find a place to hold on to, to set down her tiny feet. She found no rest. (GENESIS 8: 8, para, NIV).

Yet the dove that fluttered around aimlessly and purposelessly was less lonely than she appeared to be.

Noah, whose name means "He who will bring rest", had not forgotten the dove. He waited for her. When the bird returned, she found an outstretched hand, ready to take her into the safety of the ark. Together they were on their way to a new future. The submerged earth would be habitable again, (para). (GENESIS 8: 9-12, NIV).

When we have a special pet in our home, we experience a warm feeling in our hearts that teaches us so many things: learning to show kindness to others, being strong in difficult and harsh times in our lives, learning to forgive others for mistakes, seeing others through our Creator's eyes, seeking God's grace, learning to find peace even when we have problems, conquering our grief and helping us to laugh again and have joy in our hearts.

Even the most hard-hearted person may find humor and beauty with an animal in their midst. A loving dog or cat may be awe-inspiring and bring joy to the spirit and help you grow closer to another human being or God. They are gifts from God.

We can celebrate the bonds of heavenly love between a pet and his owner, as well as a human to another human. Oftentimes you can touch an animal with love when it is not possible with a human being. They can show you how to make friends by just being themselves. They can give encouragement even to the disappointed one. They are comforting and inspiring in their very presence and devotion.

They can teach us to be patient, kind and forgiving. God has built into all of us in varying degrees the capacity for an appreciation of beauty. He has even allowed us the privilege of participating in the creation of beautiful things and beautiful places. This is one way God brings healing to our brokenness, and a way we can contribute toward bringing wholeness to our fallen world. THAT IS THE WAY!

Praise the Lord, O my soul, and forget not all of his benefits; who forgives all your sins and heals all your diseases, who redeems your life from the pit and crowns you with love and compassion, who satisfies your desires with good things so that your youth is renewed like the eagle. (PSALM 103: 2-5, NIV).

OUR PRAYER

O Great God and Father of us all,
Shine in Thy glory upon us all in safety.
Shine in Thy glory upon us all in peace.
Shine in Thy glory upon us all in wisdom.
Keep our minds clear in Thy light.
Keep our hearts young in Thy warmth.
Keep our feet straight in Thy path.
For we are Thy children,
Great God and Father of us all.

(Source: Ann Nolan Clark, SECRET OF THE ANDES, p.11).

CHAPTER 3

KNOWING SELF AT AN EARLY AGE

When I was seven years old, my grandmother, Sadie Fountain Harper, quietly told me that her mother, Amanda Collins Fountain had to practically raise her seven children by herself in Middleford, Delaware because her husband, John Henry Fountain lived in a Camp for the Blind in Philadelphia, Pennsylvania. He was born a slave to Mary Elizabeth Fountain and Charles Smith around 1856.

John Henry was loaned as a child to a family with a small farm in Trinity, Delaware and worked for this White family. By the age of six, he developed cataracts: opacity of the lens or capsule of the eyes, causing partial or total blindness. Then he had an accident in his eye when he ran into a low hanging branch on a tree.

The White family in Trinity had no more use for a blind slave-boy, so they sent him back to his mother, Mary Elizabeth.

Mary Elizabeth, along with her whole family, was freed by her father and grandfather, William Fountain and William Charles Fountain, who lived in Maryland. The Fountain family had purchased property in Virginia, Maryland and Delaware.

Mary Elizabeth's family was given acres of land by her father and ancestors and her family was allowed to build a colonial home on it in Middleford, Delaware. It was about six acres of farm land and a large wooded area in a little place called Middleford. It was near Seaford, Delaware. This plot of land was then called the Fountain Homestead.

THE FOUNTAIN HOMESTEAD

By the time John Henry was seventeen, he had met and fallen in love with Amanda. No one knew Amanda's full name or who her parents were. She had the complexion of a White man and a slave woman-very fair - complexion. After Amanda died, her Delaware State Death Certificate revealed that her mothers name was Martha Collins. Her father's name was unknown. It was obvious that her father was white, judging from Amanda's pale coloring and extremely long straight hair.

John Henry and Amanda were married under the trees and helped build the two-story colonial -style home on the property. They moved into the Fountain Homestead. They began having children immediately. By the time the couple had four children, John Henry was totally blind and was unable to move about in the house or in the yard by himself.

Someone informed the family about the Camp for The Blind in Philadelphia, Pennsylvania. The family took John Henry to this camp where he remained for years, only visiting his family occasionally.

TRACING OUR FAMILY ROOTS

Amanda Collins Fountain had the family farm left to her by her husband's mother, Mary Elizabeth Fountain and his great-grandfather, Nicholas De La Fountaine. Mary Elizabeth was supported by her White father and ancestors: grandfather, William Fountain, Sr. and William Charles Fountain, Jr. who were descendants of Nicholas De La Fountaine; he was born in 1691 in Normandy, France married to Mary and died in Maryland, USA).

Nicholas De La Fountaine, and his all -white family moved from Normandy, France on their own ships and purchased land, farm animals and slaves in Virginia, Maryland and Delaware. (Source: Ancestry.com).

It is noted that there was a great-grandson named William Fountain and another great-grandson named William Charles Fountain. We are continuing research on the Nicholas De La Fountaine family, (later named Fountain in America) through Ancestry. Com. There were hundreds of slaves brought to the colonies by the Nicholas De La Fountaine Family and others purchased after the De La Fountaine family arrived here in America.)

The Fountain Homestead was to be a haven for family, runaway slaves and neighbors. The White Fountains had respect for their slave family members and freed all of them.

THE FOUNTAINS AND THE UNDERGROUND RAILROAD

The Underground Railroad is one of those historical mysteries and secrets. It involved slavery and the saving of slaves. It was very dangerous several centuries ago to talk about the Atlantic Slave Trade or to know where the stations were when the Underground Railroad Movement was not to be discussed openly by slaves or their masters.

The Fountain Homestead was built for the express purpose of helping all mankind. Yes, it was a hide-a-way for run-away slaves and freed slaves who were not safe from their masters.

It was kept such a secret that even today, our folks do not know how involved our ancestors were and how serious it was to know about the Underground Railroad. Even until today, my grandmother and mother tried to explain how important it was to know the details of the Slavery Movement, but not to tell it to others.

Oral history was the only means for this discourse to be revealed. The Nicholas De La Fountaine family was taught to respect women and children and try to keep them safe. They had experienced hatred and suffering in their own home country, France, and knew what it was to be persecuted against for religious and political reasons. They had many dangerous experiences in the seventeenth, eighteenth and nineteenth centuries.

What a blessing it was for our people. Our ancestors could not tell their stories, but now we can. I have chronicled my own life with some of the stories and life experiences in the 1960's, told to me by my two grandmothers in the late forties. They brought me to understand the role that slavery, race, class and gender played in the lives of African Americans and in contemporary society. In my life time, I have had experiences that were challenging, abusive, conditional, destructive and disrespectful. I have looked back many times and wondered: HOW I GET OVER?

To every thing there is a season, and a time to every purpose under the heaven. (ECCLESIASTES 3:1, KJV.)

On the other hand, the answer is, I had relationships that were compassionate, caring, and trusting. I had humane, sympathetic and God-given persons in my life.

God was in the plan. He put such families as the Fountains, both Black and White, in the midst of a dichotomy that was owning slaves and saving slaves. If Captains William and William Charles Fountain had not owned slaves, they could not have picked up slaves on their ships and taken them to the Underground Railroad stations. The run-away slaves would not have trusted White people such as the De La Fountains who were needed to tell Blacks it was ok to be secure on the Fountaine ships and in their hide-a-way barns and attics. They had opportunities to live better lives.

Conversely, White slave owners who were seeking to find their own run-a-way slaves (who were possibly assisted by Harriet Tubman and ship owners such as the Fountain family) could not distinguish or differentiate between their own slaves from the Fountains' freed-slaves or other slave owners' run-away slaves.

As I was telling my grandchildren, dichotomy means the division of two contradictory parts, opinions, or situations.

We found a Last Will and Testament (handwritten) by Nicholas De La Fountaine in the attic of the Fountain Homestead, leaving his property in Middleford, Delaware to Amenda Collins Fountain, the wife of John Henry Fountain. By this time, John Henry was living in a Camp for the Blind and was brought home occasionally to see his wife and seven children -Charles Wesley Fountain, Sadie Mae Fountain-Harper, Lettie Fountain-Banks, Clarence Fountain, Martin Fountain (called Marty), Louis Fountain, and Sylvester Fountain (the youngest child raised by his oldest sister, Sadie Mae Fountain-Harper after their mother, Amanda died.

Amanda Collins Fountain, according to her death certificate, revealed that she was born on March 12, 1861 to Martha Collins. Her father's name and birth place were unknown. Amanda died on November 26, 1920 in Middleford, Delaware. Her cause of death was listed as toxemia and collapse of the uterus. "That means a baby apparently died with her, which was not recorded," I told my children and grandchildren.

The Death Certificate had two different spellings of Amanda's last name-Founting and Fountain. It was signed on November 28, 1920 by M.C. Watson, State of Delaware Bureau of Vital Statistics.

The Last Will and Testament was found on Ancestry.com. This land in the Will was a small portion owned by the Fountain family as Nicholas De La Fountaine bought large tracts of property in Virginia, Maryland and Delaware, as well as many slaves, ships, boats and livestock when they arrived from Normandy, France. These two documents – Ancestry.com and Amanda Collins Fountain's Death Certificate are evidence of the legacy left by the Fountain family. In this family, love does not keep score. God was in the midst of all of them.

The White Fountains and the Black Fountains, (who were set free by their White grandparents),were a part of the Underground Railroad. Fight for what was right filtered down from Captain William and William Charles, who were a part of the Nicholas De La Fountaine family.

The care-givers in my family often expressed defeat and heartache at not being able to do enough or give enough for their family members.

This is what I learned from my grandmother Sadie when I was only seven years old. I am so glad she told me at that time because she became ill and died on January 15, 1949 when I was nine-years-old. With a new perspective, I learned to help celebrate family at the end of each day no matter how small the accomplishment. I wrote ideas and issues on little pieces of paper and later called them my journal. Oftentimes I remembered or recalled them silently as I fell asleep.

Other documentations of this family were the 1900 and 1910 United States Federal Census Record Report. The documents described above – The United States Federal Census Reports, Death Certificate of Amanda Collins Fountain, the Marriage Certificate of Sadie Mae Fountain Harper and Herbert Sidney Harper, and the Last Will and testament of Nicholas Fountain proves that some records were kept of and by Black families. However, some names were misspelled due to the slaves not being able to spell their names.

These documents were found in the attic of the Fountain Homestead, the old colonial home in Middleford, Delaware.

Nia Olivia Griffin, our oldest granddaughter was listening intently to my discourse. She said, "There were many mistakes made a long time ago. They were costly then and they will be costly today."

"That is right, Nia," I said.

"It was difficult to trace our heritage and find out who we really were born to, how many children were born and lived and others lost in childbirth, also when and where they were born. It has just been in the last century that Blacks have been able to keep better records and yet there is still a lot of confusion with black families' documents.

During our ancestry time and even during our time, babies were born at home. We had mid-wives come to the house to wait on the birth. Many of the Mid-wives were unable to read or write; therefore the birth place and names were not recorded. Now, most babies are born in hospitals and records are listed.

Only recently have there been breakthroughs with Ancestry.com, The United States Federal Census Records Report, Family Source, State Archives, marriage, birth and death certificates are used to trace our family roots.

The Fountains/Harpers were considered as middle - class Negroes. African Americans of pale skin or mulattoes had an advantage according to all that was taught in that day. It was believed that persons with white blood gave these persons the intelligence, refining qualities and opportunities for a good education almost equal to the "superior" race.

Annette Provine Woodard, in her book, INTEGRATING DELAWARE, states that "White relatives helped their black kin, especially if they were lighter skinned. Lighter skinned African Americans were perceived as being "Better than other blacks."

Because of my great-grandmother and grandmother's fair complexion skin coloring – partly Caucasian complexion, this fact improved the family's economic and educational opportunities and rendered them in the nineteenth and twentieth centuries as being called black aristocrats, mulatto elite, black bourgeoisie, or even middle -class.

"Prejudice is a powerful force and allowances were made for light skin people and opportunities were given to African Americans who were not so dark looking as long as they knew their place and avoided confrontation with any White person." (Woodard, p. 15).

My siblings and I were taught many things by our grandparents and parents. Remember, John Henry Fountain (Our great-grandfather) was a freed slave, and his father, Charles Smith was a slave until he was allowed to marry Mary Elizabeth Fountain. Mary Elizabeth's father, William Fountain, III, freed his whole Black Fountain family and gave them land to build and live on and livestock (horses, pigs, cattle, chickens and goats) to raise. The land was not far from William Fountain's homestead in Seaford, Delaware.

We as children were taught to protect our land, never sell it. Never abuse it. It was God-given. Our ancestors gave the land to us as a gift from God. We should protect it.

We were also taught by our grandfather, Herbert Harper, never to disgrace the family name. The Fountain Homestead was built to be a beautiful, loving place for those who entered those walls, entered the land.

Our oldest son, and his family, visited the Fountain Homestead with us. Our grandchildren, Nia and Kiara were very impressionable at that early age. They roamed the fields and woods for the few days they were there.

My sister and her husband, Nancy and Albert Kellem, along with cousins still live on the Fountain Homestead property.

I told my grandchildren, "We were always taught that you cannot help others until you can help yourself. You must first have something to give before you can give it."

We were taught that we were stronger than we knew, even though we sometimes felt weak. We have gone through agony, struggles, and heartache, and we did not know our power until the time came to use it. Our strength lay dormant within us until it emerged just when we thought we could not go on. Just when we needed it, we found that we had much more power and strength than we ever thought possible.

We were taught to be good listeners even when we could not comprehend what our elders were saying to us. We did not understand the ins and outs of the system or various services offered to us. But we were polite and said "Yes Ma'am or "No sir" to our parents and all elderly people. We did understand that somethings said to us were "good-for-us."

We must always know in our heart that our strength is coming our way to the surface.

Children need to think that you care before they care what you think. (Wes Moore, THE OTHER WES MOORE: ONE NAME, TWO FATES, p. 66, para.)

One of the real keys to victory is to cast out wrong thoughts, and replace them with right ones.

For the rest, brethren, whatever is true, whatever is worthy of reverence and is honorable and seemly, whatever is just, whatever is pure, whatever is lovely and lovable, whatever is kind and winsome and gracious, if there is any virtue and excellence, if there is anything worthy of praise, think on and weigh and take account of these things. Think or fix your mind on them. (PHILIPPIANS 4:8, para, NIV).

Anyone could come into the Fountain Homestead yard and get a drink of water from the outside pump or pick grapes from the vines and tomatoes and corn from the fields to eat.

One great lesson our mother taught us was "You are no better and no worse than anyone else."

"Try to treat all of God's children right."

A little later, I learned that everyone is a child of God and we should strive to help everyone. However, do not allow others to abuse you and take away your self-esteem. Times were hard back then and times are hard now. Times will always be difficult in this world, both morally and spiritually. We must be encouraged and encourage each other to persevere in their Christian faith and life; be sure to find your daily strength in Jesus Christ and his inspired word.

Mother told us stories from the Bible. I remember the story about Joseph who was sold into slavery to Egyptians by his own older brothers. Joseph was put into prison and God showed him how to help others when they were in need of food and water. He could not have helped others had he not had the God-given talent of interpreting dreams and rising from his own station in life to help others less fortunate. Regardless of his harsh circumstances, Joseph looked at the alternatives and was thankful for his life in Christ. Instead of complaining and asking negative questions, he as a young person trusted God and did not remain bitter with his older brothers. Yet in the end, he had to secure a place for his elderly father and offer help to his brothers.

God does not provide what we "rightfully" deserve. Many times, we are not thankful and become rebellious and complain after all we have been given. When we compare our conclusions with God's Word, the Scripture, we discover how wrong we are!

God's Word instructs us that He is sovereignly in control; He provides for and works out all the circumstances in our lives.

MORE THAN CONQUERORS

And we know that in all things God works for the good of those who love Him, who have been called according to His purpose. For those God foreknew, He also predestined to be conformed to the likeness of His son, that he might be the firstborn among many brothers. And those He predestined, He also called; those He called, He also justified; those He justified, He also glorified.

What, then, shall we say in response to this? If God is for us, who can be against us? He who did not spare his own, but gave him up for us all. (ROMANS 8: 28 – 32, NIV).

Do not be anxious about anything, by prayer and petition, with thanksgiving present your requests to God. And the peace of God which transcends all understanding, will guard your hearts and your minds in Christ Jesus. (PHILIPPIANS 4: 6-7, NIV).

Evelyn Christenson said, "When we leave our daily closet praying, do we walk out and slam the door, saying:

"That's it for today. Same time tomorrow, Lord. Same station!"

That is not what the Holy Spirit meant when He inspired Paul to write, "Pray without ceasing." (1 THESSALONIANS 5: 1-7, NIV).

Nor is it what Christ meant when He taught his disciples, "You ought to always pray, and not faint." (LUKE 18:1, NIV).

God is intimately involved with us. He works out the purposes through the events in our lives.

This is the same God who formed the world in six days and knows every hair on our heads. He is the same God who chose a people for Himself before we were born; and sent his Son to die on the cross to redeem us.

After Paul lists the armor with which we are to resist Satan, he goes on to say, "Pray always with all prayer and supplication in the Spirit." (EPHESIANS 6: 18, NIV).

The source of strength in our battle with the enemy is "Praying always". But when the line of communication closes:

WHAM! The fiery darts of Satan strike!

But that need not be the case. Let us break down the day and see how the communication system between God and us can be open twenty-four/seven.

Christianity does not make sense until we have faced the real facts of life. Christianity tells us to repent and promises us forgiveness.

"God Himself becomes a man to save man from the disapproval of God. (Lewis, MERE CHRISTIANITY, p.32).

Our God's love for his people is not determined by the circumstances in our lives. His love is steadfast and we must give him thanks and praise for His love toward us.

God gives us a chance to see what He needs us to see in His time. One day when I was reading PSALM 5, I saw a new thing that had never hit me before:

Give ear to my words, O Lord, consider my meditation. Hearken unto the voice of my cry, my King, and my God, for unto Thee I will pray. My voice shalt Thou hear in the morning. O Lord, in the morning will I direct my prayer unto Thee, and will look up. (PSALM 5: 1-3, para. NIV).

The time of the morning is not necessary; just say, "Good Morning, Lord" and give yourself up to Him. God's word speaks to us early in the morning, "before the tyranny of the urgent," before breakfast, before the school buses run, before anyone says a word to you.

PRAISE THE LORD!

CHAPTER 4

AMANDA, MY GREAT GRANDMOTHER'S LIFE

A s I continued to explain to my grandchildren, the two older ones, Nia and Kiara, as well as the younger ones, Christian-Paris, Michael, II, Amelia-Grai, Victoria, Olivia and Sophia, I gave them the benefit of my grandmother, Sadie's oral history:

She told me, "Every morning was difficult for Amanda, my mother, who was a single mom due to circumstances of her husband's unfortunate malady. She was grieving as if her husband was dead. John Henry was blind and lived in the Camp for the Blind in Philadelphia, Pennsylvania. He was able to come home periodically – annually."

As she arose from her bed each morning, when everything is quiet, Amanda's worries surfaced. She thought about her husband so far away from her, her financial concerns and her children's welfare and schooling. As her husband left for the Camp for the Blind as a young man, she did not know which way to turn.

She lived a brutal life as a slave woman but regarded her life and her journey with a sense of honesty, compassion and vivacious wit and humor.

As she prayed on her knees, she heard these words:

"Do not fear, nor be dismayed, for the Lord your God is with you wherever you go." (JOSHUA 1: 9, NIV).

By this time, as she continued to have children, she now had the responsibility of raising her seven children on her own. They were: Charles Wesley Fountain, Sadie Mae Fountain, Lettie Fountain, Clarence Fountain, Martin Fountain, Louis Fountain and Sylvester Fountain.

Sylvester Fountain, the youngest child, was the only one left with the parents, according to the 1910 United States Federal Census Report. Sylvester died earlier then the other children due to a drowning accident. This left Amanda, my great-grandmother grieving for her baby.

I told my grandchildren these things as we gathered in Delaware for a family reunion with our relatives and stayed with my sister, Nancy and her husband, Albert Kellam, who now lives on the Fountain Homestead which Amanda helped to build.

"Great grandmother, Amanda Collins Fountain and her family were an up-standing Christian family and attended church at the Methodist Church near their home. African Americans of pale skin or mulattoes with mixed blood had an advantage according to all that was taught in that day. It was believed that Blacks with White blood gave these persons the intelligence, understanding and refining qualities of the "White race."

Amanda owned her home and a large piece of property, over six acres with fields and a wooded area. She planted a garden and tended to it early each morning. She planted large fields of corn and soybeans with the help of her sons and men in the community. This was the source of the family income and livelihood. She was constantly on the go, tending her household chores early and working for White families and delivering babies as a Mid-wife. This verse often came to her:

"Be still and know that I am God." (PSALM 46: 10, NIV).

She knew that God was a busy God. He never stopped. But He cautions us to cease running here and there, stop and be still because God is always with us and He never stops.

He still flexes His omnipotent muscles and works to create calm in our chaotic daily lives.

Amanda had a skill of being a Mid-Wife. God gave her this talent and skill. She had to leave her own children when she was called to deliver babies. This was a special gift which required patience, compassion and love. It was difficult but she managed on her own. This unfailing gift was for when her heart was troubled or when she was experiencing fear and trembling. God, himself gave her peace to help others.

God gave her strength to work in her garden and help plow the fields during planting time. She delivered hundreds of babies around in the communities of Seaford and Middleford, Delaware and other towns in Sussex County. She had to walk for miles to reach her destinations, while often being pregnant herself. She may not have had the ability to give her loved one the extra measure of patience and improved health they needed or even the power to give them the peace to bear up under the struggles of life. In every event, she had confidence in God; our God stood with her and stands with us. He is more than adequate to carry us through all of life's challenges.

Suffice it to say, Amanda was led by the Holy Spirit to speak to her children about Jesus and his true and lasting love.

THE CHILDREN WANTED INDEPENDANCE

Even though they were being well trained by Amanda, her two oldest children left home as teenagers to make their own way in life. They did not wish to be farmers all their lives. Charles Wesley and Sadie May Fountain, the two oldest, left first and moved to Wilmington, Delaware, then to Philadelphia, Pennsylvania and lived in boarding houses. They were able to visit their father in the Camp for the Blind in Philadelphia. They loved their father, John Henry dearly.

John Henry Fountain needed his children and his children needed him.

Paul said, "God chose the foolish things of the world to shame the wise and chose the weak things of the world to shame the strong."

Amanda Collins Fountain prayed a lot for herself and her children and knew that God saw her needs and let her have the experience of meeting her children's needs. She let her children go away from her to be with their father. God let her experience His guidance each day. It was in the desert that "the angel of the Lord met her and said,

"The Lord has heard of your misery." (GENESIS 16: 11, NIV).

The angel of God gave Hagar (Amanda) guidance on what to do, and He assured her of what the future would hold.

Both Hagar and Amanda had different experiences and were on totally different journeys at totally different times, but they were both alone – feeling lost and forsaken. Remember, even when you are in a wasteland, God sees you and reaches out to you to trust Him, to guide you through, knowing your Creator can change the view of your current circumstances. We must respond to God, praise Him and love Him.

NO STRAIGHT LINE

One thing I am learning more and more every day and tell my children and grandchildren is that I cannot tell my family stories and history and God's purpose for us in a straight line. I want my children and grandchildren to know their ancestors through oral history as I was given my oral history from my two grandmothers – Sadie Fountain Harper and Hattie Wise (Weise) Heath. There are so many twists and turns that even I get confused at times.

One thing that I was blessed with was both of my grandmothers who gave me oral history that dated back to Africa, West India Islands and Europe, which is our family history. They were both children of freed slaves and had a picture of enslavement as well as freedom.

It must have been very painful to have the descendants of White masters and Black slaves thrown from one situation to another as White brothers and cousins intermingled with the same enslaved women which was thought of as being harsh treatment of slave women. With all the hateful things going on in the slave woman's life, she was able to be a silent listener and within herself, she was able to thirst for love and receive it through Christ.

The Old Testament book of PROVERBS frequently contrast righteousness with evil. These Scriptures contrast the reputations of wise and foolish people.

However, many descendants and off-springs of the slave women who had children by a White man were proud to acknowledge that there was white blood in their veins. Many whites and mulattoes owned slaves, but as an example of these relationships, as in the book, THOMAS JEFFERSON AND SALLY HEMINGS: AN AMERICAN CONTROVERSY, it is acknowledged that all of Sally Hemings' children were set free by their White father at an early age in what was considered prime time of their lives.

PROVERBS 10 denotes:

The memory of the righteous will be a blessing, but the name of the wicked will not.

The wise in heart accepts commands, but a chartering fool comes to ruins.

The man/woman of integrity walks securely, but he who takes crooked paths will be found out.

He who winks maliciously causes grief, and a chattering fool comes to ruin.

The mouth of the righteous is a fountain of life, but violence overwhelms the mouth of the wicked.

Hatred stirs up dissension, but love covers all wrongs.

Wisdom is found on the lips of the discerning, but a rod is for the back of him who lacks judgment.

Wise men store up knowledge, but the mouth of a fool invites ruin.

(PROVERBS 10: 7-14, NIV).

He who heeds discipline shows the way to life, but whoever ignores correction leads others astray. (v. 17).

> GOD ORDIANS IT, AND IT IS SO.

CHAPTER 5

AS DAYS GO BY

FAMILY RELATIONSHIPS

I found (through my library reading) an elderly lady whose name was Odette Harper Hines, who was born in Philadelphia, Pennsylvania around 1914. Her younger brother, Clarence Harper, Jr. was born near Baltimore, Maryland around 1915. Philadelphia and Baltimore are only a few miles apart.

My mother, Letter Harper Heath was born in Philadelphia December 6, 1908. My uncle, Clarence Burton Harper, was born in Philadelphia on February 2, 1919. I learned that both Clarence Harpers were named for two uncles, Clarence Fountain and Clarence Harper.

When I interviewed this elderly lady named Odette Harper Hines, it became more of a loving conversation between two close friends or relatives. She had her story written in a book and I had no idea that this much information would be shared about our two families, which became one large family.

Odette had her father's birth and death documented – Clarence Harper, Sr. born 1879- died 1961.

She explained that her family – the Harper family – was the only Black family in the public schools. This included Odette Harper and Lettie Harper. They knew each other and had another friend in their circle – Marian Anderson, all from Philadelphia.

She gave me an autographed copy of her book, ALL IS NEVER SAID, a narrative written by Judith Rollins. I had read this book before, and began searching for Odette. I wanted to know from her if she was related to my grandfather, Herbert Sidney Harper and my mother, whose maiden name was Harper. Odette Harper's father was Clarence Harper, Sr. and her brother was Clarence Harper, Jr.

My uncle, Clarence Burton Harper was named for my great-great uncle, according to my mother, Lettie Harper Heath. I learned that both Clarences were on the Harper side as well as the Fountain side of the family. The coincidence was too great with all the names being the same. My mother and her brother Clarence and Odette -all three Harpers- were born in the same city – Philadelphia. Odette's brother, Clarence Harper was born in another state from the other three, but not too far from each other- Baltimore and Philadelphia.

Odette had worked in World War II in England and France as a journalist. Her brother, Clarence Harper, Jr. and my uncle, Clarence Burton Harper were both in World War II. (I doubt if they knew each other or were in the same part of the world during World War II.)

Odette met Dr. James Hines in the United States Army and they married. After the war, Odette moved to Alexandria, Louisiana with her husband, who was born in Alexandria and they lived there for many years.

Odette's brother, Clarence, had died, but she was still living in Alexandria, Louisiana with her husband. My husband and I were living in Baton Rouge, Louisiana at the time that I found Odette's book.

Bertrand and his sister and brother were born in Alexandria. His sister, Darcus Griffin Merrick still lived in Alexandria. She knew Odette Harper Hines through Odette's husband, Dr. James Hines. Darcus and my husband were patients of Dr. Hines for years. It is amazing how God can put his children together in His name in His own time.

It was through this elderly lady that I learned that my mother, Lettie Harper Heath and Odette Harper Hines were cousins on both the Harper side and the Fountain side and Thomas Jefferson and his family were related to the Fountains and Harpers, as well.

All the White side of these families, the Fountains, Jeffersons and Harpers were born and raised around the same time on the east coast, France and England with their Black slaves and mingled families. They intermingled but were not allowed to marry each other. The phenomenon left bi-racial cousins and half-brothers and sisters without the benefit of marriage and family life.

Oral history and oral tradition are the only proof that we have today from our Black ancestors that there was love between the Blacks and Whites in these families. Scriptures tells us that we are to be reminded and not to be surprised when we learn new things that fit right into our lives.

Rather, we are to rejoice that God is refining in us the precious jewel of faith, which is far greater value and worth than gold. God instills in us His love. There is no need to keep silent.

Fowler pens this poem:

GOD IS EVERYWHERE

God is everywhere I look;
Sky, earth and rippling brook.
He is in the twinkling stars at night,
And the moon that gives its full, bright light.
I have found His Word to be "The Way."
And felt His presence throughout the day.
He is the rainbow's beauty after the storm;
The Maker of which Nature's laws conform.

No matter where we stay or go,
He is there to comfort and blessings bestow.
When trials assail, our burdens He will bear,
For He never ceases to love and to care.
Even the wind whispers, "God's name is love;"

While birds in flight sing His praises above.
All of life, from Him, has its start,
And now He dwells within my heart."

(Source: M. Elaine Fowler, SALESIAN INSPIRATIONAL BOOKS).

With the help of God, Love does not keep score.

MY BRIEF INCOUNTER WITH ODETTE

Even though Odette was a ninety-two-year-old famous lady who was a news reporter during World War II and thought to be a White lady with blonde hair, she was gracious and warm to me. When I showed her my mother's picture and told her my mother had died when she was fifty-one years old, she said that my mother looked like her aunts. We compared pictures and I told her that she looked like my mother, fair-complexion, slanting eyes and beautiful soft hair. Mother's hair was black before she died and Odette's hair was golden color with white strands at the age of ninety-two.

Odette informed me that she was a descendant of Thomas Jefferson and showed me documentation of it, she explained that Jefferson had slaves but had given his slave - half-white children their freedom at an early age.

I told her that my grandmother, Sadie Fountain Harper's slave ancestors were given their freedom at an early age and were given property in Delaware where my sister, Nancy Heath Kellam and her husband, Albert Kellam and other Fountain family members still live on the land.

Odette concluded that she and my mother were second or third double cousins, just by looking at the facial coloring of both of their very fair skin, slanting eyes, their mannerism and so forth. I left her house with her calling me "Little cousin."

My grandmother, Sadie was my first storyteller. My mother, Lettie was my second storyteller, musician and travel agent. They read to us when we were very young and told us stories about their parents and grandparents, John Henry and Amanda Collins Fountain. They taught us how to read storybooks, maps, magazines and newspapers.

Daddy had the PHILADELPHIA INQUIRER and NEW YORK TIMES mailed to our home in Greenwood, Delaware ever since I can remember. I was always picking up books, maps and geography points and history about Africa and America to get a better understanding of my family and myself.

GENERATIONS ALIKE

Odette Harper Hines was my third storyteller and told me all about her family life. She could trace her family tree back more than four generations to England, France and Africa.

Our family was very musical; in fact, my mother tried to teach all of us to play the piano, but allowed us to select our own musical instrument in elementary and high school. Odette told me that she and her brother, Clarence played the piano and other musical instruments.

As I was held in my mother's lap at the age of two years old and learned to "tickle" the keys, my other siblings selected their own instruments, guitars, French horn, tuba, flute, etc. All my siblings played in the high school band but me. My mother and my music teacher asked me to stick with the piano.

My mother and father's families were also from these same countries as Odette's family. I traced my mother, Lettie Harper Heath and grandmother, Sadie Fountain Harper on the maternal side of their family back to 1691 – to Nicholas De La Fountaine, who was born in Normandy, France. He moved his family to England, then to the Virginia colony in America. His family settled in several states, Virginia, Maryland, Delaware and Pennsylvania.

It is not a coincidence that traits, peculiarities, tendencies, features and names are passed down from one generation to another. Many choices and behaviors affected our lives before we were born. Our forebears lived their lives in a way that honored God their Creator and in turn laid a foundation for us to build a relationship with each other and God.

The assumption that "God the Almighty is unacquainted with the many complexities we face daily" is part of the lie that Satan promotes. Satan wants us to believe that God does not want us to succeed, or does not want the best for us.

Satan wants only to mislead us or disarrange our lives for confusion and perplexity as a daily cup of tea.

God promised that he would send a comforter to his people in the Old Testament in Isaiah 40. No less will He send a comforter, hope and peace to us now in our daily lives. He fulfilled a part of His promise with the coming of the Messiah in the New Testament. Now, He sends the Holy Spirit and faith to us.

Thus, we see that there were fourteen generations in all from Abraham to David, fourteen generations from David to the exile to Babylon and fourteen generations from the exile to Christ. (MATTHEW 1: 17, NIV).

All this took place to fulfill what the Lord had said through the prophet, Isaiah.

This is how the birth of Jesus Christ came about: Jesus' mother, Mary was pledged to marry Joseph, but before they came together, she was found to be with child through the Holy Spirit.

God continues to produce generations to eternity.

I did not know my ancestors, but I know much about them through my oral history. Their genes shaped my generation and the generations to come. How is it that generational traits and patterns repeat themselves? It is all about God and his love. Now generations later, history repeats itself. Our people took care of family, educated their children, built their own homes, started their own businesses, served in the Armed Services, loved to travel, and were leaders in the church and community.

My mother began elementary school in Philadelphia and finished elementary school in Neal Elementary School in Middleford, Delaware. This school for Black children did not go further than six grade.

She went to Rocky Mount, North Carolina to a boarding school to attend high school. Mother's uncles Robert and Uncle Burton Harper had founded this boarding school for children who could not go any further in education. High schools for Black children in the early 1920's were non-existent.

Uncle Clarence, my mother's only sibling, attended the Neal Elementary School after Mother left to attend the boarding school. He completed six grade and was sent to another town to attend and complete two other grades. Mother was twelve years older than Uncle Clarence. After that, he was drafted into the Army.

ODETTE'S EDUCATION AND FAMILY LIFE

Odette told me about her life in Philadelphia, her schooling and her church life, her love of traveling when she was young until she moved away and joined the Armed Services. Later she became a news reporter which also gave her a chance to travel a lot.

Odette Harper's story about her great -great-grandfather, William Turpin Fountain, revealed much about her family as well as my family. Odette was in the Turpin and Fountain family and was also a direct descendant of the Harper family. Odette's father was Clarence Harper, Sr. and her brother was Clarence Harper, Jr.

Odette's father and brother were named after their uncle Clarence Harper.

My grandmother was Sadie Fountain Harper and my grandfather was Herbert Sidney Harper. My mother was Lettie Sidney Harper Heath and my uncle was Clarence Burton "CB" Harper. "He was named for his great uncle, Clarence Fountain, who was my grandmother, Sadie May Fountain Harper's brother," my mother told me.

Odette researched her family and learned that the De La Fountaines changed their name from the French spelling to the English spelling when they moved to the Mid-Atlantic colonies in America. They were first and second cousins to the Harpers and Jeffersons. They lived in the same states-Pennsylvania, Maryland, Virginia and Delaware. They intermingled and procreated together. There were first and second cousins being raised together. Both the Black and White Fountains,

Harpers and Jeffersons were afraid to tell their stories, but their features and mannerisms told their stories for them.

OUR UNCLE CLARENCE

"I know Uncle Clarence," said Christian Paris, our first grandson. Bertrand and I took Christian-Paris Griffin and his great -great Uncle Clarence Harper to a zoo in Houston, Texas when Christian-Paris was around two-and a half -years old. They laughed and played together as they watched the animals play and eat.

Christian-Paris said, "Uncle Clarence kept tickling me and we both laughed." I told Christian-Paris, "Clarence Burton Harper is my uncle, your mother, Karen Griffin's great uncle and your great-great uncle. That is a good way of explaining how the generations go.

This is how my grandmother explained how my ancestors were related to me.

"I remember Uncle Clarence when we all went on a cruise together," said Michael Griffin, II, our other grandson. "He would take us down to the place where we got food and we ate together. He kept saying things that made me laugh. I liked Uncle Clarence."

Michael, you and Christian-Paris are first cousins. You have the same great-great uncle. I am the grandmother of both of you and Uncle Clarence is my mother's younger brother.

Uncle Clarence was always partial to children. He was very close to my mother and visited us often when he returned from World War II. He loved to play with my brothers and sisters and me when we were little. Now as days go by, he has gotten the chance to play with his great-great nephews and nieces.

He never had children of his own, but helped to raise his wife's children after the couple married. When we were told about Aunt Lucille's three children born to a previous marriage, we thought we had cousins to play with. By the time we met them, they were going off to college. They were much older than we were. That was OK. We learned to get along with them, anyway. Love does not keep score.

UNCLE CLARENCE'S PLAYMATES

Uncle Clarence told me a story about his life after I was grown. Middleford and Seaford, Delaware are only a few miles apart. Uncle Clarence lived in Middleford and two of his White cousins lived in Seaford. They walked the country roads and played with each other all their days and years. They all went into the Army together, only in different divisions.

Uncle Clarence "CB" Harper was drafted in the all-black Ninety-Second Division of the United States Army. The all -black troops had White officers to train them. They were not trained for combat. Black soldiers were not allowed to carry guns. They were trained for menial jobs like clearing fields and wooded areas. They also built roads and bridges.

The United States Army activated two all black divisions- the Ninety-Second Infantry Division -Buffalo Soldiers- in 1942 and Ninety-Third Infantry Division -Blue Helmet in 1942. With the little oral history that Mother and Uncle Clarence gave me, I researched many of these things later in the East Baton Rouge Parish library with help from the staff.

Uncle Clarence said that the Black soldier's basic training camps were located in Hauchuca, Arizona and they stayed there for around seventeen weeks. The harsh landscape, weather patterns and general lifestyle proved to be difficult for many of the new residents; Uncle Clarence being one of them.

There were many restrictions and humiliations of segregation in the Black divisions of the Armed Services; for instance, Black men or women could not join the Navy or Air Force at one time. However, many men, like Uncle Clarence considered continuing their careers in the military service after World War II.

Maggi M. Morehouse stated in her book, FIGHTING IN THE JIM CROW ARMY, basic training was seventeen weeks; there were fourteen more weeks of specialized training and finally eight weeks of division rehearsal or review time." (pp. 41-44 para). This totaled a year of training for the Black soldiers.

Uncle Clarence had never worked so hard in his life. Uncle Clarence could not tell us everything about his stint in the Army, but Mother and Daddy and the family did know where he was and how he got there.

At the age of seventeen, Uncle Clarence went to the Pacific Islands and stayed two years, which he never stopped talking about and bragging about when he came back home. He told us stories many times about being in foxholes and snakes were right down there with them. He told us other stories about the women in the Pacific Islands and how they loved Black soldiers. He enjoyed being with the Filipino women. The Black soldiers had been way out of the country during their young years and the young women was one of their pleasures.

After Uncle Clarence returned home and was debriefed, he and other soldiers were told they were still needed. They had caught hell in the army as well as in civilian communities near the army bases. However, it made sense to stay in the service, because it was a job and the Black men were surely respected in their own communities. Uncle Clarence stayed and rejoined the army in the reserves.

Life in the Ninety-Third Infantry Division of the United States Army was no peaches and cream matter. Uncle Clarence left home from Middleford, Delaware; after his training period, he was sent to San Francisco Bay Area, California with his Division -Blue Helmet – to await being shipped to the Pacific Theater of war.

According to Morehouse, there were many perils and struggles described in her book about the Black soldiers.

After more training, Uncle Clarence became an army engineer. His job included such backbreaking work as clearing jungles, infested mosquitoes, and other debris including dead humans and animal bodies. Building roads for trucks and other armored vehicles to pass through was another gruesome job. His first tour of duty was in the Pacific Islands, mainly the Philippines, which he spoke about constantly when he returned home.

The Ninety – Third Infantry Division was not one of the combat units. Black soldiers who were classified as engineers, wanted to be in combat and fight alongside their White soldiers for their country.

However, Uncle Clarence did fill us in with tales of being in war zones on foreign soil. As they were setting up airbases and communication systems, they experienced rifle fire, mortal fire, bombing attacks, snakes, and other wild animals in the jungles. They had to be trained to defend themselves because Japanese snipers were shooting at them.

Uncle Clarence declared that the Blue Helmet was the best division that had apparently eighteen thousand Black men on the military reservation or post of Fort Huachuca by the end of 1942. He looked on this time in his life before, during and after World War II as a milestone in his life. Also, he had something to talk about with pride and humor even afterward.

I am glad he had so much to talk about when he returned home with humor and pride. We had to listen to his jaw-jacking about all his experiences, especially all the beautiful women in the South Pacific who "loved him." There was not a humble bone in his body and we enjoyed listening to his stories as they inspired us. He was over twenty-one years old when he left the service and we were small children. Uncle Clarence was always at our house, playing with us and letting us ride in his small car with him. He was always a joy and delight to his nieces and nephews.

As time went on, Uncle Clarence married Aunt Lucille McSears (her first marriage name) and built her a new house in Middleford. He helped raise her three children, Mary, Viola and Jack McSears and sent them to Delaware State College (University).

He received a great position at Dupont plant in Seaford, Delaware. He knew most of the men who worked there from childhood. Later in life, Uncle Clarence learned that several of the White men who worked with him were his cousins. They had the same grandfather and great-grandfather.

The family had a good life together on the Fountain-Harper Homestead. My parents and grandparents got along well with Uncle Clarence and his family. We are still fortunate because our Black ancestors from slavery time had property given to them (even though they had to work for it); and since the sixteenth century to the present time in the twenty-first century, our family, the Fountains and Harpers have maintained our property and new generations of John Henry and Amanda Collins Fountain are still living there.

From Nicholas De La Fountaine, to his granddaughter, Mary Elizabeth Fountain, to John Henry Fountain (the blind son) and Amanda Collins Fountain to the grandchildren and new generations, the family always wanted us to have a place to come home to. The older Fountains willed the property to the younger members and trusted them not to sell the land. Uncle Clarence lived on the property all his life.

He especially inspired my three brothers, George, Jr., Daniel and Joseph, who were excited about the Armed Services, and later joined the United States Navy. They lived full lives in all types of circumstances.

Uncle Clarence had little White boys that he played with as a child. Little did Uncle Clarence know that the White boys were his cousins because they had the same grandfather and great-grandfather. The White boys whose mother was a Fountain and their father was a Brown, knew about their kinship, but Uncle Clarence was not aware of their blood relationship until much later.

I was searching for my family history. I was not finding anything about them in books or other-wise. Anyway, I found Odette's book, ALL IS NEVER SAID, by Judith Rollins in my search. Beginning with Sadie Fountain Harper, a lightbulb came on in my head when I looked at Odette's book. Number one, her picture was on the front cover of her book. She looked like my relatives, especially my mother. I was joyful at searching for Odette to see if she was related to or knew my grandfather, Herbert Sidney Harper, or his parents, Delcia Sanders Harper and Steven Harper.

Apparently, I realized that my mother and Odette had two last names that were the same – Harper and Fountain. Odette's grandfather was Peter Harper; her other grandfather was Durock Turpin. Her mother's maiden name was Turpin. (This source is from Ancsrtry.com and Odette's book.)

I met Odette and had a long beautiful conversation with her. Several months later I called to interview her further, but she had had an accident. She was walking across Lee Street in Alexandria, Louisiana and a car struck her. I learned from my sister-in-law, Darcus Griffin that she was in the hospital. I attempted again to contact her with no success. I thought maybe she had died.

In researching my grandmother's married name and my mother's maiden name again, (Harper), I ran across Odette Harper Hines' name once again by googling the Harper name on Family Search.

Odette Harper Hines was listed in the United States Census Bureau Record as being one hundred years old and still living in Alexandria, Louisiana.

More research into Odette's ancestors revealed that Sarah Jane Turpin, born in 1868, was Thomas Jefferson's great-aunt. Sarah was married to William Fountain.

"Odette had learned of her relationship with Thomas Jefferson many years ago before it was popular to reveal relationships between White and Black persons," she told me.

My mother and Odette were direct descendants of the Fountains, Turpins, Jeffersons and Harpers. They were godly people, with love for one another.

GOD BLESS!

CHAPTER 6

OBTAINING WISDOM AND UNDERSTANDING

We are speaking to our current moment. A self-centered approach to life may be satisfying for a while, but it lacks the true fulfillment of maturity, love and sacrifice. Our Creator knows and understands us perfectly, far better than we know ourselves. We can assume that He is able to predict our behavior more extensively and accurately than we can do, because our present character does not predict or determine our future.

Our Creator Himself, who dwells within us in the person of the Holy Spirit, intercedes for us in our weakness with words that cannot express our needs and groans. He searches our hearts and knows the mind of the Spirit.

The Spirit intercedes for the Saints in accordance with God's will. (ROMANS 8: 26-27, NIV).

Establishing a gallery of superb ideas in your specialty and determining how it relates to influence others, gives self-mastery, courage and criticism to yourself and others. If we embrace our destiny as it is given, we will discover God's purpose for us in this new generation.

Historically, prophecies pertaining to be understood by individuals are examples of the Lord establishing certain circumstances ahead of time. An individual's character becomes more predictable over time. The more we persist in a chosen path, the more that path becomes a part of who we are.

Many of our people have always been hard-working, dedicated, highly sensitive and zealous people. They come bearing gifts in spite of their own circumstances. There are times in the lives of all God's children when we are called on to suffer. While believers of Christ are sustained in their suffering by hope and praise, we are also given strength during our weakest hour in a most special way: God's love intercedes for us. All the things we are, make us human. This includes hurting, struggling, anger, loving, helping and serving which are both settling and beneficiary.

There was a very sensitive (unknown) woman who wanted to give something special to the Lord before he was taken away. She was full of wisdom and understanding. She had a great deal of spiritual discernment as well. She had heard of Christ's execution and believed it. Even so, without invitation, she gave a gift of love. As Jesus was eating at the table of Simon the leper, she came and poured a very expensive perfume on his head.

The disciples, Christ's chosen men, became indignant and scolded her when they saw her anoint the Lord in this manner.

"Why this waste?" they asked. "This perfume could have been sold at a high price and the money given to the poor."

But Christ said to them, "Why are you bothering this woman? She has done a beautiful thing to me. When she poured the perfume on my body, she did it to prepare me for burial." (MATTHEW 26: 8-9, NIV).

Her reason for giving this gift to Christ was not understood by these leaders of the church and the disciples, but Christ understood. He appreciated her outpouring of love and made a promise like no other in Scripture.

Christ said, "Wherever this gospel is preached throughout the world, what she did will also be told in memory of her. (MATTHEW 26: 13, NIV).

Just as this woman's gift was misunderstood by the leaders of the early church, many people and churches today criticize others for trying to share their special gifts. It is comforting to know that our gifts are often acceptable, and appreciated by the Lord when given in love. Christ understands our motivations and accepts what we bring. With his love for us, Christ does not keep score:

As He looked up, Jesus saw the rich putting their gifts into the temple treasury. He also saw a poor widow put in two very small copper coins.

"I tell you the truth," he said, "This poor widow has put in more than all the others. All these people give these gifts out of their wealth, but she out of her poverty put in all she had to live on." (LUKE 21: 1-4, NIV).

Give careful thought to the paths for your feet and be steadfast in all your ways.

In other words, make level paths for your feet and take only ways that are firm. (PROVERBS 4: 26, NIV).

You cannot help someone else unless you can help yourself.

The purpose of Proverbs is "to attain wisdom and discipline; for understanding words of insight; for acquiring a disciplined and prudent life, and doing what is right and just and fair; as well as for giving prudence to the simple, knowledge and discretion to the young," says Solomon, son of David, king of Israel. (PROVERBS 1: 1-4, para, NIV).

Let the wise listen and add to their learning; we do not have all the answers and therefore must embrace humility. We should respect the purpose of our humanity and understand that a deepening of change and faith take time.

And let the discerning get guidance because we need to learn to better embrace our pain and other emotions. Emotions bring clarity about what we need and want.

We have proverbs for understanding, and proverbs and parables are the sayings and riddles of the wise. (PROVERBS 1:5-6, NIV).

MORE OF FAMILY LIFE

"Am I my brother's keeper?" (GENESIS 4: 9, NIV).

"No. He was his brother's brother. Zoos have keepers, bees have keepers, prisons have keepers. Only families have brothers.

A STORY ABOUT A BROTHER

I thought about the fact that some things, such as the value of human life, is non-negotiable. There is a book by Jeffrey C. Stewart called THE NEW NEGRO: THE LIFE OF ALAIN LOCKE. This nine-hundred-and-thirty-two-page book (932) denotes that pluralism allows people to look at the world through different eyes and move through stages of consciousness by holding together opposites and differences, and recognizing that some things cannot be compromised or bartered. Let us think about energy, and our emotions as a kind of energy.

What have we learned about energy, perhaps from a physics class, perhaps when you were in high school, as I did?

"Energy cannot be created or destroyed; it can only be transferred or transformed," said Amadi, in her book, WHY DO I FEEL THIS WAY?

She says, "It can also be helpful to think about our emotions as a kind of psychological energy that flows throughout our body when something triggers it. Sometimes we feel or experience sadness, fear or hurt. Consequently, we feel heavy, or lethargic, as if something is weighing us down. That is negative energy and when it is moving through our body, it is hard to miss.

Otherwise, we may experience joy, excitement or love. This energy causes us to feel light on our feet, free of burdens and filled with all things good. Our emotions, our smile and other signs of emotions denote how we feel about ourselves and how others feel about us.

These emotions of energy connect us to God, others and ourselves.

TWO FAMILIES GREW UP TOGETHER

There were two families who grew up around each other – the Locke Family and the Fountain/Harper Family. My grandfather, Herbert Harper and his two brothers, Robert and Joseph Burton Harper went to Bible College and became teachers, ministers and directors of their own boarding school in North Carolina. They were thoroughly involved in their children and other's education and welfare.

Dr. Alain LeRoy Locke, born in Philadelphia, Pennsylvania, was widely known as the Father of the Harlem Renaissance Movement and was an exceptional philosopher, critic, theorist. He was a champion of African American art, and had taken his participation in the FINKELSTEIN ANNUAL CONFERENCE seriously. He presented two papers which allowed him to redefine "Pragmatism and Cultural Pluralism."

Of the two papers he presented, "Cultural Relativism and Ideological Peace," have been the most innovative in sharing and charting his answers.

My mother and her family interacted with the Locke family. Mother, too, was born in Philadelphia in 1908 and she and my grandparents knew the Locke family.

What is so special about the Locke family and the Harper family interacting with each other? Dr. Locke was close to the age of my grandparents and they always admired his achievements and accomplishments. My mother was allowed to talk and listen to Dr. Locke's philosophy.

Moreover, my mother always allowed us to interact with her peers and friends as her parents did with her. Mother wanted us to emulate high achievers and have as many heroes as possible. With this background and these role models, we were to get a good education, knowledge and understanding, walk and live a good life and be a better influence in the world. She wanted us to identify our skills and talents and use them to help heal others. We were to help heal others by understanding ourselves and others.

THE LOCKE FAMILY

The Locke family were such persons that my grandparents allowed their two children to interact with them. Therefore, my mother sought to raise us in the same fashion. She wanted us to be healthy, physically, mentally, spiritually and peacefully. As Mother was taught, she wanted us to involve ourselves in self-improvement. Healing ourself will help us to walk and live differently in the space that is called our world and be a better influence in the world; be a better model for our children; be a better model for our family and our friends. Show them what authentic and true healing looks like. This was our mother's initiative.

Kimberly Jones, in her book, HOW WE CAN WIN: RACE, HISTORY AND CHANGING THE MONEY GAME THAT'S RIGGED, denotes, "The most revolutionary thing you can do right now is self-improvement. Heal yourself! Be better!"

"In the face of our history, healing and understanding self is a revolutionary act. Naming the place where we are not healthy but reaching for health is the choice to move beyond devastating history.

If we were to have a true reconciliation commission, it would require unpacking this history and presenting the receipts of the harms that have been done. We need to feel more than, rather than less than life." (p.87-89, para).

There were many differences in the Locke family and the Fountain/Harper family. Yet there were so many similarities. Both were educational-minded, both were middle-class Negro families, they both believed strongly in the African American people and challenged Blacks to fully embrace their cultural heritage. They both exalted the virtues of self-expression.

Although there were aggressively assimilationist thinkers that disagreed with Locke, he was invited to teach at Harvard, which was one of his life-long dreams. Locke broke a significant race barrier when he became the first African American student to become a Rhodes Scholar.

Despite this incredible achievement, racial discrimination hindered Locke's efforts to complete post-graduate study abroad in Oxford, England. Although he was rejected at the University of Oxford, he received admittance at Hereford College and later University of Berlin.

Locke returned to the United States and began teaching at Howard University in Washington, D.C. for four years. After this period, he applied and received admittance at Harvard University and earned a Ph. D. degree in philosophy.

Locke narrated inclusion, self-determination, universalism and pluralism as characteristics of the world. He was talking about himself. The people were getting a taste of a Black academic subjectivity they had only heard of; inclusion came with a price just as democracy did.

THE FOUNTAIN/HARPER FAMILY

My grandfather, Herbert Harper was one of three brothers who completed high school and Bible College at the turn of the twentieth century. They were also builders as well as educators. Their parents, Delcie and Steven Harper, took the team approach to educate their children and teach them in the way they should go.

They were taught to look to the light and not fear the darkness. We must assess our capabilities and summon strength each day and accept ourselves as strong, resilient persons because of who we are and whose we are, knowing that God loves us unconditionally and does not keep score.

There may have been differences on a number of issues which could have divided the families and community life. In an effort to find common ground between them, one family member, my grandfather said, "Since we are all believers, we should focus on our unity in Christ."

Instead of passing judgment on one another, he encouraged them to "do what leads to peace and mutual edification." (ROMANS 14: 19, NIV).

My ancestors were taught that education and the ability to reason and make good choices were the key to having a decent, wholesome life.

No matter where we are or what we do in life, we can help ourself to inevitably make our own decisions and be self-sufficient. We must prepare our new generations for real freedom. Imagine that despite wanting to be free and educated, we would need to justify seizing our freedom and self-worth over the investments others have made on the structure of power that has forced us to be another's servant.

How important is it to love yourself, respect yourself?

You must have self-respect for yourself because God has enough love for all of us.

A book written by Ruth Tucker, A SELF-IMAGE IN THE IMAGE OF GOD, explains that "It was through the creation of man and woman that God has offered Himself and his fullest self-revelation. As we reflect on who God is, we see a picture of the image we carry in ourselves. (para).

Joan Rae Mills wrote in a Review:

NO SCHOLAR

This thick young lad,
A shock of black hair
Hiding his eye,
Bent over his paper,
Wringing out labored words.
He was alone by himself,
With nobody with him, he wrote.
No scholar, yet a teacher,

For though I cannot recall
The character he described,
It makes my mind,
It makes me think of you, my Lord,
Hanging between heaven and hell,
Heartstrings stretched so tight,
They snapped, so forsaken that you cried,
OH, MY GOD!" to empty, silent skies.
All alone by yourself,
And nobody with you.
FOR ME.

Because we have put our hope and trust in the living God, who is
the Savior of the world, what can be better than to serve him. (1
TIMOTHY 4: 10, NIV).

CHAPTER 7

KNOWING FAMILY

am indebted to God and everyone who has shared their life with me. The actions, thoughts, observations and feelings of these grand – spirited people cannot be overstated.

Neither time nor space allows me to acknowledge and thank all the persons for the countless acts of support and encouragement (as well as criticism) I received from individuals who walked with me and talked with me all my days. A labor of love has gone into this book which made it all the sweeter by the many hands that made it a reality.

I have written and published thirty-one books about my family and put together three photograph books in four and a half years and I am so proud of the people mentioned in these books because it feels as if their hands were on the pen and computer with mine.

First and foremost, let me acknowledge and thank my God-given mother, Lettie Harper Heath and my father, George Wesley Heath, Sr. who with the help of God, gave me life. I was blessed to have grandparents and ancestors who survived many adversities in their lives until they passed away. I owe a tremendous debt of gratitude to them; I mention a few: Sadie Fountain Harper and Herbert Sidney Harper, as well as Hattie Wise Heath and William "Will" Heath, Jr. They shared many experiences with us by interacting with my siblings and me. Our parents and grandparents encouraged us to choose hope and faith instead of fear and dismay. It appeared that their love for us was their first priority. As I experienced their love, I realized that happiness is not dependent on money or wealth.

As Habakkuk in the Scripture said, "Though the fig tree does not bud and there are no grapes on the vines, yet I will rejoice in the Lord and be joyful in God my Savior." (HABAKKUK 3: 17-18, NIV).

When He gave us a new commandment, Jesus said, "Love one another, as I have loved you." (JOHN 13: 34,NIV).

Our three children, Rev. Bertrand Griffin, II (Rev. Kotosha Seals Griffin), Karen Michelle Griffin Phenix, (Keith B. Phenix), and Dr. Michael Gerard Griffin (Tracie Haydel Griffin) and Jason Massenburg, who is Michael's best friend, have always been our pride and joy even when they were young and required much attention and care.

I cannot leave out my eight beautiful grandchildren: Kia Olivia, Niara Janelle, Christian-Paris Bertrand, III, Michael Gerard, II, Amelia-Grai Addison, Victoria Olivia, Olivia Christina and Sophia Morgan – all Griffins. They are number one on our spiritual priority list.

Apparently, Jesus was saying "Love is the main thing on which we should concentrate. It is the best thing we should commit our lives to. Therefore, in our hearts, we will know that love does not keep score.

I am thankful for my six siblings: Phyllis Heath Pepper (Willie Alex Pepper- both deceased), George Wesley Heath, Jr. (Corine Mitchell Heath – deceased), Daniel Louis Heath, Sr. (Lois Randell Heath both - deceased), Daniel Heath, Jr. (Tenika Goines Heath – both deceased), Danea Heath, Joseph Burton Heath (Barbara Dennis Heath), Nancy V. Heath Kellam, (Albert Lee Kellam, Jr.), Hattie E. Heath Purnell, (Gerald Purnell – both deceased). These are the siblings that offered me much love, support and challenges.

Bertrand, I and Marian Griffin's grandchildren include: Nia Olivia, Kiara Janell, Christian -Paris Bertrand, III, Michael, II, Amelia-Grai Addison, Victoria Olivia, Olivia Christina, and Sophia Morgan – all Griffin

Our personal love journey gives us confidence before God and enables us to receive from him what we ask for in prayer. (1 JOHN 3: 18-23, para, NIV).

There are cousins that I grew up with and have tried to keep in contact with. They are Janet Nock Moreno and family. Janet sent me documents and ancestral material for my first book, CULTURAL GUMBO, OUR ROOTS, OUR STORIES, and dared me to write a book from this material. I did. Martin Nock (Stephanie), her brother requested that Janet (his sister) help with Ancestry.com as she was also doing research on the family history.

Their grandmother, Annie Wise (Weiss -different spelling), Jones and my grandmother, Hattie Wise (Weiss) Heath were sisters. These two sisters lived near each other along with another sister, Mary Etta Wise (Weiss) Heath and other siblings. Mary and Hattie Wise, two sisters, married two Heath brothers. All three Wise (different spelling, Weiss) sisters attended Hampton Agricultural Institute and received training to be mid-wives. They all lived in Painter, Virginia on land given to Grandmother Hattie by an unknown White woman.

Annie Wise Jones and her family moved to New York for a period of time but some of the family returned to Virginia.

Whenever we visited our grandmother Hattie in Virginia as children, we had cousins to play with: Leonard (deceased), Joyce, Jeffery (deceased in infancy), Martin, Janet, Evelyn, Norman, and Elfemel – all Nocks.

There were Heath cousins, Evelyn and John Heath, and others who were older then we were: Douglas Heath and wife (both deceased), Esther Heath (deceased), Jacob Heath(deceased) and Dr. George Edward Heath (deceased), (Kim and family) and younger cousins, Sandra, Paul and Iris Johnson, Great Aunt Annie Wise (Weiss) Jones's grandchildren.

Then I recently learned that Dorothy Smith Collins and her family who are members of our St. Mark United Methodist Church family share the Heath name with us. She has Heaths in her family and I, being a Heath, have Smiths and Collins in my family. We have declared that we are close cousins and are still researching our names through Ancestry. com.

There is a special cousin around my mother's age – Odette Harper Hines whom I met late in life. She gave me oral history about my mother's family which proved to be a part of her family, also. This was invaluable to me as it dated back over a century. She was born in 1914 and lived to be over one -hundred years old as was in our Ancestry.com chart and Odette's book, ALL IS NEVER SAID, by Judith Rollins.

The cousins who lived near our grandparents, Sadie Fountain Harper and Herbert Harper in Middleford, Delaware are: Virginia Fountain Freshwater and (John Freshwater -both deceased). Their children are Lucille Freshwater Harmon (James Harmon), John Freshwater, IV (deceased), Medford Freshwater (Star Ann Freshwater), and Jackson Freshwater. We can include Mother's first cousins: John Banks, Clifford Banks, Amanda Banks Batson (Otha Batson, both deceased) & Mable Banks.

I am appreciative of Bertrand, my husband and his cousin, Rose Brown Kelly. I say thank you to Rose for listening as a small child as the old folk talked about family history.

My oldest sister, Phyllis Heath Pepper had two children, Mary and Willie. There are several generations in this branch of the family. Willie Alex "Billie" Pepper, Jr. (deceased) and Terri Brown Pepper and their five children, Arshawon, (deceased) Tikia, Lentia, Willie, III, and Jermaine and new generations lived with their grandparents. (names given by Terri for this book).

George Heath, (Corine-deceased), my oldest brother's children are Jerome Heath (deceased – never married) and Gloria Heath Martin (Michael Martin), and their children: Michael, Jr. and Rita.

Other nieces and nephews are Francine Heath and Linda Cannon, who are Daniel Heath's daughters, (Lois Randall Heath -both deceased) children and Whitney Foucheaux Cannon, (Daniel's granddaughter),

Daniel and Lois's son, Daniel Heath, Jr. (all three – Daniel, Lois, and Daniel, Jr. are deceased). Daniel Jr. has one daughter, Danee Victoria Heath.

Joseph Burton Heath, Sr., our youngest brother, (1). Mamie Heath, (2) Barbara Heath) have four children: Valerie Heath Garcia and children; Bobbie, Enrika and Alberto Garcia, and Joseph Burton Heath, Jr. (Tonya Heath) and one son, Tyler Joseph Heath, Malcolm Dennis and Eddie Dennis.

Nancy Virginia Heath Kellam, younger sister (Albert Lee Kellan, Jr.) had no children.

Hattie Elviria Heath Purnell, youngest sister, (Gerald Purnell-both deceased), are parents of Crystal Renee Purnell.

Rev. Amos James Griffin, Sr., my husband Bertrand's brother and Nettie Harris Griffin (both deceased) had children, Amos James Griffin, Jr. and Delasper Griffin Sanders (Warren Sanders-deceased), and Randall and Samanthia Byrd Cunningham and their children.

Thanks to our Gillespie cousins, Sandra and Francis (deceased) and the younger brother, Allen Levi Gillespie for their help with genealogy charts and to Bessie Berry Lawrence and Sallie Gillespie Newman, (Jewel J. Newman-both deceased) and children: Brenda Cooks, Linda Cooks Narcisse (Johnnie Narcisse and children), and Edwin Cooks (Rosalyn) and Diana Cooks for invaluable service and family information.

To my first to fourth grade teacher: Mary Daniels and my high school English teacher, Elizabeth Dix, I must give a special thanks. I am fortified by all the knowledge they gave me. Their lessons in life have been a blessing to me. Several other high school teachers: John Parker, Pauline Walker, Monroe Hearn, John Walker were exceptional teachers and special to me.

As I reflect on the loving, generous spirit of my parents, grandparents and teachers and how they led by example, I remain grateful. My family and teachers made every effort to forgo their own needs and share what they had/have with us. How much more does God show mercy and loving kindness for his world.

I am especially honored to acknowledge many special friends and distant relatives who have been supportive of me over the years. They are my seminary friends, Rev. Dr. Leslie (deceased) and Roszeta Norris, Bishop Alfred and Mackie Norris, Bishop W. T. and Ruth Handy (both deceased), Rev. Robert and Helen Williams, (both deceased), Rev. Dr. George W. C. and May Calvin Belton, (both deceased), Rev. Dr. Donald and Marcia Avery, Rev. Dr. Jesse L. Douglas, Professor Julian (deceased) and Loretta White and children, especially our god-child Whitney White, and Dr. Johnathan and Geraldine Roberts and children.

To my precious church members and friends who are all family at St. Mark United Methodist Church, the Senior Pastor, Rev. Simon Chigumari, the ministerial Staff, retired Chaplain Bertrand Griffin, and retired minister, Rev. Glorious Wright, my class leader, Catherine Martin (Semmie), Eunice Simmons and Sophia Ennin and children (from Ghana), and Melvin and Sylvia Sanders.

Let me say thanks to my lovely Sorority sisters of Alpha Kappa Alpha. They are all family: Karen Griffin Phenix (daughter), Sanettria Glasper Pleasant (Cousin), Janifer Peters, Lorita W. Frank, Susie Boudreaux, Gloria and Carmen Spooner, Lovenia Deconge-Watson, Katina Semien (former South-Central Regional Director), Marvis Henderson Lewis, Sandra Temple Hall, Judy Pitts Reed, Geraldine and Joni Roberts, Kismet Gray, and Julia B. Purnell (Sixteenth Supreme Basileus (deceased).

Thanks to Lear Chase, our grandchildren's great grandmother and James Hayden, our grandchildren's "Papa" for family information and encouragement.

I am thankful to my husband, Bertrand Griffin of sixty-one years for his indulgence and patience as well as his love. He entered my life many years ago and has never left my side. All these persons are close to me and I love them dearly. Love not only blesses others, it blesses the one doing the loving. Concentrating on being a blessing to others and committing ourselves to others brings joy, excitement and challenges. The single most determination made is to love and not keep score.

As I explain to my children and grandchildren: these are your generational ancestors. My relatives and friends are your relatives and friends. I want my children and grandchildren to understand that instead of wanting to be successful and powerful, they should know that true power and success is love. Instead of being selfless, thank God for His eternal compassion and love.

> ## TO GOD BE THE GLORY; I LOVE YOU ALL.

CHAPTER 8

LOVE IS SWEET HARMONY

How can man live without God, who gave him his very life? Do we know what love is? There are several phases of love. God, the one we turn to in prayer, and who calms us in time of strife is our first love, our first phase of love. Even as an infant, we experience love and return it.

"Pleasure is sometimes mistaken for joy, but joy is part of God's love. It comes from giving back in return for the things we received from above. Seeking harmony without seeking God is like rivers that cannot find the sea. Why search for what is in everyone's reach: Our God is sweet harmony. (Source: Margaret Peterson, Salesian Inspirational Books, p. 5).

His love endures forever. (PSALM 107: 1, NIV).

"Let them give thanks to the Lord for his unfailing love." (v. 15).

I remember a plaque on our living room wall from the time I was a little girl as I was growing up. The plaque stated:

GOD IS LOVE.

I would think, "I must learn to love."

What prompts me to reflect on Jesus Christ? As members of Christ, we come in many shapes and colors, widths and lengths, uneven edges and all. Moreover, some of us glitter for the Kingdom in prominent places, while others serve faithfully in accent positions. Why are we still one body, led by one Spirit? We are following one Christ of the world.

There is one body and one spirit; just as you are called to one hope when you are called; one Lord, one faith, one baptism; one God and Father of us all, who is over all and through all and in all. (EPHESIANS 4: 4-6, NIV).

One young girl on a Lakota Indian reservation describes LOVE:

"Love is the climax of my happiness,
and the pinnacle of my pain.
Love is the fire in my heart
with an eternal flame"

(Source: Isabelle, 10th grade, Red Cloud Indian School).

PERSPECTIVES AND PERCEPTIONS

Later, I learned that life is all about perspectives and our own perceptions are enriched by seeing circumstances and events through different phases of love. There are always special opportunities and expressions of joy that give us different layers of experiences as we develop our own traditions and memorable occurrences in life.

We are all a masterpiece in God's sight. An inspiration in God's sight: no careful definite lines, a dash of glitter, overlapping shapes, uneven edges of free strokes, dominant colors of white, black, brown, yellow, and pink, beloved symbols created with love. The Artist blesses us each day by adding light and cheer to our lives. Our common hope is Heaven; one day we will all gather in the same place: past, present and future, and worship Jesus Christ our Savior of the world.

Then I saw a new heaven and a new earth, for the first heaven and the first earth had passed away, and there was no longer any sea. I saw the new city, the new Jerusalem, coming down out of heaven from God, prepared as a bride beautifully dressed for her husband.

And they heard a loud voice from the throne saying, "Now the dwelling of God with men is with men and He will live with them. They will be his people and God himself will be with them and be their God. He will wipe every tear from their eyes. There will be no more death or mourning or crying or pain, for the old order of things has passed away." (REVELATION 21: 1-4, NIV).

The angel who talked with me had a measuring rod of gold to measure the city, the gates and its walls. The city was laid out like a square as long as it was wide. He measured the city with the rod and found it to be 12, 000, foursquare in length, and as wide and high as it was long. He measured its walls and it was 144 cubits thick, by man's measurement, which the angel was using. The wall was made of jasper, and the city of pure gold, as pure as glass. The foundations of the city walls were decorated with every kind of precious stone. .... The twelve gates were twelve pearls, each gate made of a single pearl. The great street of the city was of pure gold, like transparent glass. (REVELATION 21: 15-20, NIV).

God, Christ and the Holy Spirit – three in one- want this for everyone – Sweet Harmony!

As Amy Carmichael reflects in WOMEN'S DEVOTIONAL BIBLE, "If I am inconsiderate about the comfort of others, or their feelings, or even their little weaknesses and frailties; if I am careless about their little hurts and miss opportunities to smooth them away; if I make the sweet running of household wheels more difficult to accomplish, then I know nothing about Calvary "the cross" love. (p. 630, para).

In the book of 1 Corinthians, Paul reminds his followers they were missing one essential component. The believers possessed many spiritual gifts, but lacked love. He encouraged them to always infuse their actions with love. Remember that God's plan always calls for love which trusts, protects, hopes, and perseveres. (1 CONINTHIANS 13: 1-7, para, NIV).

Sinning is against God. However, there is nothing you can do that God will not forgive you for. Guilty actions are against a person. If you confess your sins and guilty actions to each other and pray for each other so that you may be healed, the prayer of a righteous man or woman is powerful and effective. (JAMES 5: 16, para., NIV).

Man is sometimes being accused of being so heavenly-minded that he is no earthly good. He gets caught up in studies of the end - times or other church activities, and ignores the needs around him.

When problems are brought to our attention, we contend ourselves with feeling sorry about them while doing nothing. We can easily identify with the Israelites' tough life in the wilderness because life can be hard. (DEUTERONOMY 2:7, para, NIV).

But do we see the other parallels? Instead, we create our own itinerary turning from God like the Israelites. We also grumble about getting our own needs met. In our daily fretting, we often forget God's purpose. The story of the Israelites is repeated over and over again in our own lives. And sympathetic thoughts or kindly musings are not true compassion.

God assures us that if we follow his path, He will deliver us into a better place. He will provide for us and we will lack for nothing that we need. (PHILIPPIANS 4: 19, para, NIV).

We need to follow God's roadmap instead of whining and complaining. If we let our Maker direct our path, we will journey in joy with Him at the wheel. (PSALM 119: 35, para, NIV).

What are we fretting about? We must clothe ourselves with compassion and help meet others' needs, not to continually satisfy our own selfish desires; as our Maker showers us with comfort through His word and through other believers; we in turn are to redirect the stream of His mercy to others. We are not to hoard God's love, but to overflow with the good news of his compassion to all. Sharing one's goods is how people relate to each other. Humbly sharing with others helps us to serve them better.

Clothe yourself with humility. God apposes the proud but favors the humble. Therefore, humble yourself under God's mighty hand, that He may lift you up in due time. (1 PETER 5: 3-6, para, NIV).

The more familiar a situation is, the more valuable or smooth it should be. As we reflect, the hard thing to understand is that faith and love are the sure things in our lives whereby growing up means we must grow to be more like a child, trusting simply in the goodness and complete knowledge of our Father who has our best interest at heart.

Suffice it to say, God conquers evil with good. He does that by pouring out His limitless grace upon us so that if we sin, His grace becomes greater than our sin.

The law was added so that the trespass might increase. Where sin is, the lesson of perspective allows us to enter into episodes and happenings that alter the lives of the world and its inhabitants forever. We join the humble people who welcome what we need most – a new perspective.

"Within my heart a burning bush,
Within a mountain smoking;
This flesh of mine a temple veil,
The wondrous Presence cloaking;

Within this broken earthenware,
A high and holy treasure;
Oh, mystery of mysteries!
Oh, Grace beyond all measure.

"The Lord is in His holy house,
Mysterious habitation.
I feel his presence here within,
And offer my oblation.

Keep burning, incense of my soul!
Keep cleansing me, O Lover!
I want to serve and praise my God
Forever and ever.

(Source: Anne Ortlund, WOMEN'S DEVOTIONAL BIBLE, p. 1100).

"Compassion is active and requires action."

(Source: Barbara Bush, wife of President George H.W. Bush, para.)

True compassion (love) is personal and active involvement expresses God's merciful heart in words and deeds.

"With the divine power he possessed, Jesus could have met the multitude's needs merely by forming a thought or speaking a command. He could even have done it from heaven without coming to earth. But his compassion caused him not only to come and live and die among us, but also to touch the lepers, (MARK 1:40-41,NIV) and blind men, (MATTHEW 20: 34, NIV), and take little children in his arms, (MARK: 10: 13-16, NIV).

MY CHOICE TO ACCEPT LOVE

When I was twenty years old, a senior in college, and had everything to live for, my mother died after two months of lying in a hospital bed in a coma. She was a brilliant woman with many talents. She completed her degree in music at Cheyney State college, and a degree in education at Delaware State University. She was a teacher, a writer, a poet, a musician but first of all, a great mother to us and compassionate wife to our father. She was a humble person and loved all persons and was greatly loved.

Her death was a moment in my life that dramatically changed the rest of my life forever. I was especially close to my mother, and took her death very hard. In my loneliness, I searched for answers to so many painful questions: why did God let my mother die at the age of fifty? Where was He when she was taking her last breath? In fact, where was I? In college, in class.

My mother had taught me to read Scriptures every night since I was a little girl. I had to begin making all my decisions and choices on my own after she was gone. I had to make a choice. I could turn from God, blaming Him for my mother's death or turning to Him, accepting his offer to love me and comfort me.

As I read more and more, I stumbled on a phrase that stuck with me: God is a "Father to the fatherless" (PSALM 6: 5,NIV), and a mother to the motherless, (para). I began praying constantly, "If You will be my mother, I will be your child."

I began once more bringing my gifts to the alter and to realize that we have to navigate good and evil together. Death is conquered by life. We will have both in our lives but hang on, there is always hope. We want normal to come; normal is not coming, but Jesus is. Stay connected and cling to him. We will grow again. Therefore, we must not be afraid of Satan's drives.

What good is a man if he cannot help keep someone else out of hell?

It is written, "I believe, therefore I have spoken."

With that same spirit of faith, we know that the one who raised the Lord Jesus from the dead will

also raise us with Jesus and present us with you in His presence. All this is for your benefit, so that the grace that is reaching more and more people may cause thanksgiving to overflow to the glory of God.

Therefore, we do not lose heart. Though outwardly we are wasting away, yet inwardly we are being renewed day by day. For our light and momentary troubles are achieving for us an eternal glory that far outweighs them all. So, we fix our eyes not on what is seen, but by on what is unseen. For what is seen is temporary, but what is unseen is eternal. (2 CORINTHIANS 4: 13-18, NIV).

Anna L. Waring wrote this poem:
In heavenly love abiding,
No change my heart will fear;
And safe is such confiding,
For nothing changes here.
The storm may roar without me,
My heart may low be laid,
But God is round about me,
And can I be dismayed?

Wherever He may guide me,
No fear shall turn me back,
My Shepherd is beside me,
And nothing shall I lack.
His wisdom ever wakes,
His sight is never dim,
He knows the way He takes,
And I will walk with Him.

Our Creator is ever present. (para).
Green pastures are before me,
Which yet I have not seen;
Bright skies will soon be o'er me,
Where darkest clouds have been.
My hope I cannot measure,
My path to life is free,
My Savior is my treasure,
And He will walk with me.

(Source: WOMEN'S DEVOTIONAL BIBLE).

Plan your work for today and every day. Then work your plan. Going above and beyond, take responsibility for yourself and others, aim high and lead the way and strive for excellence. Success begins with yourself; quality is your own responsibility. To receive success and happiness, you must do the right thing. Don't try to fool anyone. Help others to grow. Never stop believing. Also being careful is important. But follow your dreams and PRAY.

LOVE PRECEDES DISCIPLINE

After praying these thoughts over many years, I realized that my Creator has been faithful to His word, protecting me and providing for my every need. I will never regret my decision to trust God.

As I rounded the curve in the road, I was learning to really make my own choices and decisions. My experiences underscored the importance of those moments of decision-making as a young adult of twenty – years old. I made a significant choice. Moments when the choice to walk with God, or to go my own way, has had consequences for my entire life. I have felt His closeness and compassion, as my Father draws closest, whispering love and hope in my heart. Now I know, LOVE DOES NOT KEEP SCORE!

For days and years, I was deep in thought. I had experienced pruning before and knew there was surely more to come. Pruning is real and painful. As I considered what God had cut away from my life, I realized that what had been pruned away was not the complete story. Whether the pruning happens to a person or a grapevine, what is left is as important as what has been cut away.

God said, "Never will I leave you; never will I forsake you.

So, we say with confidence, "The Lord is my helper; I will not be afraid. What can man do to me? (HEBREWS 13: 5-6, NIV).

Through Jesus, let us continually offer to God a sacrifice of praise - the fruit of lips that confess his name. And do not forget to do good and to share with others, for which sacrifices God is pleased. (HEBREWS 13: 15-16, para., NIV).

THE LOVE OF GOD!

I know that God loves me. I wish that I could say that all is well and I could laugh in the face of all adversity. Yet, there is something that I can do; something deep inside my heart. Even though I sob into my pillow at night, then lay awake unable to breathe through my nose, wondering what will happen to me next, God's love gives me the courage to get up each morning and make it through another day.

I hold on to these words when I feel abandoned and totally alone: "Never will I leave you; never will I forsake you!"

God allows us to go through challenges and hardships so that we can be molded into who He called us to be. Sometimes it is easy to praise God for the victories and triumphs in our lives, without acknowledging that the growth in our character often comes through times of struggles. What could possibly be delightful about hard times?

The prophet Zephaniah, early in Josiah's reign and before his reforms, (2 CHRONICLES 34: 1-13,) prophesies about a coming devastating day of the Lord. But he promises a wonderful future to those who humble themselves - seek the Lord and live righteously. He addressed His people who were in trouble. There was so much corruption among them as is now in the twenty-first century. Zephaniah announced that God's judgment was coming soon. So, remember that a day of judgment is coming, but you can escape by turning to the Lord, Jesus Christ. (ZEPHANIAH 3: 1-8, NIV).

I have cut off nations; their strongholds are demolished. I have left their streets deserted, with no one passing through. Their cities are destroyed; no one will be left – no one at all. I say to the city, surely you will fear me and accept correction. (v. 3:7).

Then I will purify the lips of the people, that all of them may call on the name of the Lord and serve him shoulder to shoulder from beyond the rivers of Cush, my worshipers, my scattered people, will bring me offerings.

On that day, you will not be put to shame for all the wrongs you have done to me, because I will remove from this city those who rejoice in their pride.

Some of our hidden strengths come from knowing where our home is. What did the Israelites feel was joy when they went back to Jerusalem after being exiled. (para).

We were like men who dreamed.
Our mouths were filled with laughter.
Our tongues were filled with joy.

(PSALM 126: 1-2, para, NIV).

In the Scriptures, James instructs us to "consider it pure joy" when we "face trials of many kinds" (JAMES 1:2, NIV).

I hold on to these words in such times that I feel homesick, desolate, unwanted, forlorn and empty. Satan uses these occasions to tempt me to fall; but God uses the same occasions to make me stronger. When I am willing to reach out to God and His reassuring words, He faithfully holds me up.

MATTHEW 1: 23, "the virgin will be with child….and they will call him Immanuel, which means "God with us."

By staying grounded in the Living Christ, we can persevere through any challenge, growing stronger and allowing the fruit of the spirit to blossom in our lives. (GALATIANS 5: 22-23, NIV).

I am thankful that God holds me up, especially in my most vulnerable moments and His love never keeps score.

GOD BLESS YOU IS MY PRAYER!

CHAPTER 9

GOD WORKS IN OUR LIVES

G od comes through for us in times of trouble, giving help to the helpless and hopeless. When we are desperately in need of help, CHECK OUT GOD!
Let us look at Elijah in his great time of need.

Elijah was afraid and ran for his life. When he came to Beersheba in Judah, he left his servant there, while he himself went a day's journey into the desert. He came to a broom tree, sat down under it and prayed that he might die.

"I have had enough, Lord," he said. "Take my life, Lord. I am no better than my ancestors."

Then he lay down under the tree and fell asleep.

All at once an angel touched him and said, "Get up and eat." He looked around, and there by his head was a cake of bread baked over hot coals, and a jar of water. He ate and drank and lay down again.

The angel of the Lord came back a second time, and touched him and said, "Get up and eat, for the journey is too much for you."

So, he got up and ate and drank. Strengthened by that food, he traveled forty days and forty nights until he reached Horeb, the mountain of God. There he went into the cave and spent the night. (1 KING 19: 3-9, NIV).

TAKING ADVICE

The Bible has much to say about taking advice. Proverbs denotes, "The wise listen to advise and only a fool fails to heed it. (PROVERBS 12:15, NIV).

A truthful witness gives honest testimony, but a false witness tells lies.

Reckless words pierce like a sword, but the tongue of the wise brings healing.

Truthful lips endure forever, but a lying tongue lasts only a moment.

A prudent man keeps his knowledge to himself, but the heart of fools blurt out folly.

The Lord detests lying lips, but He delights in men who are truthful. (PROVERBS 12: 22, NIV).

PRESCRIPTION FOR DISCOURAGEMENT

Many times, we have felt discouraged and said as Elijah did, "I have had enough, Lord."

God sends an angel to show that you are not alone. When lonely and discouraged, ask for his help. Trust Him and he will respond with whatever you need. He works through the Holy Spirit. Let the Spirit speak to your heart and He will show you his ways.

In John 13:21, the Scripture ushers Jesus into trouble in the spirit. In an act we can scarcely comprehend, at the Last Supper in his friends' – Mary and Martha's home, Christ served Judas, his betrayer, bread.

The account reads: "As soon as Judas had taken the bread, he went out. And it was night." (JOHN 13: 30, NIV).

When it seemed as though the darkness was winning, God faced His darkest hour and defeated it. In our dark nights, He walks with us. It will not always be night.

And then there was Peter as a perfect example. The Lord tells Peter he will deny him three times before morning. (MATTHEW 26:33-35, para, NIV).

There were particular for-ordained activities that we only need to believe that God the Father knew and revealed to Jesus about Peter's character. In that day, anyone who knew Peter's character could have predicted that under certain highly pressured circumstances, he would act the way he did. Peter had just made the typically proud claim to Jesus: "I will never desert you."

But Peter, as other Jews believed, had always believed that the Messiah would be a military leader who would not suffer but would vanquish his enemies. This explains why Peter appeared so courageous when the miracle-working Jesus was around, but turned into a complete coward after Jesus was arrested. Peter's false dream of what Jesus was going to do, and what Peter, himself, would be alongside Jesus was shattered.

From that time on, Jesus began to explain to his disciples that HE must go to Jerusalem and suffer many things at the hands of the elders, chief priests and teachers of the law, and that he must be killed and on the third day be raised to life.

Peter took him aside and began to rebuke him. "Never, Lord!" he said. "This will never happen to you."

Jesus turned and said to Peter, "Get behind me, Satan! You are a stumbling block to me; you do not have in mind the things of God, but the things of men.

Then Jesus said to his disciples, "If anyone would come after me, he must deny himself and take up his cross and follow me. For whoever wants to save his life will lose it; but whoever loses his life for me will find it. What good will it be for man if he gains the whole world, yet forfeits his soul? For the Son of Man is going to come in his father's glory with his angels, and then he will reward each person to what he has done. I tell you the truth, some are standing here will not taste death before they see the Son of Man coming in his kingdom. (MATTHEW 16: 21-28, para, NIV).

Moreover, God saw past Peter's false bravado and knew the effect Jesus' arrest would have on Peter. The Lord lovingly used this knowledge to teach this valuable lesson about love and servant leadership to Peter, a future pillar of the Christian church. God was a part of the orchestration of the events that happened that night.

Three times Peter had his character squeezed out of him so that, after the resurrection, he might three times have Christ's character squeezed into him. (para).

It is no coincidence that three times the resurrected Christ asked Peter "Peter, do you love me?" Thus, he is telling Peter to feed his sheep after each refrain and concluding with a prophecy about how Peter would die a martyr's death just as He did. (JOHN 21: 15-19, NIV).

GREAT IS THE LORD

Great is the Lord and He is most worthy of praise; His greatness no one can fathom. One generation will comment your works to another; they will tell of your mighty acts. They will speak of the glorious splendor of your majesty; and I will meditate on your wonderful works.

They will tell of the power of your awesome works; and I will proclaim your great deeds.

They will celebrate your abundant goodness and joyfully sing of your righteousness. The Lord is gracious and compassionate, slow to anger and rich in love.

The Lord is good to all; He has compassion on all He has made. (PSALM 145: 3- 9, NIV).

We must listen and trust him and his answers are pure and right. He loves you as he leads you to a life of holiness daily. God is ageless and loves us unconditionally and exuberantly with a love that never fails or falters.

A CHILD'S DISCOVERY

A child was sitting on her grandfather's lap and patting his head.

"Grandpa, what happened to your hair," as he was completely bald.

"I lost it as years went by," said the grandfather.

Pulling her hair out of its braids, she said, "I'll just have to give you some of mine," as she hugged him.

Love never keeps score as Jesus Christ showed us that God's plan was unfolding as He ordained it. This child loved her granddaddy so deeply that she was willing to give up a part of herself.

Joyce Meyer, in her book, REDUCE ME TO LOVE, said, "When we make a true commitment to walk in love, it usually causes d huge shift in our lifestyle. Many of our ways, our thoughts, our conversation, our habits, have to change. Love is tangible; it is not just an emotional feeling, a spiritual thing that cannot be seen or touched. It is evident to everyone who comes in contact with it."

A love journey does not come easily or without personal sacrifice. Each time we choose to love someone, it will cost us something.-time, money and effort. That is why we are told to count the cost before we make the commitment. (LUKE 14:25-33, para, NIV).

Lepers were the standard outcast of Jesus' time on earth. They were some of the pictures of fallen people in a fallen world. They lived a life of shame, isolation, sorrow and anguish. Suffice it to say,

Matthew provides this picture and background for Jesus' extraordinary encounter with a leper.

A man with leprosy came and knelt before Jesus and said, "Lord, if you are willing, you can make me clean."

Jesus violated every social and religious prohibition of the day as he healed the leper by touching him. This was one of the things that was absolutely not done for a leper.

Jesus reached his hand and touched the man. "I am willing," he said. "Be clean! Immediately the leper was cleansed of his leprosy.

THE COST OF BEING A DISCIPLE

Large crowds were traveling with Jesus, and turning to them, he said,

"If anyone comes to me and does not hate his father and mother, wife and children, his brothers and sisters – yes, even his own life – he cannot be my disciple.

Suppose one of you wants to build a tower. Will he not first sit down and estimate the cost to see if he has enough money to complete it? For if he lays the foundation and is not able to finish it, everyone who sees it will ridicule him, saying, "This fellow began to build and was not able to finish." (LUKE 14: 25-30, NIV).

WHAT CAN BE BETTER?

What have we learned about Christ that we want someone else to know?

Timothy was a child when his mother, Eunice and grandmother, Lois taught and influenced him in his faith. He was a young adult when he

met the apostle Paul who invited Timothy on a mission journey because he saw the potential in Timothy's service for God. (2 TIMOTHY 1:5, para, NIV).

Paul became Timothy's mentor in ministry and life. He encouraged him to study, and put his faith and trust in God.

Paul wrote, "We have put our trust in the living God, who is the Savior of all people. Jesus is our hope and the Savior of the world. What can be better than that!" (1 TIMOTHY 4: 10, para, NIV).

LEARN ABOUT CHRIST!

CHAPTER 10

A DEFEAT LED TO VICTORY

n Matthew 6: 10, Jesus is telling his disciples to pray to the Father
with an understanding of growing in oneness with God. We must
have the same attitude of heart that Jesus had in mind when he
taught his disciples to pray to the Father, "Your will be done on earth
as it is in heaven." (NIV).

Jesus himself expressed that same attitude a few hours before his
death. He concluded an agonizing prayer session in Gethsemane – a
time when He even asked the Father to let him avoid the cross with
these words: "Nevertheless, not my will, but Yours be done." (LUKE
2: 42, NIV).

This surrender, after an intense, honest struggle, kept him in a
spirit of oneness with his Father.

OUR DEFEATS AND VICTORIES

My husband, Bertrand and I are witnesses to many defeats and victories.
In February, 1963, I was preparing to leave the Atlanta University
School of Social Work and return home to Delaware to teach. I had

studied at Atlanta University for one and a half years and was about to complete my final semester. I had just returned to Atlanta from doing my field placement in Cincinnati, Ohio. This field placement began in August 1962 and concluded in February, 1963.

When I returned to Atlanta University, I learned that I had lost my two-year scholarship the last semester. I was to study and complete my last three courses, which included writing my thesis, and two courses on doing research and perfecting my writing skills. But I had no means to pay my fees for the last semester of my graduate study. I only had to finish writing my thesis and take a final examination to conclude my Master's Degree at the Atlanta University School of Social Work.

I learned much later that my supervisor at the Social Work agency in Cincinnati, Ohio wrote a letter to my Dean at the School of Social Work, requesting that I do another semester at the Cincinnati agency. My dean took this to mean that I had not completed my work there.

This supervisor, Mr. Sells, was in the hospital for two months and, also bedridden at home due to a serious accident. He only returned to the Cincinnati Social Work agency two weeks before my "field placement" assignment was completed.

Little did I know that God was setting the stage for my victory in life. Where could I turn for comfort and understanding of what was happening to me. It was not defeat but success and overcoming my lose.

My mother had said to me many times when I was upset, "Success is the best revenge." I took that to heart and trained my own children and grandchildren to think that way. My oldest son, Bertrand, II, repeats this saying to me often. He has had many successes and failures.

Despondent at the point of losing my scholarship, I informed Bertrand Griffin, my fiancé, of my plans to return home to Delaware and get a teaching job to earn enough money to finish my Master's degree in Social Work. With my scholarship given to a freshman male student, I had to move out of the resident hall and leave the campus.

Bertrand did not want me to leave Atlanta. He said, "Marry me now so we can be together. We can work something out. When he saw that I was procrastinating, he said, "Marry me next Saturday or give me back my ring." (We laugh about that statement all the time).

I was hurt by his statement, but I accepted his second proposal. I was about to do the unimaginable, marry someone I knew only slightly, had seen only three times and had only written to him a period of seven months while I was away from him in Cincinnati performing duties as a student in what seemed like another country, a real cold country.

Following Bertrand's suggestion and wisdom, that next week-end we got married on March 23, 1963. We had thirty dollars between us, (my money). He had spent his on a bouquet of flowers and the marriage certificate for our wedding. After our small wedding and a larger reception sponsored by our pastor's wife, we had a week-end honeymoon in a barrowed apartment given to us by seminary friends who moved for that period to give us space.

We first walked to a bank on Monday after the wedding and placed our money into a joint account. Then we both had dormitory rooms we had to move out of and went to stay with one of Bertrand's seminary friends. We were almost homeless with suit cases of clothes.

After we moved out the two different dormitories, Bertrand went to the Dean of the Gammon Theological Seminary where he was a student and requested an apartment in the Gammon Apartment building. This was granted to him. However, we had to wait for over a week before we moved because the apartment had to be cleaned and painted.

I went with Bertrand to the same Dean, Dr. John Winn, and requested help in finding a job in the city of Atlanta. This was granted and I received a job working at the YMCA a few days later. I worked one night and realized that I could not work there. I would have to work every night, plan programs for young men and teen -age boys. My husband would have to go with me every night and stay until midnight. I would have to work from two o'clock in the afternoon until mid-night. Bertrand had to study every night and write his thesis.

I gave up that job, explaining that I could not accept it and never returned. The next day Dean Winn called me to his office and told me he found out how strenuous the job at the YMCA would be on both my husband and me. He offered me a scholarship to attend the Gammon Theological Seminary at the Interdenominational Theological Center.

A full scholarship!

Time and time again, we have learned over and over again that our human knowledge will never be enough to rescue us from pain and suffering and evil. (PROVERBS 4: 14-15, NIV).

Despite our best knowledge and remarkable insights, we really have no idea what makes us stumble. Wisdom teaches us what to do with understanding. True wisdom, which we desperately need, comes from God. Our knowledge always falls short, but His wisdom provides what we need.

Hermut Thielicke wrote "Thou understands my prayer better than I understand it myself." (Source: ROMANS 8:26, (KJV).

Thou knowest most whether I need hunger or bread. Whatever may come, I will say, "Yes, dear Lord." (MATHTHEW 15:27, KJV).

For I know that in everything, no matter what it may be, "Thy will" gives me fulfillment-beyond my asking and my comprehension.

Jesus said to his disciples, "My food is to do the will of Him who sent me." (JOHN 4: 34, NIV).

And we are echoing the Lord's prayer in Gethsemane. Whether or not He gives us bread or a job or a mate or a child, or a scholarship, His will must be done. His way is best.

Dr. John Winn, President of the seminary, offered me a full scholarship and registration fees for that semester. I readily accepted, happily paid my fees with the seminary scholarship and began attending classes on the quarter system at Gammon Theological Seminary with my husband. I was given a reduced study program because I was starting late and had to catch up to the other students. I worked hard, prayed a lot and succeeded in completing my course of study that Spring semester.

That is why we must get wisdom and get understanding and pray a lot. The next semester, I took a full course of study at Gammon Theological Seminary.

Dr. Norman Vincent Peale said, "When pain strikes, we often ask the wrong questions, such as "Why me? The right questions are:

"What can I learn from this?"

"What can I do about it?"

"What can I learn in spite of it?"

There were several glitches to this wonderful turn of events. Many of us carry scars that others cannot see or understand. There was no family to lean on: my mother had died two years earlier, my three brothers were in the Navy but had their own families and living expenses, my two younger sisters were in middle school and high school and my father was working out of town and at home only late at night.

There was no money between my husband and me to eat and travel to class. The old Gammon Apartment building was way across town in Atlanta from the Interdenominational Theological Center where classes were held.

My oldest brother had just sent me twenty dollars because I had just lost my glasses. I could not ask him for more help because he was in the Navy with low pay and had a wife and several children.

My husband did not want to ask his family for financial help. They had given him money to assist him in getting back in the seminary that Fall and Spring semesters.

"Life can be difficult and you may have many trials. But when you put your trust in God's hands, you can embrace life's trials. You will know that He can transform you and your faith will produce the beautiful fruit of endurance." (Peale, para).

Over the years, we just may be in the wrong place at the right time. We had practically nothing, but we had a place to come in out of the cold and a place to lay our heads.

We continued praying and were encouraged by the way David prayed to the Lord.

Without being asked, my mother-in -law, Annie Griffin, knew we were having financial trouble. Later I learned that she had bought my wedding ring. But I did know this fact at that time.

Then, she sent us food and money along with it. She also sent us a Sears card to buy household items and clothes. We did not have to ask for help. We were grown and did not want to act like children.

Susan L. Lenzkes said in the form of a poem:

THAT'S A MOUTHFUL:

Don't look now, Lord!
I don't want you to see me,
Standing here with my big foot
Crammed in my mouth.

Don't worry, child,
If I didn't love you
Just as much with your
Foot in your mouth,
I would hardly ever get a
chance to love you.

Bertrand did not want to ask for help but received these blessings anyway; his mother went to their Methodist church they attended in Alexandria, Louisiana, and asked for donations for him to continue in school. This was such a blessing. We tried with all our might to focus on the loving care of our precious mother, who knew her son needed help in his first weeks of marriage. Our earthly mother and heavenly Father, knew that they could lead us to brighter days. We asked God to help us live our lives aligned with His will. We began our marriage to live a blessed life of purpose and perseverance. We were looking ahead to our future and doing everything we could to achieve our goals.

We look back on those days, sixty-one years ago of marriage with its usual ups and downs. There were so many moments of anguish and pain, but more moments of gratefulness and joy. Early mornings can be painful. When everything is quiet, worries surface.

It was in the desert that "the angel of the Lord" met Hagar, an Egyptian maidservant of Sarai, (who was carrying Abram's child and was being mistreated by Sarai) said, "The Lord has heard of your misery."

The angel of God gave Hagar guidance on what to do. And He assured her of what the future would hold. She learned the name of God-El Roi – the God who see you. (GENESIS 16: 4-13, para, NIV).

There were financial concerns and studies to worry about. It was difficult but I knew God saw us and gave us strength and saw our needs. He let us experience His guidance each day.

The apostle John describes our future as "a new heaven and a new earth. (REVELATION 21: 1, NIV).

We thanked God every day and believed in His power to help us. Things began to open up for us as God helped us to believe in our goals and gave us the courage to pursue our goals according to His will.

He is the one you praise; He is your God, who performed for you those great and awesome wonders we saw with our own eyes. (DEUTERONOMY 10: 21, NIV).

Thank God that comfort and love are always available to us.

> SUFFICE IT TO SAY, LOVE DOES NOT KEEP SCORE.

PART TWO

WHAT'S LOVE GOT TO DO WITH OUR LIVES?

CHAPTER II

HISTORY REPEATS ITSELF

We know only in part, and we prophesy only in part: but when the complete comes, the partial will come to an end. (1 CORINTHIANS 13: 9-10, NRSV).

Many people say that history repeats itself. Often, I feel that my relationship with God and people has not changed very much over the years. But looking back, and establishing a reference point, I can see there have been quite a few changes, although at times they may have been slight.

My relationship with God is closer now, my knowledge of God's way is greater now than it was, but not as complete as it will be.

The process of being perfected is like a gradual sunset that has a slow transition in hues. The process and changes are there, but we need to be still and see the chances in order. Day by day, little by little, we see with a new perspective and know God better. We acknowledge how far we have come and see how far others have come.

MOTHER! MOHER!

An elderly woman, Dorothy, was sitting on her porch at her son's home. The son, Lonnie, came home from work and asked, "Mother, why are you so quiet? You usually are jolly and frivolous and fun-loving when I come home."

The mother replied, "God is leading me beside still waters." (PSALM 23: 2, NRSV).

"Mother, you are stronger than you know; I know father is constantly on your mind, especially since he died two months ago. I know you are going through heartache and struggles, because I feel the hurt, too. You are on a different journey -feeling lost, lonely and weak. But remember you have a great Provider who protects you and guides you. We have gotten through many touch times that has changed our lives for the better. We often do not know how much strength and power we have and we think we can not make it through the night. But joy comes in the morning. Do not give up; your strength is on the way."

"It was great sacrifices to care for Daddy as you were his main care-giver. But do not forget the great things and times we have had together. I am here to tell you that at this very moment, no matter what you are going through and how you feel, abandoned and unwanted, friendless and rejected, God knows how strong you are, and He will pick you up from your burdens and see you through this dark hour."

Give thanks to the Lord, for He is good; His love endures forever. Who can proclaim the mighty acts of the Lord or fully declare His praise?

Blessed are they who maintain justice, who constantly do what is right. Remember me, O Lord, when you show favor to your people, come to my aid when You save them; that I may enjoy the prosperity of your chosen ones, that I may share in the joy of your nation and join Your inheritance in giving praise. (PSALM 106: 1-5, NIV).

Lonnie continued, "We need quiet time to contemplate still waters because oftentimes, we need to be thus led by God. Our lives become turbulent, our way rocky and rough. Our Maker can bring into our lives such quiet moments. Sometimes we do not know our own strength until our time to use it. It lies dormant within us and emerges only when we need it most. When we do need it, we find that we have much more power than we think we have. God sees and God cares. He can bring our strength to the surface. You will look back one day and see just how strong you really are."

The son was holding his mother's hand and squeezed it as she squeezed out a tear. Lonnie was showing his love and God's understanding to his mother. She felt both.

"God is in charge of all things," Lonnie said. "God's Word and Spirit can comfort our grieving hearts so that we will be able to say like the psalmist:

"The Lord is my strength and my song. He has become my salvation. (PSALM 118: 14, NIV).

I may walk before the Lord in the land of the living; I am His servant. Praise the Lord!

Lonnie felt like he was preaching to his mother as she had taught him many things about God and His saving grace. He was an only child now that his younger brother had died from the tragedy of a "hit and run" accident. He was a teenager, thirteen - years- old, and felt secure until this tragedy hit their family.

He prayed hard many nights because he felt that he partially caused the accident. His brother and he were running on the sidewalk and Lonnie ran across the street. His brother, Norman, only eight-years-old, darted across the street with him and was struck by a speeding car. The car kept going and Norman died on the spot in Lonnie's arms. The family suffered greatly from this tragedy. Lonnie was forced to reach deep into his spiritual well-being, but he came up lacking.

He felt that God had abandoned him. He wanted God to remove the pain, but it would not go away. He was carrying a deep scar and sense of responsibility that others could not see. He had much more compassion for others but could not heal his own mental health issues.

Lonnie could not depend on tangible miracles to ease the heartache, but simply discover the magnitude of God's love and learn to know God on a deeper level. He could not depend on daily circumstances for proof of the Savior's love and approval. He needed to learn that the love of God transcends both good and bad circumstances. Then he found a Scripture that spoke directly to him:

I have loved you with an everlasting love; I have drawn you with loving kindness. (JEREMAIH 31: 3, NIV).

His mother had taught Church School at their church for many years and as a young man, he too had taught children about the Bible. He thought he really understood how much God cared for them.

Whatever is true, whatever is honorable, whatever is just; whatever is pure, whatever is lovely, whatever is gracious, if there is any excellence, if there is anything worthy of praise, think about these things. (PHILIPPIANS 4: 8, NIV).

The loss of one son, the loss of a mate and the thought of now being a single parent is enough to keep Dorothy sobbing forever. She must find the courage to continue with life.

Dorothy told Lonnie, "I feel like I could cry forever. I miss your Daddy so much and Leanard, your brother, too, that I hurt inside. I wonder if my life will ever be the same again. I have lost a child and now a dear husband and feel comfortless and overwhelmed with grief.

I know that God's Word gives hope when we feel utterly alone and hopeless. We can take comfort in knowing that our Creator does not allow a trail in our lives that is too great for us to bear. (1 CORINTHIANS 10: 13, NIV).

We can be assured that death does not conquer those who die in Christ. (1 CORINTHIANS 15: 22, 53- 56, NIV).

She knows that joy will follow her sorrows.

God wants us to participate in this love relationship because it is the foundation of life. God's love is everlasting, unchanging, forever. We can continue to believe it even though we have lived through hardships and trials, we must never lose our awareness of God's love for us.

Restore to me the joy of your salvation. (PSALM 51: 12, NIV).

You will grieve, but your grief will turn to joy, and no one will take away your joy. (JOHN 16: 20-22, NIV).

The Psalmist turns to the only one who will dry all our tears; the one who carries all our sorrows; the man acquainted with grief. (ISAIAH 25: 8, 53: 3-4, NIV).

Even the terrible destruction and the traumatic aftermath of death form those who mourn under His lordship. His Word and Spirit will comfort our heart as we call on the Lord's name.

David wrote in Psalm 6:

O Lord, do not rebuke me in your anger,
Or discipline me in your wrath.
Be merciful to me, Lord, for I am faint.
O Lord, heal me, for my bones are in agony.
My soul is in anguish.
How long, O Lord, how long.
Turn, O Lord, and deliver me;
Save me because of your unfailing love.
(PSALM 6: 1-4, NIV).

We can be encouraged by David's actions as he responded to his pain. During his overwhelming suffering, he cried out to God. He wrote of his own struggles, penning raw and honest words. He was in agony, anguish and was worn out from groaning. His bed was wet from drenched tears.

"How long," he cried?

Dr. James K. Dew, Jr., President of New Orleans Baptist Theological Seminary, ruminated in his book, LET THIS MIND BE IN YOU, "The world is filled with greed, pride, and selfishness, and it is terribly broken as a result. As servants of the Lord, we are called to enter into this brokenness. This calling requires humility, compassion, and servanthood in those who do God's will." (p.10, para.)

Pouring out his heart, David prayed for healing and mercy. When we bow before our Way-maker with our needs and our requests, we think we are the initiators. It may be that all prayers and supplications are in direct response to Him.

David was confident that God would hear his cry and would act in His time. Because of who our Creator is, there is hope and restoration for us. God can give us peace of mind and rest in our soul.

"Behold, I stand at the door and knock" is the key that opens the door to prayer. How does Christ knock? Through the conditions and circumstances of our experience and needs that drive us to Him in prayer.

Our perspective is like looking through a pinhole. We cannot see the whole picture. If we could, we would see that what we long for may not be good for us or for those we love.

HANNAH'S STORY

Hannah of the Old Testament knew what it was like to feel rejected by God. (I SAMUEL 1: 1-18, NIV.)

Sometimes it seems that God has put us on hold; however, He may be doing great things in our lives. However, our deepest most cherished request is not being granted. We know He is still there, but He is simply not responding.

Hannah was barren in a day when childlessness was considered a sign of God's displeasure. Conversely, the other wife of Elkanah, Peninnah, had borne Elkanah several children. To make matters worse, Peninnah took cruel pleasure in mocking Hannah's barrenness whenever the family made the annual trip to the house of God to offer a sacrifice. Hannah's distress lasted for years even though she was a devout and faithful woman of God. She prayed and prayed; yet God did not answer.

In God's time, God gave Hannah a son. She became the mother of Samuel who in time would become a priest and prophet who would change the course of history. (I SAMUEL 1: 19-20, para, NIV).

In God's time, Hannah's sense of spiritual rejection was changed to joy. In an overwhelming song of praise to God, Hannah showed that her deepest longing was not for a son, but to know that she was accepted and approved by God. (1 SAMEUL 2: 1-10, para, NIV).

For every generation to come, Hannah's bitterness was turned to joy. Her experience shows that what counts is not whether God immediately answers our prayer. The whole issue is whether we are humbly waiting on God's wisdom and timing.

WISDOM AND TIMING

When Hannah's story and experience is combined with the rest of the Scripture, we are able to see some of the many reasons for deferring not to our emotions but to the wisdom of God.

P. T. Forsythe wrote, "We shall come one day to a heaven when we shall gratefully see that God's great refusals were sometimes the truest answers to our prayers."

Jesus taught his disciples the prayer of patience. If you are right with God and He delays to answer your prayer, we must not misjudge or think of Him as an unkind friend. Just keep at it -prayer, that is.

KEEP AT IT; THAT IS, PRAYER!

CHAPTER 12

GET OVER YOURSELF

((My prayer is not for them alone," Jesus said. "I pray also for those who will believe in me through this message."

It is time to get over yourself. It is time to take off your shoes. You are about to move onto holy ground. Sit at Jesus' feet and learn of him. Give all you have and all you are worth to share his concerns, his love and be anxious to accomplish his purposes.

GOD TALKS WITH GOD

Above all else in the Holy Bible, John 17 is the only lengthy conversation ever recorded between God and God. When God the Father talked to God the Son, there was a long discussion between them and this literature was written by human beings on earth.

Jesus took his eleven disciples aside and prayed for them. Jesus prayed to God, "I am coming to You now, but I say these things while I am still in the world, so that they may have the full measure of my joy within them. I have given them Your word and the world has hated them.

They are not of this world any more than I am of the world. My prayer is not that you take them out of the world but that You protect them from the evil one. Sanctify them by the truth; Your Word is truth. As You sent me into the world, I have sent them into the world. (JOHN 17: 13-19, NIV).

Then he prayed for all believers. My prayer is not for them (the disciples) alone. I pray for those who will believe in me through their message, that all of them may be one, Father, just as You are in me and I am in You. May they also be in us so that the world may believe You have sent me. I have given them the glory that You have given me, that they may be one as we are one.

Father, I want those You have given me to be with me where I am, and to see my glory, the glory You have given me because you have loved me before the creation of the world.

Righteous Father, I have made You known to them and will continue to make You known in order that the love You have for me may be in them and that I, myself may be in them. (JOHN 17: 20-26, NIV).

When God the Father discusses issues with God the Son, He is mainly interested in the following: the glory of the Father and the glory of the Son, the well-being of believers; their protection, unity, joy and their sanctification, and the salvation of the world; that all may believe that God loves them and yearns for them.

We must get over ourselves and be zealous to put Him first. Forget all other competition with Him and as God said, "Remain in me" (JOHN 15: 1-11, NIV).

One thing that man fears the most is the unknown. What is unknown to us is our greatest adversary. Oftentimes, we do not know which way to turn.

As children, we use to say, "What you don't know won't hurt you." That is the greatest untruth ever told. Right now, there is so much uncertainty in the world. Day after day, month after month, Americans and people around the world have a low morale as they become busier and busier. There are so many broken people in the world and they affect others to become broken. We never think of broken pieces that can be made whole. God took our brokenness away with His perfect son, Jesus. He broke Him in order to make us whole. That is God's way.

It is quite clear that there is significant confusion and chaos in our communities, our nation and in our world. It is not due to infrastructure as much as it is due to factions. We are fragmented by many issues now more than ever before. We need to make connections between each other as we are in trouble spiritually.

Someone said, "Friendship is essential to the soul." As we trek through the wilderness, we need family, mentors, friends and the Love of God because we cannot walk or talk alone. The main calling is to trust God, deepen our love between our neighbors, ourselves and God.

Things and circumstances are changing in our lives. No matter how frustrating our lives are, we need to ask for help. At the same time, we must develop a spirit of independence and creativity. With the help of God, we must develop more understanding of ourselves and others.

Zora Neale Hurston, the author of several books, once said "There are years in our lives that ask questions and there are years that answer them."

It is not always easy to face adversity and be patient with yourself or proud of yourself. There is a time to embrace and a time to refrain from embracing. (para).

We may not be able to give our loved ones an extra measure of improved health or patience they need. It may not be within our power to give them peace and hope they desperately need to bear their burdens. But we must be led by the Spirit of God to speak to others about Jesus, the giver of true and lasting peace.

We have one purpose in life for existing. We are all connected to those who have gone on before us and will come after us. We need each other to survive because we are all of God's creation – one body.

We are designed to fit God's purpose and live in harmony and friendship. I tell my grandchildren all the time, "Friendship is the window of the soul."

Share your concerns for the well-being of your fellowman, (your fellow believers). Share your concerns for this needy world! Reach out to others!

As you share concerns with others, give your time, your gifts, yourself. Move into the heart of God and be "in sync" with him.

We must have confidence in what God wants for us. Our goal as the believer in Christ is to become one on the heart with God. When we come to him in prayer, we need to be honest with ourselves about whether our desires are His desires, whether His will is His will.

All of us are given air to breathe as a gift from God and must value ourselves and all others.

How do we as mere humans grow in this oneness with God? Certainly, we can never share in His complete understanding of all things. Yet as we pray for our daily needs, for our spouse and children and friends; as we pray for healing, or employment or guidance, we must do so with the same attitude of heart that Jesus had in mind when He taught His disciples to pray to the Father: "Your will be done on earth as it is in heaven." (MATTHEW 6: 10, NIV).

Thomas F. Lee stated in his book, THE HUMAN GENOME PROJECT, "No organism except Homo sapiens know anything of its history. The faint stirrings of instinct, operative in us are the only vestiges within all other creatures that evoke the past. The study of history as we see it, is sometimes tedious but richly instructive. Such history must be viewed in the context of a long history or tradition. It is important to realize that the unraveling of the secrets twisted into the double helix of DNA (deoxyribonucleic acid) has only just begun; discoveries will be made, technologies will improve and attention will be diverted from one gene to another as the pieces of the mosaic fit together." (p. 299).

Man is special to God. He needs to know about himself. He needs to know his history, his traditions and his worth. He needs to question fearlessly his past; challenge his beginning, starting with his universe and moving to himself. He must search better to understand himself, his diversity, and bio-diversity, his inclusion/exclusion which creates justice and injustice as well as sin and guilt in the world.

We must protect our purpose for life, not our traditions. We must consider our own natural abilities and enjoy these abilities more and learn how we can use them differently, if you have been miraculously healed of your ills. If you believe in Jesus, he has healed you spiritually. He has rescued you from your sins.

Myles Munroe, in his book, SEASONS OF CHANGE, UNDERSTANDING PURPOSE IN TIME OF PERPLEXITY, states, "Tradition may change, but purpose is permanent. The traditions of men, regardless of how sacred you may think they are or how long they have been in effect, are usually not worth dying for. Generally, traditions mean the passing down of elements of a culture from generation to generation or a body of unwritten precepts. (p. 47, para).

The English word TRADITION comes from the same Latin word that denotes trade or transaction. Trade implies an item that has been patterned. That is why you can trade it. Whenever a business or individual develops a trade, they have patterned something that they wish to export to other persons or businesses.

Even though most cultures, religious systems and businesses have something that is good and worth trading, their interest must be led by the Holy Spirit and rooted in the prudent interpretation of God's Word.

Jesus told the Pharisees and Scribes that they emasculated our Creator's purpose for themselves by the insistent keeping of their traditions. We today have lost many of our traditional values and understanding of them and should discord them.

Get over yourself because the love of God does not keep score. My mother, Lettie Harper Heath, taught us that the desire to have knowledge will transcend the fear of knowing what is good or bad, good or evil. True to our past and true to our human nature, we will continue to learn how this awesome universe functions.

I picked up a book much later in life, by Charles Robert Darwin, THE ORIGIN OF SPECIES. He was born in 1809 in a small English town called Downe and published his "abstract" in 1859, detailing certain findings and theories concerning the "descent with modification" of living organism. His thesis was simple and buttressed by twenty-seven years of observations and experimentations. This bold man, a fifty – year - old biologist in poor health, stated that "living organisms have changed gradually from simple organisms over the course of time, resulting in the complexity of forms which we see and others have become extinct. The following principles are possibly emphasized by his research:

"All organisms vary one from the other. Many of these variations are to some degree inherited. Among the survivors of organisms, there will be those that may have inherited variations that have facilitated their adoption to their local environment. When scientists speak of seeking the code within our genes as a key to analyzing how human beings function, they do not do so with the intentions of denying what are deep mysteries such as the source of creativity, the sense of justice and the stirring of love." (para).

If somehow, we are able to recreate all the qualities of perfect man and perfect woman into one being, we have perhaps a faint idea of who God is. As we reflect on who God is, we see a picture of the image we see in ourselves individually. Unfortunately, that image of God often bears no resemblance to our own self-image. The reason for this is perhaps because many of us suffer from a low-self -esteem. (Ruth A. Tucker, A SELF IMAGE IN THE IMAGE OF GOD, (p. 1, para).

In 1871, Charles Darwin stated that "the weak members of civilized society propagate their kind."

Further, Dr. Thomas Lee denotes, "Billions of years have resulted in many millions of species, most of which are extinct. The living organisms on this planet now represent the tips of the branches of an enormous evolutionary tree. Every moment, our world is changing. Only one species, going by the name of Homo sapiens, has developed over the last 450, 000 million years, the ability to reason." (p. 25-26, para).

What builds a healthy self-image is when one reaches out selflessly to someone in need and gives no thought to a reward. Then a person can have a self-image that truly reflects God's image.

Talking with God is intended to be a spirited interaction between us and a living, loving Being with whom we have an intimate and growing relationship. It is hard to listen to God when we are doing all the talking.

PRAY, THEN LISTEN TO GOD.

CHAPTER 13

HOW LATE IS THE HOUR?

Without even turning on her bedside lamp, Immaculee Ilibagiza, in her book, THE BOY WHO MET JESUS, stated that she reached for her pen and paper and began jotting down the images that were still burning in her mind and taking root in her heart. She had just had a dream about a young man who was one of a million innocent victims slaughtered during the Rwanda's horrific 1994 genocide.

Segatashya's voice drifted into her dream "across the lightless abyss as if floating upon a calm breeze." (p. 1).

It was mid-November of 2010, and Segatashya had been murdered many years before. It may have been a dream, but "What I was feeling was a vivid, real and lifelike feeling as anything I had experienced during my waking hours," said Immaculee. "What Segatashya said was an urgent and passionate message."

In her dream, she was gliding above the ground as her heart pulled her toward the voice of Segatashya, which led her out of the darkness into a golden circle of light. The young teenage boy was sitting on a long bench speaking to a crowd around him.

Immaculee was happy to see Segatashya because she had known him when they were both children. He was one of the visionaries who "claimed to be having divine apparitions."

In essence, the visionaries delivered messages of love, instructing us on how to live better lives closer to God's will.

"They told us that by following the inspirational advice of those messages, our world would become a more peaceful place and our souls would be better prepared for the day when we meet Jesus at the end of our lives and called to account for our time on earth."

(Source: Ilibagiba: p.12-13).

These messages are for the entire world. They can heal our bodies, and hearten our souls. They can provide us with courage, comfort and the strength to transcend even the bleakest periods of personal sorrow and despair. Jesus came to Segatashya and shared comforting words while he himself was suffering during his own personal tragedy.

Before Jesus came to Him, Segatashya had no idea who Christ was. "That's because Segatashya was a poor, illiterate, African peasant boy who was also a pagan. He had never been inside a church or school before 1982. Therefore, his innocence made him an ideal candidate to receive messages from our Lord because he asked possibly the same questions we would ask if we met face to face with Jesus.

His questions were: "Why is it so important to love God?"

"Between God, the Holy Spirit, Mary and Jesus, whom should I love more?"

"The Bible says I should love You, Jesus, more than I love my parents."

"How can I do that, when I don't know you?"

"Why should I love my enemies, when God doesn't love his enemy, Satan?"

God answered these questions by sending lightening and thunder. We ask for miracles. God sends us miracles through unborn babies, and many other visitations.

One of the priests, Father Rwagena, in the African town of Kibeho, in Rwonda led processions of people through the towns and as they assembled, he recites such words:

"God will never deny you mercy if you have a true conversion in your heart. Jesus is telling me to tell you that life on earth lasts only a moment; but life in heaven is eternal. So, you must pray.

Remember that those who pay lip service to God and cry out, 'Oh Father, bless me!' without meaning it from their heart, or repenting for their wrongdoing, will not go to heaven.

It is those who truly love God and do his will by performing loving deeds who will be welcomed into the Kingdom of Heaven – not the pretenders and hypocrites." (p. 34).

Remember to pray with sincerity; the only way into heaven is through prayers that come from the heart. Millions of believers in that country were slaughtered. Many were ushered into heaven and have returned to tell about it, such as Segatashya. He was presented into heaven and received his assignment to speak for God.

It is a reflection of what the writer of Hebrews is saying. As we continue our journey in life, we need to "throw off everything that hinders us and the sin that so easily entangles us." (HEBREWS 12: 1-3, para, NIV).

We need to travel light to press on; as some of the mysteries of life can be the most rewarding and pleasing experiences of one's lifetime. When we are faithful to Him and receptive to his will, He will change our lives, transform our hearts and make us new again.

May my lips overflow with praise, for you teach me your decrees. May my tongue sing of your Word, for all your commands are righteous.

There are some things we cannot change but we need to get to know ourselves more and more. I feel that this poem was written for someone such as myself:

INVICTUS

Out of the night that covers me,
Black as a pit from pole to pole,
I thank whatever gods may be
For my unconquerable soul.

In the fell clutch of circumstance;
I have not winched nor cried aloud.
Under the bludgeonings of chance,
My head is bloody but unbowed.

Beyond this place of wrath and tears,
Looms but the horror of the shade,
And yet the menace of the years,
Finds and shall find me unafraid.

(Source: INVICTUS, William Ernest Henley.)

MY HEAD IS BLOODY BUT UNBOWED;
GOD DOES NOT KEEP SCORE!

CHAPTER 14

THIS MESSAGE IS FOR EVERYONE

T his message is for everyone. One day someone stood up and spoke out in public to people about Jesus; "God made it clear; this message is for everyone."

All Scripture is God-breathed and is useful for teaching, rebuking, correcting and training in righteousness, so that the servant of God may be thoroughly equipped for every good work. (2 TIMOTHY 3: 16-17 NIV).

"It was a great day: sometimes called the birthday of the church. The great wind of God's Spirit had swept through Jesus' followers and filled them with a new joy and a sense of God's presence and power."

(Source: Wright, PAUL FOR EVERYONE, p. ix).

Peter, the leader of the new church, who a few weeks earlier had been crying like a baby because he had lied and cursed and denied even knowing Jesus, found himself on his feet explaining to a huge crowd that something had happened which had changed the world forever. What God had done for him, Peter, he was beginning to do for the whole world: new life, forgiveness, new hope and power were opening up like spring flowers after a long winter. A new age had begun in which the living God was going to do new things in the world – beginning then and there with the people who were standing there with him, listening to him.

> *"This promise is for you," he said, and for your children and for everyone far away. It is not just for the person standing next to you. It is for everyone." (ACTS 2: 29, NIV).*

"Within a remarkably short time, this narrative came true to such an extent that the young movement spread throughout much of the known world; one way in which the "everyone promises" worked out was through the writings of the early Christian leaders. These short stories and letters about Jesus were widely circulated and eagerly read. They were never intended for either a religious or intellectual elite. From the beginning they were meant for everyone."

(Source: Wright, p. ix).

AFTER HATRED, LOVE

Paul was one of the teachers of love, after he taught hate. After all his shananigans, and playing with people's minds, he fell on his face and learned his lessons of love. That is as true today as it was then.

Oswald Chambers is quoted as saying, "We are at this moment, as close to God as we really choose to be."

We must celebrate making our relationships a priority by plugging into His word and taking time to share our innermost thoughts and goals which may enhance every aspect of our lives.

Sometimes we see prayer as nothing more than a ritual. A common hindrance to confident, praying is the feeling that no one is listening. We feel like the wife who is talking to her husband while he is reading the sports page of the newspaper. We may lose the sight that God is truly interested in us. Prayer is intended to be a spirited interaction between us and a living, loving Being with whom we have an intimate, growing relationship.

At one time there was a woman who came to church looking for spiritual direction. The pastor asked her what she hoped for in spiritual direction.

She answered, "I want help in understanding what is coming from God and what is coming from here: pointing to her head."

She was saying, "How can I discern what is coming from God and what is coming from me? What's distraction and what is not? What should I pay attention to?" (Martin, LEARNING TO PRAY, p. 226, para).

HOW DO I KNOW IT IS GOD?

In a good person, Satan seeks to cause gnawing anxiety, to sadden and set up obstacles. In this way the evil spirit is finding a way to unsettle your thoughts by false reasons aimed at preventing your progress.

A simple way to understand is that if you are feeling despair, hopelessness or uselessness, this is not coming from God because, as Ignatius understood, these feelings lead to preventing of progress in life.

Beware of the universal language of negative statements about yourself, such as, "Nothing will ever get better," or "Everybody hates me," or "I will never be able to change."

This is a sign of the evil spirit. "Catch yourself when you use these terms and try not to listen to those impulses."

(Source: Ignatius of Loyola, p. 8, para)

We must develop confidence in listening to God. Oftentimes we feel that God is not listening but we need to focus on Him. It is hard to listen to God when we are doing all the talking.

In time, with generations to come, our experience would show that what counts is not whether God immediately answers our prayers. The main issue is whether we are humbly waiting on God's wisdom and timing.

LOVE AND FORGIVENNESS GO TOGETHER

Love and forgiveness go together, they co-relate. As I said earlier, it is difficult to ascertain or figure our origins and genealogy as human beings or as a slave. From the very beginning it was prohibited for slaves and the enslaved peoples to trace their background or find their relatives.

Nevertheless, it is very obvious that blacks and whites came together, had common-law marriages and had children together. Many mixed-race children resulted from rape of a white man on a Black women or a couple of mixed-race parents falling in love and forgiving each other for their misdeeds.

Oral tradition, although confusing, had a significant role to play in our history and our stories. No clear-cut records were kept or documented to prove the dates of birth, marriages, deaths and name spelling of indentured servants or slaves.

As Saul promoted hatred in the earlier part of his life, he had to fall flat on his face to receive the blessing and the gift of love for another race of people or human beings.

Do not remember the rebellious sins of my youth. Remember me in the light of your unfailing love, for You are merciful, O Lord. (PSALM 25: 7, NIV).

I went to visit my sister in Delaware and went to church with her that Sunday. When I walked in the door, someone shouted my name, only they said Phyllis, my older sister's name, not mine. Surprised, I looked around and saw two ladies sitting on the back row talking. Church service had not started, so I walked back to them. One of them said, "You are Phyllis, you play the piano."

I responded," I play the piano and organ, but I am not Phyllis. I am Marian, her younger sister."

"You probably do not remember us. We are the girls who told on Phyllis, that she was pregnant and should not march in the graduation line. We told the principal the day before graduation and Phyllis got pulled off the "march -in" line. Phyllis was denied the privilege of participating in the graduation ceremony."

One of them, Norma, said, "I was pregnant, too, but I told on Phyllis to keep the heat off of me. Right after I marched in the graduation, I had a miscarriage so I never let anyone know I was pregnant. We were hoping you did not remember us."

"I remember your faces but I sang in the choir for graduation. Phyllis was a senior and I was a freshman. I went down to the choir room that night and came on the stage with the choir. Later, as my family drove home from the high school graduation, Phyllis was not in the car with us. I learned later that she did not march in the graduation, but went home to Bridgeville with a friend. I was given no more information by my mother."

"We were hoping that you did not remember us, because we were real stinkers in those days. The one named Maggie said, "I was pregnant too and was trying to cover up for myself, as well. I had my baby and she is grown now. I often think about Phyllis Heath. She was real smart. It was not my business to tell on Phyllis."

"That was then, this is now," I said.

I said, "You know God gives and gives, then He forgives! We as people get and get, then we forget. Our Master provides for our every need and we return His favor by forgetting about other's needs. God has forgiven your sins if you prayed about it. He is a forgiving God.

My younger sister, Nancy had asked me to play the organ that morning because their organist was ill. I went straight to the organ, warmed it up and began to play.

To that day, I did not know the ins and outs of what happened at Phyllis' graduation, but I forgave these ladies for Phyllis, because she was dead. They should have atoned for their misbehavior, from high school. I wanted to relieve the guilt feelings from their minds. I reminded them that we all have done things that we regret in our younger days.

I remember the incident without the details, but Jesus does not remember our sins and guilt. He has the ability to blot out our sins from His memory. This is beyond my comprehension but so is the scope of His love. Through the lens of His love, He sees me and you, then and now.

Jeremiah 31: 33-35 says "This is the covenant I will make with the house of Israel after this time," declares the Lord.

"I will put my laws in their minds and write it on their hearts. I will be their God, and they will be my people."

No longer will a man teach his neighbor or someone teach his brother, "Know the Lord, because they will all know me, from the least of them to the greatest," declares the Lord.

"For I will forgive their wickedness and will remember their sins no more."

Diane Head, in WOMEN'S DEVOTIONAL BIBLE said, "Sometimes I think my life is like my linen closet -constantly in need of cleaning, discording, rearranging and straightening. There are always a few undesirables that need to be discorded – gossip, yelling, gluttony, complaining, bitterness, fretting, jealousy, worry, pride, uncommitted struggles, impatience – all jammed way back into the corners of my closet.

Unfortunately, linen closets never clean themselves. Likewise, we cannot, by our own power, change our own lives. To bring about a permanent change of heart, we need more power than our tired, human selves can muster.

We must open the door and allow God's life-changing power to enter in, step by step, moment by moment. "He can open doors no one can shut; and He can shut doors no one can open," says my niece Terri.

He will enter in and do a good work in us. Dead-wood is cut out and a great discipline can enter in! Be prepared!

If we embrace what life has in store for us, if we embrace what is given, we will discover God's purpose for us in this new generation.

Historically, many indigenous persons have always been hard-working, dedicated, highly sensitive and zealous. However, there are so many products of oppression and brutality that have instilled in us timidity, dependency, and lack of self-confidence.

We do not trust our Creator enough to give us what we need so that we can embrace what life has in store for us. Many new possibilities may hold an exciting destiny for us. We often fail to realize our capacity to be leaders and embrace our God-given talents.

The culture we live in carries with it "the dehumanizing element that fosters dependency and robbing individuals of their creative development. This debilitating system also robs individuals of their ability for productivity."

We need to swing open wide the closet doors to our hearts and let God exert His resurrection power, tenderly and quietly cleaning and straightening our lives. There is hope for your future. He is love and love does not keep score.

Jesus said, "I have loved you with an everlasting love, I have drawn you with loving kindness."

The magnitude of His love even though sorrow and tragedy may step in, will revolutionize my life. I realize more and more that his love is everlasting and is the foundation of my life. God loves us perfectly, totally and eternally. He does not keep score.

A LOVING GOD IS ALSO A FORGIVING GOD!

CHAPTER 15

KINDNESS IS A GIFT

K indness is a gift from our Creator. It is a universal language every man, woman or child understands.

We often ask our why questions; and instead of giving us answers, God gives us Himself, the Comforter. In Luke 11, He explains himself:

> So, I say to you, ask and it will be given to you, seek and you will find; knock and the door will be opened to you. For everyone who ask receives, he who seeks finds, and to him who knocks, the door will be opened. (LUKE 11: 9-10, NIV).

> Which one of your fathers, if your son asks for a fish, will give him a snake instead? Or if he asks for an egg, will give him a scorpion? If you then, though you are evil, know how to give good gifts to your children, how much more will your Father in heaven give the Holy Spirit to those who ask Him! (vv. 11-13).

> Today we live in a world of darkness in which our secular problem-solvers are beginning to stumble. In spite of our "social-conscience," there is evidence of ignorance, illiteracy and dark imaginings.

Romans 2: 1 tells us that we as Christians are "a light for those who are in the dark." (LUKE 2: 1, NIV).

But we say, the world is so big and our lamp is so small. Yes, but we can light some part each day. Look at the star-struck heaven. Each star looks so small in a distance.

"Yet," June Muster Bacher said, "put together, these tiny jewels can light the darkest night."

Each of us is a star or a lamp, and we can make this world a better, brighter place. It all begins with the desire expressed in Michelangelo's prayer:

"God, grant me the desire to be more than I can ever accomplish."

C.S. Lewis once said, "praying for others is a "sweet duty."

After we pray for others, we must be reminded to pray for ourselves. By this time, our own needs will be put into proper perspective and we will be able to pray for ourselves more effectively.

We must think and pray: "Light your lamp. Let God send you in a new direction each day. Meet someone at the crossroads of his or her life. Give your bright face, whether you feel it or not. Gladness and joy will come."

Luke said, "No one lights a lamp and puts it in a place where it will be hidden, or under a bowl. Instead, he puts it on a stand, so that those who come in may see the light. Your eye is the lamp of the body. When your eyes are good, your whole body also is full of light. See to It then, that your body is not darkness. Therefore, if your whole body is full of light, and no part of it dark, it will be completely lighted, as when the light of a lamp shines in you." (LUKE 11: 33-36, NIV).

A kind spirit and a gentle nod benefits those individuals who are growing to succeed as human beings. It is good that one has a strong belief and conviction that all God's children should acknowledge their humanness and yield to the spiritual guidance and THE WORD.

There is a story told many time that we have heard since being children. It is the Christmas legend about the inn keeper who was kind enough to help a young couple when they had nowhere else to turn. We tell it each Christmas to our children and grandchildren.

Writer Walter Wangerin, Jr. imagines the journey this way:

"They were bound for Bethlehem, the city where King David had been born one thousand years before, because Joseph was descended from the house of David.

Mary rode the donkey. Joseph had made a rolled saddle to support Mary's back. She had nearly reached the term of her pregnancy. She was breathless and tired, having ridden on a donkey for some eighty miles, swollen hands and wrist, ankles and feet. Her long hair had lost traces of its beauty, as Mary was determined to go with Joseph to bear her child in the city of his father David.

It was in Bethlehem, a village about five miles from Jerusalem from the foothills of the Judean desert. (Marian Griffin and her husband, Bertrand and family members and a tour group of over two hundred fifty from The United Methodist Church in Louisiana visited this area in January, 2008).

In the early century, Mary and Joseph found the small community flooded with pilgrims who had come for the Census. The inn was groaning under the weight of overflow capacity, and there was no place for the young couple to sleep, let alone give birth to a child. The city of David was without shelter for the young woman who was ready to deliver.

THE BIRTH

"This son, promised by an angel, conceived by the Holy Spirit, affirmed by the then-unborn John, carried in the womb to Bethlehem and surrounded in birth by farm animals and shepherds – was the One whose name would be called "Full of Wonder", a miracle. (ISAIAH 9: 6, NASB).

Joseph apparently served as Mary's mid-wife as they delivered their baby. Joseph gives the child to his mother and she must have experienced every wonderful emotion felt by each new mother as well as felt overwhelmed by the realization that this child was the Son of God. Mary, an ordinary normal first century Jewish girl, embraced these thoughts and with obedience accepted the extraordinary implications of God's extraordinary plan for her life. (para).

"Mary treasured all these things, pondering them in her heart. (LUKE 2:19, KJV).

Over two thousand years later we are still in wonderment:

"When Mary birthed Jesus, 'twas in a cow's stall.
With Wise men and farmers and shepherds and all.
But high from God's heaven, a star's light did fall,
And the promise of ages it then did recall.

(Source: Bill Crowder, WINDOW OF CHRISTMAS, Para.).

While they were there, the days were completed for her to give birth. And she gave birth to her firstborn son; and she wrapped Him in cloths and laid him in a manger loaned to them by the innkeeper. (LUKE 2:6-7, para, NEW AMERICAN STANDARD BIBLE).

But for the innkeeper, there would have been no sympathy or compassion for the young sixteen- year -old mother. The innkeeper was considerate, kind and thoughtful. He was kindhearted, sensitive, and perceptive as well as understanding. He was in tune to all of humanity and sent a message throughout the world. This story shows the love and kindness of God which permeated and filtered through the times to eternity.

Knowing the love, strength, and wisdom shown to Mary and her child is sufficient for all of us. God's words are here for all of us, ready to draw us close, quiet our fears and empower us. His words are wise, comforting and eternal.

Should we find it hard to sleep tonight or tomorrow night, just remember the homeless family who had no beds to lie in.

WE ALL NEED HIS LOVE. AMEN.

CHAPTER 16

A JOURNEY ON FOOT

Many years ago, in the early days of our country, a weary young traveler, Daniel, set foot on the banks of the Mississippi River. At that time there was no bridge to cross over. It was winter time and the water was a hard freeze. The young man, Daniel, had to get across the mighty Mississippi River before nightfall. His family was on the other side.

Could the layer of ice hold his weight? Was it strong enough to hold him up? As he pondered this idea, terrified, he crept slowly on hands and knees across the frozen surface, fearful that he may not see the other side.

He hummed an old Negro Spiritual:

Oh, wasn't that a wide river;
That river of Jordan, Lord, wide river.
There is one more river to cross.

Verse 1
The river of Jordan is so wide,
One more river to cross;

I don't know how to get on the other side;
One more river to cross.

Verse 2
Satan is just a snake in the grass,
One more river to cross,
If you ain't mighty careful,
He will hold you fast;
One more river to cross.

Suddenly, he heard the familiar sound, a horse-drawn wagon - clop, clop with the sound of the horses' feet. When the other man in his wagon passed by, singing merrily, the young man realized that the horse drawn passenger was obviously familiar with these weather conditions, and had no doubt at all that the glacial "road" was strong enough to hold him up.

Many of us are like Daniel, the young traveler; with fear and trembling, we move along.

One thing that man fears most is the unknown. We find ourselves lapsing into the discouragement of circumstances and long for the kind of faith and power that would give us control over our physical conditions. What is unknown to us is our greatest adversary. Who or what is our adversary? Do we know our adversity? Perhaps not!

Our adversary may use other people or institutions as instruments to accomplish its (his or her) purpose.

In the Scriptures, James was calling on his readers not only to read and reflect on God's instruction, but also to do what it says.

"A complete faith," James noted, "means both knowing Scripture and putting it into action."

Who is wise and understanding among you? Let him show it by his good life, by deeds done in the humility that comes from wisdom. (JAMES 3: 13, NIV).

Do not merely listen to the Word, and so deceive ourselves. Do what it says. Anyone who listens to the Word, but do not do what it says is like a man who looks at his face in a mirror and after looking at himself, goes away and immediately forgets what he looks like. But the man who looks intently into the perfect law that gives freedom, and continues to do this, not forgetting what he has heard, but doing it, he will be blessed in what he does. (JAMES 1: 22, NIV).

Consider it pure joy, whenever you face trials of any kind, because you know that the testing of your faith develops perseverance. Perseverance must finish its work so that you may be mature and complete, not lacking in anything. If anyone lacks wisdom, he should ask God, who gives generously to all without finding fault, and it will be given him. But when he asks, he must believe and not doubt, because he who doubts is like a wave of the sea, blown and tossed to the wind. (JAMES 1: 2-6, NIV).

Matthew denotes, "Temptation and testing are two sides of the same coin. Satan uses an occasion or a person to tempt us to fall; God uses the same incident to try and make us stronger."

Then Jesus was led by the Spirit into the desert to be tempted by the devil. After fasting forty days and forty nights, he was hungry. The tempter came to him and said, "If you are the Son of God, tells these stones be become bread."

Jesus said, "It is written, man does not live by bread alone, but on every word that comes from the mouth of God." (MATTHEW 4:1 - 4, NIV).

Jesus is our constant companion, no matter where we are. He is with us in our present troubles and even prepares a place for us to live with Him forever.

Despite the uncertainty and change we might experience as citizens on this earth, we can dwell permanently in our fellowship with Him every day and everywhere. (JOHN 14: 3, para, NIV).

So, why do we so often forget that God is our keeper, will keep His promise and will bear the weight of our every load. God has promised no harm will befall us. (PSALM 91: 10, NIV).

PSALM 55: 22, states: "Cast your cares on the Lord and He will sustain you; He will never let the righteous fall. As for me, I trust You, Lord."

Our adversary has clearly been identified by our Creator:

For we wrestle not against flesh and blood, (human beings), but against principalities, against powers, against the rulers of darkness of this world, against wickedness in high places (demonic beings and forces). (EPHESIANS 6: 12, KJV).

We need more understanding of ourselves and others. It is not always easy to face an adversity and be patient with ourselves or be proud of ourselves.

Paul, in his letters to the church in Corinth states: "We are one body with many parts. The body is a unit, though it is made up of many parts, and though all the parts are many, they form one body." (1 CORINTHIANS 12:12-14, NIV).

Paul appeals to us for all times that all of us should be in agreement and harmony and that there should be no divisions among us, as in strife and confusion, but we should be in the same mind and same purpose.

As we are one body with many parts, each part has a function, but all parts of the body with working parts causes the whole body to be healthy. When one part is unhealthy, as one political party is against another, neither party can function properly.

When one part is unhealthy, hurting or suffering, then the whole "body" suffers. The whole "body" functioning properly makes the church, community, nation or world healthy and freedom abides among us.

Someone said, "Friendship is one of the essential ingredients for the soul."

As we walk through the wilderness of our lives, we need friends, mentors and the love of God because we cannot walk it alone. Our main calling is to trust God to deepen our love for others, our neighbors, our community, our nation.

Things are constantly changing in our lives and no matter how frustrating our lives are, we must develop a spirit of independence and creativity.

We have one purpose in life for existing. We are all connected to those who have gone before us and will come after us. We need each other to survive because we are all of God's creation and are one body. We are designed to fit God's purpose and live in harmony and friendship. Friendship is love and a part of the soul. We must look for love and encouragement in our daily walk. No matter how hard we try, we cannot fully comprehend God's ways. Rather than exhaustingly trying to solve life's mysteries, trust God! He will always lead you to a better life. Just trust that He knows what's best for you.

> ## TRUST GOD!

CHAPTER 17

TAKE CARE OF YOUR BODY (DON'T EAT THE WHOLE HOG)

"Don't eat the whole hog, Miss Griffin," said Arica. Arica Lavigne is one of my Cherubim Family Choir mothers at St. Mark United Methodist Church. She is teaching her three children, Jaxson, eleven-years old, Aubrey, five-years-old and Joy, their angelic little two- year- old, to eat meatless meals and glutton-free food. Jody and Arica Lavigne's children are very lively and sweet. Aubrey, at the age of four started singing solos with the Cherubim Choir; now he is five years old and can project his voice like an elephant.

When we celebrated our Cherubim Family Choir's fifty-first Anniversary last Saturday and Sunday, on October 21-22, 2023, Arica offered to prepare the food for the children's repast after their program at St. Mark United Methodist Church. This taught me much about this family which is so brilliant and precious to me. They sing together and they work and play together.

I happily accepted Arica's offer because we were also planning to have a Food and Water Distribution project for the community the Saturday before the Anniversary Worship program on Sunday.

We are trying to teach our children at an early age to have a generous heart and consider others.

Since maturity for us means taking on God's nature, you and I are called to grow mentally in our knowledge of Christ' spiritually in traits like goodness, self-control and perseverance; we must practically explore new ways to love, offer hospitality and serve each other through our gifts. (2 PETER 1-8: para, NIV).

Giving food and water as a project for the Cherubim Family Choir is one way of helping the children practice thoughtfulness toward the poor or strangers in their lives. Teaching them to pray and work with their hands is a good way of gathering early, divvying up tasks and working together, even with the children working in the community in a single day. This is a good deed for the church and each member of the Cherubim Family Choir was a part of it.

Even children make themselves known by their acts, by what they do is pure and right. Train up a child in the right way and when he is old, he will not depart from it or stray from it.

The Lord knows how to deliver the godly person out of temptation. (2 PETER 2: 9, para, NIV).

The children should set their hope in God; and not forget the works of God, but keep his commandments and should not be like their ancestors, a stubborn and rebellious generation.

That day as we were planning our activities for the Annual Cherubim Family Choir Anniversary, I learned that the Lavigne family were vegans; they do not eat meat. Arica explained that she and her husband, Jody Lavigne had decided to not to ruin their three children's health by serving them meat.

That was a lesson I had learned as a child because my mother did not let us eat much meat. She taught my siblings and me to help her in her garden by planting and picking vegetables when we were young. She wanted us to not eat meat, but eat plenty of vegetables and fruit.

However, we did have farm animals to care for and help with frequently; and we had meat sometimes. But she was always admonishing us not to eat much meat because our father worked hard everyday and needed most of the meat.

Moreover, my husband, Bertrand and our three children, Bertrand, II, Karen and Michael love all kinds of dishes made with meat. So, it was after I was grown that I cooked meat almost every meal for our family.

The Sunday Arica was to serve her meatless meal, her choice was red beans and rice. I told her we usually served the children at the church, hot dogs and chips, a sweet drink and cup - cakes or cookies.

I was thinking about what V. Staneseu reported in ANIMAL STUDIES JOURNAL – White Power Milk, "Many people across the globe lose the ability to digest milk when they leave the breastfeeding period of infancy – we call them "lactose intolerant" instead of "lactate persistence."

Some people from Northern Europe have a mutation that allows them to produce lactase into adulthood, perhaps an adaptive trait gained via natural selection by that population when diary foods were more abundant than other foods and those who could digest milk had a better chance of surviving and reproducing.

Arica said, "Oh no, Miss Griffin. My children cannot eat meat and I do not want to hamper other people's children from growing improperly with improper food. I would rather not serve them anything."

Linda C. Grazulis said in SALESIAN INSPIRATIONAL BOOKS, "Children are tiny gifts from God, sweet miracles of goodness and love; sent to teach us valuable lessons, like patience, delivered from the heavenly realm above. God sent these wee souls to us to cherish, nurture and attend. So enjoy each passing moment and make time with them to spent.

I was thinking, "Arica Lavigne is my brand- new boss, and she knows how she wants to raise her children."

"Okay, Arica, have it your way - red beans and rice, it is!"

"But can I bring some kind of meat?" I asked.

"Miss Griffin, I will make some sausage on the side."

COMMON'S STORY

I had recently read a book by COMMON; AND THEN WE RISE: A GUIDE TO LOVING AND TAKING CARE OF SELF. COMMON is a multi-award-winning performer and musician - Oscar, Golden Globe, Emmy, and Grammy awards winner. He is an actor and producer and author of several books, ONE DAY IT WILL ALL MAKE SENSE and LET LOVE HAVE THE LAST WORD. (NEW YORK TIMES bestsellers.

He has appeared in critically acclaimed films and TV hits and has had much success and accomishments.)

"His book AND THEN WE RISE, A GUIDE TO LOVING AND TAKING CARE OF SELF is about his journey, a call to action as he has seen the value of taking care of himself, taking one positive thought and turning it into a lifetime of positive vibrations.

His mother made incredible soul food and as a young person growing up in Chicago, COMMON loved fried chicken, and pork and his folks were always getting together eating soul food.

Then he learned through rap music by listening to KRS -ONE (a rapper), rapping about a vegetarian: "no goat, no ham, or chicken or turkey and hamburger." (pp. 19-21).

A GREAT CHERUBIM FAMILY CHOIR CELEBRATION

Listening to Arica and Jody about the food they were exposing their children to, as COMMON at age sixteen listened more to rap music and learned to eat right, he thought, "Oh, man, I love myself."

We had a beautiful worship service during our anniversary which celebrated all the children in the church, as they marched in, read the Scriptures, prayed the prayers, with special music and one soloist, Aubrey Lavigne (who sang "THERE IS NONE LIKE YOU," a children's moment, and a special guest speaker, Rev. Linda Smith, who spoke eloquently to and about children.

Afterward, Arica and other ladies of the church served us a delicious meal of Red Beans and Rice with one small piece of sausage on the side of the bowl.

I went back into the kitchen after all the children and adults had been served and asked Arica, "May I have more sausage?"

"Yes, Miss Griffin, you may have more sausage for you and your husband; but don't eat the whole hog! Do not eat it all at once!"

I thought about COMMON's book and how rap music changed him by what they taught. You can learn from anyone, sometimes positive issues and sometimes negative issues. The rapper was calling himself "an intelligent brown man, a vegetarian, no goat, no ham...." Hearing the rapper made COMMON at sixteen feel like he was encouraging and reaffirming him to be his greatest self and be proud of who he was.

I made that a promise not to eat all the sausage at once. It is more fruit and vegetable for us as well as my young choir family. Fruit can be thought of as nature's candy. It is a "Good- for- you" way to eat sugar. We must make food a great protector of our health.

Suffice it to say, my husband, Bertrand and I are still laughing and giggling about that statement Arica made. "Don't eat the whole hog!"

Bertrand does not eat pork anymore except sausage and once and a while, chitterlings on New Years Day.

Arica and Jody's lesson to me is a beautiful example of how we can come alongside those who have new ways of doing things. We may not understand someone else's way, but we do not need to understand everything in order to love them well by simply being with them. Jesus is our lead teacher.

When you believe in Jesus, He knows your every need and He will always be your friend. You cannot say, think or do anything that will change your friendship with Jesus. You are not always right in your thinking or doing; but trust in God and take heart; he will forgive you and help you live a better life.

Suffice it to say, the only way to truly forgive is by remembering. "We cannot make a simplistic connection between forgiving and forgetting. True forgiveness requires a careful look at what has actually happened." (Source: Gary Inrig, THE RISK OF FORGIVENESS: WHAT IT MEANS TO FORGIVE, p. 17).

He is indeed more creative than any human being's imagination; He is the absolute Sovereign One over all of creation and history. Arica's lesson to me is a one -of-a kind experience and I will continue to remember it all my life.

However, you must make your own decisions and choices. Consider your own natural abilities.

It occurred to me that my mother and Arica were on the right path to start their children out right on their eating habits; eating the right foods is important when you are young and when you are old.

The significance of self-care for your family as well as your self is multifaceted. Foremost among these strategies of correct eating is the act of setting boundaries. Asserting one's limits is an exercise in self-respect and a declaration of personal worth.

"Like a tranquil oasis in a desert of demands, it may provide the family with a space to replenish their energy, nurture their emotional health, and fortify their mental well-being. It is a treatment to their inherent worth and a recognition of their humanity beyond societal roles. (Leiba, PROTECTING MY PEACE, p. 100, para).

How might you enjoy these abilities more and how might you use them differently especially if you have been miraculously healed as the lame man who sat at the temple gate begging for money?

The lame man asked Peter for money and Peter gave something more precious and durable. He gave him healing.

PREPARING FOR OUR SPECIAL DAY

As we continued to prepare for our two-day anniversary, Aubrey, Arica and Jody's middle child, seemed to always be hungry. As we were placing fruit in the baskets for "family food distribution," Aubrey asked me if he could have an apple. I told him yes, "But let's go wash it" giving it to him. He surprised me when he asked, "Is this apple glutton-free?"

"I said, "This apple is good for you, wash it and eat it." When Aubrey returned from washing the apple and taking a big bite out of it, I was digging a piece of licorice candy out of my purse. He asked "Is that candy "glutton-free," too, Miss Griffin?

Arica came up beside us and started laughing. Her child knew food terminology that I did not even think about. She was teaching her children how to take care of themselves. These special parents were teaching their children how to trust the adults in their lives. They are teaching expressively affectionate preschoolers.

WHAT LOVE DOES

This is what love does. It does not always make sense to outsiders looking in because we want justice, especially if someone we love is the one who is being betrayed. Children as well as adults need not be afraid to live lives of faithfulness, praise and surrender to our Maker. Goodness supplies our needs and mercy blots out evil. God's kind goodness and loving mercy follow us always.

We need more of that, because children do not trust adults. They are taught not to talk to strangers and not trust others. We are reminded that we are not trapped by the Law or our Culture because we are invited to pursue the way of love and redemption.

So, take Jesus with you as your friend, because He is merciful and wants what is best for you. If you believe in Jesus, he has healed you spiritually. He has rescued you from harm. Jesus is the YES that we need as food for our hungry souls.

God is being patient with us. (2 PETER 3:9, para. NIV).

And if God is being patient with us, can we not pass on some patience to others? Of course we can; because before love is anything else, love is patient. (I CORINTHIANS 13:14, para, NIV).

COMMON adds a little "food for thought" for his soul. He said, "after reading AWAKENING THE BUDDHA WITHIN, I did not have to be Buddha to understand that the practice of love is important. That is the same thing Jesus spoke about. I believe that people from different spiritual and natural practices are in tune with God. I do not knock that because that is their path to their higher being." (p. 152-153).

Later, Arica explained that some of her relatives had illnesses that resulted from eating improper food and she did not want her children to pattern after them because they had the same genes. Knowing our family's health helps us to understand what decisions to make and teaches us to correct some eating habits and problems.

Arica and Jody are teaching their children to be encouraged. Peace comes as we realize that God does not extend his favor to persons who deserve; but to those who need it. Oftentimes, we pass over children and children do not understand many concepts.

LOST IN SIGHT

There was a situation whereby a middle school class was being taught to follow rules and take care of themselves. They were paired off, taken to a wooded area near a lake and given a compass. They were given instruction to navigate around the lake and through the woods and meet the bus on the other side in three hours. They were not allowed to take a watch or their cell phones.

Unfortunately, the two students who were in the fray knew nothing about compasses. They wandered about for several hours and got thoroughly lost. Finaly, as they became frightened and dismayed, they suddenly heard the bus horn and saw in the darkness the lights of the bus. The bus driver turned on the headlights and started honking his horn because two of his students were lost.

When they finally made it back to the bus, the other students suppressed laughter and were very happy to see their classmates.

The student, Norman, who told this story, confessed that he never did learn how to use a compass but used another type of compass – THE BIBLE – to use, read, study and learn the directions of life. The wisdom of the scripture guided him in daily decisions and led him to safety many times.

DO NOT GIVE THE LEFTOVERS

At times, it can be tempting to give God and other people our leftovers or something improper, instead of a wonderful gift. We praise God and expect Him to give us His all, yet we offer Him our crumbs. We must reach out to someone else and help shoulder and build together to do God's work. What God has for us to experience and accomplish is like feeding the multitudes as in what Jesus Christ did.

> *The Israelites sometimes gave God their damaged goods. When He spoke through the prophet Malachi, He rebuked the Israelites for sacrificing worthless animals, blind, lame and diseased animals, when they had strong healthy animals to offer. He reprimanded and forgave the Israelites. However, He announced His displeasure for the people keeping the best for themselves.*

> *But love does not keep score. God will purify and refine them like gold and silver. Then the Lord will have men who will bring offerings in righteousness. (MALACHI 3: 3, para, NIV).*

Arica and Jody Lavigne are giving their children their best as God wants us to give our best to Him every day. Their best is good food, proper eating, and proper training. These are their gifts to their children and their God.

GOD CARES AND SO DO WE.

LAVIGNE FAMILY

- Mother: Arica Lavigne
- Father: Jody Lavigne
- Daughter: Joy
- Sons: Jaxon, Aubrey

CHAPTER 18

MY SPECIAL ELDERLY FRIEND

This incident of family eating habits reminded me of moments with my Ninety-Plus special lady, Eleanor Seals Miles. She requested that I establish a group for elderly members of our church so they could secure attention from the younger church members. She felt that the older members of the church at St. Mark United Methodist church were being overlooked and forgotten.

Well, Eleanor Miles made it to one-hundred-four-years old before she died. She had almost perfect eyesight with her one pair of glasses on. It was her hearing that was shot!

If you came into her room at any time and she did not have her hearing-aid in her ear, and she could not find it at that moment, she could not talk to you and she started fussing. She would not talk and she could not answer the phone.

I have called at times and she did not have her hearing-aid on.

Eleanor would say, "Look, I cannot talk to you, because I do not have my hearing-aid on. She could see who was calling her! Remember, she had perfect eye sight, with or without her glasses.

"GOOD BYE!" She slammed the phone down in my ear.

I was one of her care-givers, her executor and I wanted to know why she was so agitated. I would drive over to her house, which was twenty miles away, use my key to open her door and walk in her house, shouting, "It's me, Eleanor, It's me, Marian."

I knew she had a gun under her pillow because she told me regularly that she would shoot anyone who came into her house unannounced. I did not want to startle her if she was asleep and her sitter was not there. Whenever I entered her house, I announced myself. "Hey, Little Rat," I said. She would answer back, "Hey, Big Rat."

It was funny to me; I started laughing and she would start laughing and we would look for her hearing-aid. She lost it every day. It occurred to me that she just needed my company and I had to show up and talk to her. Even if her sitter or nurse was there at the time, she needed friendly company at the moment, not professional help.

Arica was right to start her children out right, because eating the right food is important when you are young and when you are old.

It occurred to me that my mother was very serious about food and what we ate. She gave us mostly vegetables and fruit and not much meat.

"Save the meat for your Daddy," she always said, "because he has to be strong to go out and work for us every day."

Bill Cosby adds his taste to the doctor's orders for my friend Eleanor in his book, TIME FLIES. Bill is a classic comedian and was always pointing up things that his father said after he got old.

Whenever I would go to the doctor with Eleanor, she would get a "doctor's sermon and orders."

"Dr. Bernard says, "You have to cut down, Miss Eleanor."

"Cut down on what?" she answered.

"Are you eating food?" the doctor says.

"Yes"

"Well, cut down, especially on the stuff that has taste. Stop eating salt, sugar, egg yokes, red meat, whole milk and almost everything else. Try to build your meals around parsley, but with no barbecue sauce, of course."

She asked the doctor, "Is chicken okay to eat?"

"Yes, but without the skin."

"It doesn't look good that way," Eleanor told the doctor. Oftentimes I would be in the doctor's office with her during her discourse with her doctor and I could not help but laugh at their conversation.

"Then close your eyes and add lemon juice," Doctor said.

"At your age of over a hundred, you know the lemon juice has become the seasoning for everything, the all-purpose seasoning for the fish you eat, with no salt and the chicken you eat with no oil and the eggs with no yoke."

"With no lemon juice, you might not even know when you are eating because tastelessness has become the heart of your cuisine. You must sit down to heaping plates of celery and radishes, cauliflower and boiled beets, broccoli and watercress."

Bill Cosby adds to the doctor's orders for Eleanor's meals. He said, "My mother stated to us kids, "Eat your spinach and drink your milk."

"By feeding me like this, my mother had no doubt that I would live to be one hundred and five, belting bullies all the way while defending the flag." (Cosby, p. 91).

Bill said, "My grandfather used to say, "Do not worry about senility. When it hits you, you will not know it."

"He was right," Bill said. He lived to be ninety-eight years old and spent the last fifteen of them thinking he was Frederick Douglas.

So, with love, Dr. Bernard was teaching Eleanor Miles, my old lady, "You are what you eat."

The longer you live, the less you should eat, according to Eleanor's doctor.

Eleanor is learning not to eat much. She asked me to start cooking for her instead of eating so much Meals on Wheels food and restaurant food that her "new" grandson would bring her.

Randall Cunningham moved across the street from Eleanor and they became very close, loving neighbors. He visited her every morning, bringing her a carry-out plate of food before he went to work as a Constable. Eleanor, Randall and I became very good friends and he started calling Eleanor "Grandma" and called me "Auntie."

So, Eleanor gained a grandson and I gained a nephew. Eleanor had no children, so church members wanted to know how she had a

Grandson. They adopted each other. He became her guardian angel and helped her to move around.

"What's love got to do with it?" sang Tina Turner.

Randall, as many others do, take their work for God, their family and others seriously, passionately even. The significance of self-care and caring for others is multifaceted. He told me that Eleanor reminded him of his grandmother and he missed her terribly. When he got married to Samanthia, I am sure they had their "New Couple" weebies and whows, but Randall still had time for Eleanor and her elderly boyfriend Frank, whom he took care of as well. Frank hung around Eleanor for years, but her friends finally met him on her one hundred – forth birthday.

Loving, caring and forgiving others may provide us with a space to replenish our energy, nurture our emotional health and fortify our spiritual well-being. You cannot help others until you first help yourself.

We too need to heed the advice of trusted loved ones and rely on the wisdom and power of God in all we do so we will have the energy to do a good work with our family and neighbors.

Suffice it to say, they are honoring Christ through their own sacrificial gift by giving their family and other families the nutrition and basic needs they require to grow and thrive.

The King will reply, "Truly I tell you, whatever you did for one of the least of these brothers and sisters of mine, you did for me." (MATTHEW 25: 40, NIV).

LOVE HAS EVERYTHING TO DO WITH IT!

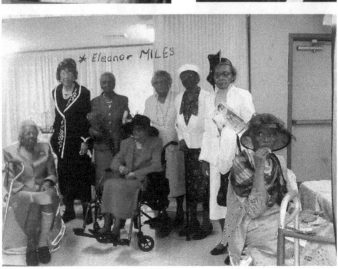

ANCESTORS

CHAPTER 19

INDEPENDENT MOBILITY

My neighbor, Maggie's daughter, Letisha, had a challenge as a toddler. The child at eighteen months was not walking. She would stand up and plop back down. When she tried to walk, she would hold on to furniture or someone's hand but would not let go. Apparently, she had a great fear of falling.

Our daughter, Karen had been walking, holding on to furniture and our hand since she was nine months old. She independently let go and walked on her own by the time she was ten and a half months old.

Now Karen is walking across the room and outside on the sidewalk with us at the age of one year old.

My neighbor was disturbed by this, and I dare say, even jealous. We wanted our children to be the best and do the best that they could. Infants and toddlers have meltdowns just like we as adults do, but thank God for his endless patience with our immaturity and fearful moments.

Letisha's pediatrician said her legs and everything were fine. She just had to get over her fright of moving about on her own. With the support of Karen and our family, Letisha learned to walk on her own and her mother was happy about it. We are all sent by God to help and support one another in times of stress. Finally, she developed independent mobility.

I thought about Peter when Jesus summoned him to join him on the dark murky water. Peter moved right along, not hesitating. He had no fear.

During the fourth watch of the night, Jesus went out to them, walking on the lake. When the disciples saw him walking on the lake, they were terrified. "It's a ghost!" they said and cried out in fear.

But Jesus immediately said to them, "Take courage! It is I. Do not be afraid."

Peter said, "Lord, if it is you, tell me to come to you on the water."

So, Jesus said "Come."

"And when Peter had come down out of the boat, he walked on the water to go to Jesus."

But when he saw the wind, he was afraid and began to sink. He cried out, "Lord, save me."

Immediately Jesus reached out his hand and caught him. "You of little faith. Why did you doubt?"

And when they (Jesus and Peter) climbed into the boat, the wind died down. Then those who were in the boat worshipped him, saying, "Truly you are the Son of God." (MATTHEW 14:25-33, NIV).)

At first, Peter did not question Jesus or waffle about whether the water was too deep, too cold or just plain scary. He took a leap of faith. Then he was frightened by the wind. But whatever fears he had, disappeared when he saw the Lord's outstretched hand.

Jesus calls us to do things we could never imagine ourselves doing, even when we are frightened. It is not easy to live life as a people -pleaser. As I grew up in our large family, I was the third child of seven children. I was never petted as an only child or the baby because my mother was pregnant with the fourth child a few months after I was born. My desire to please my parents as well as my siblings has persisted even into my adulthood.

Audre Lorde stated, "Caring for myself is not self-indulgence. It is self-preservation."

Even small children must conquer their fears and needs to want love so badly that they are willing to do things for others to get by. When we get caught up in pleasing people, we stray from pleasing God.

The fear of not being loved by others is not of God's design. We must reach out to Jesus in openness and vulnerability. Jesus is saying "COME" to me with outstretched arms and I will love you.

We must teach our children to trust and have faith in God. For God has not given us a spirit of fear, but of prayer and of love and of a sound mind. As we pray and teach our children, and find prayer partners, we must pray that Jesus will help us conquer our multitude of sins and love deeply. It may take time, but Jesus is always with us every step of the way. (para).

After all, love each other deeply, because love covers over a multitude of sins. (1 PETER 4: 8, para, NIV).

You and your Lord are the architect of your own life. You have strength that is powerful and enduring. You must seek to grow in faith, to learn to see the bright side of dark moments. You must try to relinquish your fears and struggles.

The flowers appear on the earth, the time of singing has come and the voice of the turtledove is heard in our land. (SONG OF SOLOMON 2: 12, NIV).

TRUST IN THE LORD!

CHAPTER 20

LOVE IS BLIND

When I was a small child, I often heard my mother and others say, "Love is blind. Naturally, I thought, "You can't see love; you can only feel it." Then, when I was fourteen and in high school, I read a book about Helen Keller. I learned that she was blind and deaf.

"Helen Adam Keller was born in Tuscumbia, Alabama on June 27, 1880 with no disabilities. Healthy and precocious until nineteen months, she suffered a mysterious illness that left her completely deaf and blind. Helen's frantic parents were led to consult several doctors about her condition.

Among them was the eminent Dr. Alexander Graham Bell in Washington, D.C. As a teacher of the deaf, Bell had invented the telephone in 1876 in the partial hope that it might serve as a hearing aid.

Kate Keller, Helen's mother learned of a book by Charles Dickens who wrote of his first visit to the United States. In Boston, he met and wrote about Laura Bridgman, a fragile deaf-blind girl who had been stricken at approximately the same age as Helen. Laura had been partially educated by Dr. Samuel Gridley Howe, the first director of the Perkins Institution and Massachusetts Asylum for the Blind in Boston.

Laura's learning of finger spelling and other methods led the frantic Kellers to consult several doctors about Helen's condition. Twenty-one-year-old Annie Sullivan's name was given to the Kellers for the sake of helping Helen learn and grow. At the age of seven, Helen met Anne Sullivan and immediately began to fight with her.

"The first meeting of Helen and Annie in the door-yard of the Kellers' home proved to be a disaster. Mrs. Keller attempted to restrain Helen's impulsive movements but the child paid no attention to these signs. Helen's face grew red to the roots of her hair, and she began to clutch at her mother's dress and kick violently. It was only the beginning. Annie Sullivan soon lost two teeth.

The struggle continued between the two blind individuals as they were sequestered together in the Keller's garden- house, away from Helen's indulgent parents. Two days later, after this close encounter, Helen half understood now that the finger games Annie was playing with her, promised some form of passage through the "dense fog" of deaf-blindness that enclosed her. This new lure tempted her out of herself, but the violence continued. Annie would hold Helen's hands tightly until she became calm. This tactic worked and increasingly Annie was able to teach Helen new activities and words and eventually language.

Less than a year after their four-week war, a published account of Helen's learning to talk with her fingers made Helen Keller and Annie Sullivan famous. Helen began writing THE STORY OF MY LIFE at an early age under the watchful eye of her teacher, Annie Sullivan and the Perkins Institution. "Helen was admitted to Radcliffe College in 1899 which represented a private examination, a public triumph. This encouraged the idea of a book about Helen's education." (p. xv).

Doubleday Book Company was chosen (against Scribner) to publish her book in March 1903. There are three reprints of the original edition (in different layouts and order) of her book. Three authors, Helen, Annie Sullivan and John Macy showed the record that "one member of the trio was deeply impaired and needed help to find the world. Yet, the impairment came to serve all of them as an enhancement in responding to the world.

Helen's thoughts were, "I do not know if Mother Nature made me. I think my mother got me from heaven, but I do not know where that place is." (p. 205, para).

It was evident that it was impossible to keep from her the religious beliefs held by those with whom she was in daily contact.

Suffice it to say, the book is Miss Keller's and is final proof of her independent power even though her thoughts were, "My teacher (Miss Sullivan) is so near to me that I scarcely think of myself apart from her."

"I feel that her being is inseparable from my own, and that the footsteps of my life are in hers. All the best of me belongs to her, there is not a talent, or an aspiration or a joy in me that has not been awakened by her loving touch." (p. 39, para).

It seemed as if Miss Sullivan's love for Helen and Helen's love for Miss was like a mutual love of God for his children.

To love Him with all your heart, with all your understanding and with all your strength, and to love your neighbor as yourself is more important than burnt offerings and sacrifices. (MARK 12: 33, NIV).

AMERICAN BRAILLE

"In 1931, thanks to Helen Keller's plea of standardization, English braille was accepted as the world's standard alphabet for the blind." (Notes, p. 413).

IS LOVE BLIND

Is love blind. Are miracles still entrenched in love? The rapidity of teaching and learning was matched by the rapidity with which the news went forth about this deaf-blind girl.

I remember reading and hearing about Helen Keller from my mother when I was a child and could understand Mother's interest in her because of the love and caring for her beloved blind grandfather. As a teenager, I was intrigued by Helen Keller's life and story.

My mother's grandfather, John Henry Fountain was also blind but not deaf. Mother had a very close relationship with her grandfather and would read to him. She had one book about Helen Keller which she read to her grandfather constantly.

Blindness connected the dots for all of us and is one of the miracles written about in the Bible which Jesus was truly concerned about. He healed blindness as well as a multitude of other illnesses and sins as he did not keep score about others' tragedies.

Then Jesus said to him, "Get up! Pick up your mat and walk." At once the man was cured; he picked up his mat and walked. (JOHN 5: 8-9, NIV).

I read mother's book and secured others from the school library and the book-mobile which rode into our church-yard once a month. Helen could not hear; she could not see, but she was my hero. (Source: Helen Keller, THE STORY OF MY LIFE, edited by Roger Shattuck and Mother's oral history).

WE ALL HAVE A HERO! GOD!

PART THREE

PERILOUS IN NATURE

CHAPTER 21

A HIGH PRICE FOR LOVE

I have a special person in my life, whom I recently met, mainly by telephone. Terri Brown Pepper is the oldest child in her parent's family; born on August 16, 1961 in Sussex County, Delaware.

I talked to her for a few minutes in person while visiting my family home in Delaware decades ago. Terrie was a teenager, pregnant with her second child. Much later in life, I was informed by my sister, Nancy Heath Kellam, that Terri's first child, Arshawon, had died. I called Terri in sympathy for her and her children.

Since then, I have gotten to know her and love her dearly.

She is my niece who married my nephew, Willie Alex "Billie" Pepper, Jr. (who was my oldest sister, Phyllis's son).

These two young people were teenagers. As they stayed together in my parent's home in Greenwood, Terri had several children by my nephew, Willie, Jr. She had to raise them by herself with the help of my parents, because my nephew was hardly ever home. He was always out trying to find jobs and find himself.

Willie, Jr. was an "empty-nester," and floated from his mother's relatives (our parents) in Delaware to his father's relatives in Florida.

Both sets of parents and grandparents had patience with him because from infancy he was sickly. Willie, Jr. attended several elementary and high schools due to his "moving around" so much. In high school, he suffered from bullying, gang issues, drugs, teen sex, cheating, racism, disrespect for authority, weapons on campus and concerns about study habits and exams. He was often late for class and had not completed class assignments.

After high school, he moved on to get training in JOB CORPS. This upped his motivational skills and self-esteem.

He was constantly seeking new jobs but he drank heavily and would only help take care of his children periodically. He did meaningless things for his wife, Terri Brown Pepper and their five children, Arshawon, Tikia, Lentia, Willie, III. and Jermaine; yet his wife and their children loved him dearly.

In his early adult period, he was at the crossroads of his life, dealing with the choices of being the popular "thug." He was dealing with personal identity issues. His choices, decisions and actions affected not only his life but the lives of everyone around him. His mother, Phyllis as well as his wife, Terri were concerned about him, but he became disrespectful to them both.

An individual does not have to live long before sensing that he/she has inadequacies, imperfections and weaknesses -emotionally, physically, mentally and spiritually. Willie, Jr. was unique in his own way. He was a "Mr. Know It All" who was not living up to his scholastic and academic potential. He had poor study habits. He often found himself in the wrong place at the wrong time.

He was very handsome with fair complexion, blonde hair and dark green-hazel eyes. He was a body builder. Some would say that he was a "Lady's Man" without even trying because he was friendly and quiet. Constantly surrounded by girls and women, this made him seem disrespectful to his wife when other women approached him. He suffered from conflict resolution which "landed" him in trouble.

Willie, Jr. was a street-wise person who had a very unstable home life from his early childhood to his adult life. He had to deal with many issues and challenges on his life's journey because he was moved around so much – from pillar to post!

He was on "a journey of a thousand steps, a continual practice of carving out spaces for rest, honoring emotional realities, constantly engaging in self-care, and nurturing the harmony of physical and mental health. Yet, in this journey lies the beauty and strength of individuals, the resilience embedded in their spirits, and the boundless potential that unfolds when they prioritize their holistic health and well-being." (Leiba, p. 108, para).

Willie, Jr. seemed to realize that he was the focus of pain, shame and sin, and often found himself in unforgiving situations that made life terribly unpleasant for him. Occasionally there was domestic violence in the home. Terri was the victim until she learned to fight back. She also learned to forgive her husband for his infirmities towards her. She had to learn how to hold others accountable for their behavior. This required that she had to carefully and prayerfully determine the nature of the other person's behavior and not ignore it. She learned to speak directly to her husband, not about him to others.

The goal of this type of encounter was not to express her anger but to encourage reconciliation, repentance and restoration and to protect others who were being victimized by this behavior.

Terri had to make a commitment to herself to do what she had to do to feel better. Forgiveness was for herself, not for anyone else. However, Jesus did not forgive us for His sake, but for ours.

Julie Schwartz, in her book, FIGHT RIGHT, stated that "most of us blunder into conflict without knowing what we are really fighting about and then quickly become overwhelmed by physiological responses we cannot control and emotions we do not anticipate.

A major problem is, we have not been taught how to fight right. We do not get "Fighting 101" in high school before we launch into our first relationship. No matter how many relationships we might have had, or how many years we have been partners, many of us are still feeling our way, trying to figure it out as we go and we make lots of mistakes.

Conflict is human and necessary. With kindness, clarity and a deep understanding of the struggles couples go through, this narrative shows us that we each have a conflict culture, born of how we were raised and how we experience past relationships." (p.9, para).

Suffice it to say, couples must learn how best they can work together and really understand the situation, "and escape the win-or- lose mentality in favor of a collaborative approach: calming down, staying connected and really trying to understand each other so that the fights can bring the couple closer together." (p. 10, para).

Conflict is connection. It is how we figure out who we are, what we want, and who our partners are becoming and what they want. It is how we bridge our differences and find out similarities, our points of connection.

There also is a thing called "know thyself" that is so critical to a couple's togetherness.

Phylicia Rashad, TV star on the Bill Cosby Show said, "Loving one's self is not hard when you understand who and what you are. It has nothing to do with the shape of your face, the size and color of your eyes, the length and texture of your hair, or the quality of your clothes. It is so beyond all these things, and it is what gives life to everything about you. Your own self is such a treasure."

Even in our fallen world, God cares for those who experience the liabilities of human existence and frailties.

God knows how we are formed; He knows that we are dust. (PSALM 103: 14, NIV).

In Genesis it is revealed, "Then the Lord God formed a man from the dust of the ground and breathed into his nostrils the breath of life, and the man became a living being. (GENESIS 2: 7, KJV).

GOD IS OUR CREATOR.

CHAPTER 22

WHEN WILLIE, Jr, WAS BORN

I was graduating from high school and preparing to go to college when Willie Alex "Billie" Pepper, Jr. was born on May 31, 1957. He was born in Greenwood, Delaware at my parent's home. Phyllis and her husband had returned home to recuperate from working in Florida. She suddenly went into labor and had her baby three months early.

I was in the process of graduating from high school and Mother asked me to go visit my aunt Lucille and Uncle Clarence Harper and help them out as Auntie was sick.

I learned much later that my sister Phyllis and her husband Willie, Sr. came to our house and Willie, Jr. was born almost immediately. Willie, Jr. was a premature baby and was born at home at three months pre-mature, and was taken immediately to the hospital in Milford, Delaware. He remained in the hospital for several months because he had not fully developed as an infant.

My older sister, Phyllis and her husband, Willie Alex Pepper, Sr. and their daughter, Mary who was a year older than Willie, Jr. came to our parent's home to live for a while in Delaware before returning to Florida to live with Willie's family.

I was in college by then and my two older brothers, George and Daniel Heath were in the United States Navy. The three younger siblings, Joseph, Nancy and Hattie Elviria Heath were in elementary and high school. They knew what was happening at home in Greenwood, Delaware.

The whole Heath and Pepper family was struggling by the time Willie, Jr. was born. This infant child got off to a very rocky start.

Just like today, things do not always work out the way we want them to or in the good guy's favor. Sometimes we feel like we are living under a course -both personally and societally. We wonder about God's silence, become skeptical and ask the question, "God, are You there? Do you still care about me?" We are in a mess down here.

But the angel said to him: "Do not be afraid, your prayer has been heard. (LUKE 1:11, NIV).

After generations and generations of silence from heaven, God has finally spoken again. If you have heard, (or if you are Zechariah and Elizabeth who wanted a child thousands of years ago), He has spoken to you and not just about your particular situation, but in one short message, God announces through his angel the remedy not only for personal suffering for you and not only for tribal suffering your people have endured, but an end of suffering for the whole world.

Doubt and mistrust limit our participation but does not stop God's plan. I have heard it said, "This is too good to be true."

Doubt is understandable. Our doubts and fears have led us to a place of discouragement and hopelessness. From a human perspective, we feel that we have waited a lifetime for answers to our problems.

God had allowed a sick child to come into the world, and the whole family is hurt. Through our struggles and pain, we must learn that gifts are not earned. They are given through faith and trust in our Maker. The most important issue in life is to know what our Creator has for us. LOVE! He has only love for us and love is what makes us get out of bed each morning.

When we realize that a great gift such as a child is given, it shows us the love of the Giver is perfect. This is what love does. It does not

WHEN WILLIE, JR, WAS BORN

make sense to those on the outside looking in. The timing is perfect. We must find joy in the midst of our disappointment.

LOVE IS SUFFICIENT.

CHAPTER 23

LIKE NEW TURTLES

Willie, Jr., like new born turtles, was at a great risk when he was born. He should have lived to write his own story. He should have written about himself and his life. What struggles an infant has may never be known. We do not know who cared for him when we were away from him; who loved and held him while he was in the hospital for so many days?

Willie, Jr. was in the hospital for over three months. Our parents, Lettie and George Heath, visited him as much as they could.

It is awfully important how we treat each other, talk to each other, love each other. We must learn to respect each other and follow in Jesus' foot -steps. This is a great responsibility if we are the care -giver of another person.

There are questions about Willie, Jr.'s young life and those family members around him that draw a blank to me. I was not there. When I first saw Willie, Jr. and his older sister, Mary, I was a freshman in college, eighteen years old. Willie, Jr. was apparently six months old.

Phyllis and her husband, Willie, Sr. had returned to Florida to live and had left Willie, Jr. and Mary with my mother and father, Lettie and George Heath to raise. Mother was home alone trying to care for a year-old baby and a pre-mature infant while my younger siblings were in high school and elementary school.

Our mother was a Juvenile diabetic sufferer from birth and sickly herself, therefore there were many challenges when she was trying to raise her own children, let alone two small grandchildren. While at the Heath family home in Delaware, these children were loved and valued by their grandparents and aunts and uncle.

The three younger Heath children, Joseph, Nancy and Hattie Elviria, were in school all day, and Mother was alone with these two grandchildren. She carried them everywhere she went, to church, (she was the musician at our church and played for many different programs, including funerals), the supermarket, the beauty shop and her club meetings. There were times in her life that Mother was worn out, down-hearted and depressed, thinking, "I have raised my children, now I have to raise my grandchildren."

Yet, while Mother faced trials and felt discouraged, she was assured by God that He cared and delivered her from her troubles. Jesus knew what it felt like to feel brokenhearted and misunderstood. He still understood the feeling of rejection and exerted his comforting presence in Mother's life.

GOD CARES FOR US!

CHAPTER 24

EVOLUTIONARY SURVIVAL

W hen I came home from college my freshman year before the Thanksgiving holiday, I met Willie, Jr. for the first time, he was langly and puny-looking. I wanted to quit college and come home to help Mother raise my niece and nephew.

I told my mother, "I would like to adopt Billie, and take care of him."

Mother said, "Phyllis will never let you adopt her child, so let things stay as they are. You go back to college."

As I looked at my niece, Mary and infant nephew Willie, Jr., I thought, "She is doing fine but he's not going to make it."

He is like the tiny turtle racing to the sea for survival. He has no help from mother or father, or siblings, only God and grandparents.

SURVIVAL IS EVOLUTIONARY.

It is possible that the Creator has established laws we know nothing about; this is what makes miracles possible.

The Tree of Life is a map of the earth's evolutionary history; it will always be incomplete; not only because we do not know all the living species there are to know, but because we certainly do not know most of the 99 percent of species that have gone extinct in the nearly four-billion years on this earth. The life span of most species is short, at least in evolutionary terms, but despite their unassuming appearance, there was and is an astonishing diversity of species within that unicellular life. We do know that life gives rise to life; and other creatures living today were always alive through the countless ancestors of all living things. (Source: Chakrabarty, EXPLAINING LIFE THROUGH EVOLUTION, p, 127-128, para).

God is able to make things happen, because He is not bound by "natural laws." He is the creator of the laws of nature and has the prerogative and power to work outside them.

In the game of life, we each receive a unique set of unexpected limitations and variable questions. How will we respond to the hand that we are dealt?

For even the Son of Man did not come to be served, but to serve. (MARK 10: 45, NIV).

There will be times in our lives when we feel helpless. There will be lessons learned through obstacles placed in our way, whether we are adults or children. Nevertheless, every day of our lives, God is working in us and through us; we will experience set-backs and curve-balls thrown at us.

> These words were spoken by the Son of Man on a day when his disciples needed a proper perspective on servanthood and when a blind man cried out for help. (MARK 10: 36, para, NIV).

> The Son of God, surrounded by endless requests for help and weary from miles of walking, looked the man straight in the face and asked, "What do you want me to do for you?" (MARK 10: 51, NIV).

Jesus saw the burden another person carried and offered to help with the load. This is unconditional love. Love does not keep score.

Those words Jesus uttered, "What can I do for you?" might revitalize our relationships with our family and friends.

Jesus was willing to share in our humanity not only to secure our right relationship with God but to enable us to trust Him in our moments of trials and struggles. When we face temptations and hardships, we know we can lean on Him for strength and support. He is our Way-Maker and He is able to help us. God in His loving kindness and infinite wisdom comes to meet us:

In putting everything under Him, God left nothing that is not subject to Himself. We see Jesus, who was made just a little lower than the angels; now crowned with glory and honor because he suffered death, so that by the grace of God, he might taste death for everyone. (HEBREWS 2: 8-9, NIV).

Mother Teresa said, "Prayer enlarges the heart until it is capable of containing God's gift of Himself. Ask and seek and your heart will grow big enough to receive him and keep him as our own. Wherever God has put you, that is your vocation. It is not what we do but how much love we put into it.

Jesus will meet you wherever you are and he will help you. He is not intimidated by past failures, broken promises or wounds. He will make sense out of your brokenness. He will be the Lord of your life today, not next Monday or next month, but now.

You can see that all things are possible with God. So many times, it is daring to put your best foot forward and even when you are not sure of how things will turn out, you know you have a God and there are things he wants you to do. In God you move and breath and have your being. Look to your heart for what you really want and what will bring you closest to following God's will.

Whether you turn to the right or to the left, your ears will hear a voice behind you, saying, "This is the way; walk in it." (ISAIAH 30:21, NIV).

God wants your service and your heart. Make time to focus on Him. Keep silent and be joyful; enjoy His presence. His Spirit can speak deeply to your heart as He shows His ways. Listen and trust Him as He answers you. Show Him what you got! Show Him what you can do!

MEETING WILLIE, Jr.

I was in college at Delaware State College (later University) studying classical music; I had received a scholarship in music. When I first saw little Willie, and realized his slow start in life, I wanted to strive to make things better for him. I wanted to bring love and understanding to the forefront and help him and other children in a different way.

I was told that Willie, Jr. weighed less than three pounds when he was born. At that time, he not only was under-weight, but he was ill and had problems breathing. He was rushed to a hospital eleven miles away, as he was born at home. My parents were trying to save my nephew's life. His life was a thread as he was pre-mature and my sister did not have a doctor or mid-wife to help with the birth. Upon arrival at the Milford Memorial Hospital, the doctor took one look at Willie, Jr. and consulted with other doctors. They gave this little tyke about two weeks to live. He remained in the hospital for months.

After the several months were up, one of his doctors, Dr. Bentley felt that he was well enough to go home and allowed him to be carried home with strict orders about his feeding and his health. The doctor still gave Willie, Jr. only six months to live but felt that he would be better if he were at home.

Upon my first peep at Willie,Jr. he was nothing more than a little pink fluff with blond hair and green eyes. While he was in the hospital, only Phyllis could see him for the first two weeks; than his father could go in the room where pre-mature babies were.

My older sister, Phyllis and her husband, Willie Alex Pepper, Sr. were traumatized by the slow progress of their baby. After Willie, Jr's birth on May 31, 1957, Phyllis and Willie left to return to his home in Florida within three weeks. The doctor told Phyllis there was nothing she could do for her baby. All they could do was see him in the NICU, but not be able to hold their baby. As they saw their baby slowly making progress, they felt that Willie, Jr. would get good care from the hospital staff and his grandparents and so, his parents returned to Florida to their jobs. Willie, Jr. saw his parents about ten months later.

After Willie, Jr. was released from the hospital, Phyllis came and took her baby home to Florida. They set up a pattern, the children came in the winter and stayed until summer at Mother and Daddy's house. She never knew when the children's parents were coming. I was away in college when the children were brought back the second time. So, I saw them only a few days.

Phyllis and Willie, would go back to Florida for months to a year and work. Then they would come and pick the two children up and let them live with them for a short time in Florida; only to bring them back to my parents' home. The tykes had a stable life at our home in Delaware. Mother cared for them during the day and my two younger sisters, Nancy and Hattie Heath played with them and fed them during the evening. They were in high school and came home each day and their main focus was on the two children.

Willie, Jr. was always quiet and needy. The three women - my two younger sisters and my mother - made every effort to attend to the needs especially to this child. A rocky road occurred because this child was snatched from one home to another. There is such a thing as children's rights.

I can imagine there was another side to this story. Being a preemie makes parents add a whole new layer of fear, doubt and vulnerability to their lives as well as their infant child. Besides having to be brand new parents, they had a crash course in neonatal care. They were taking an educational path they never thought they would need. They were tired and fearful of their baby's progress. After the first five weeks of Willie, Jr.'s NICU stay, his parents surrendered their stay to the hospital staff because the staff knew what they were doing. The parents left and missed a lot of their baby's growth and milestones.

We later learned that the parents felt guilty and powerless because their baby was not improving, and were not cognizant of Willie, Jr.'s doctor's boundaries. The parents left and returned to their home in Florida. The doctors developed a plan for Willie, Jr's care. The grandparents returned home and came back every day to see the little fellow.

(Source: Oral history from Nancy Heath Kellam and Milford Memorial Hospital).

LIKE MOTHER, LIKE CHILD

Mother had told us many times that Phyllis was her smallest baby. She weighed less than three pounds when she was born. As humans we tend to focus on the differences between us, no matter how small those differences are; but we are all more similar to one another then we are willing to believe. We are beginning to realize that science describes gender, race, sex and other attributes on a spectrum. We focus on our differences because there are so many similarities. There are hard truths in our DNA, but there are also mysteries, and even miracles.

I was told by my mother that she herself weighed just three pounds when she was born. Her first child, Phyllis was under three pounds and Phyllis had a baby that weighed under three pounds.

"The reason for paucity of DNA from ancestors is that the DNA remaining from every previous generation is essentially halved with each passing generation. You get half of the DNA in your genome from your mother and half from your father; and your brothers and sisters get different halves. In sifting through evolutionary history of generations, one may discover some puzzling facts. Our recent ancestry can be pretty perplexing, especially as DNA testing becomes commonplace.

I talked to my children and grandchildren about DNA and had them do more research on the matter.

There was much to be learned through researching my mother and my grandmother and great-grandmother. They did not have DNA to research, but we do.

Aside from the fact that they were among the past generations from my generation, they were the beginning stories of future miracles and mysteries of new generations. We do not choose our human family; we do not choose our ancestors.

So, it seems that oral history proves that my mother was born as a pre-mature infant; her first child, Phyllis, was a pre-mature infant; and Phyllis' son was a pre-mature infant. Special care apparently had to be given to each of these infants. My mother knew that she was a special baby; her child was a special baby and Phyllis' baby was a special child.

When I stumbled up on some of this history, and remembered my grandmother's oral history from the time I was seven -years old, I realized that although there were turbulent and treacherous times in our generations, there were caring and compassionate members placed in our midst so that we could carry the torch. Each generation carried its share of the burdens as we have been blessed to travel through historical synthesis. It is now our obligation to stay true to ourselves and refuse to give in to the challenges of life.

CHANGES

When I was a sophomore in college, I changed my major from classical music to psychology and sociology, thinking that my career should be in caring for sick and troubled children. I gave up my music scholarship my mother helped get for me, (as she was a classical music pianist, and knew many people in her field). I never told her. I was looking at careers in the social sciences and decided on social work.

I was wondering if I was using my time and energy wisely to help others? Was I going to positively impact another person's life just with music or interact with someone as an opportunity to make someone's life brighter?

My Spanish teacher, Miss Jayne Patrick and I talked in class and in her office when she learned that I wanted to become a social worker. She informed me that there was a School of Social Work at Atlanta University in Georgia. She had attended Atlanta University in her field of foreign languages and encouraged me to apply at her school. I secured an application from Atlanta University, when I was a senior in college, but realized that I did not have the finances to attend that graduate school. Still, I was determined to go into that field. My mind was on my first niece, Mary and my first nephew, Willie Alex "Billie" Pepper, Jr.

Studying in my new career, I was learning in child psychology that between the ages of infancy through three, children are traumatized by many things. Both Mary and Billie may have been experiencing traumatic moments in their lives which would affect and present troubles for them in later life.

They call these children the "terrible two's" when they "act out." I can imagine that Willie, Jr. acted out all the time because my mother said he was "More than a handful." His movements were slower than the normal one- and two-years old child. But these young children are our most vulnerable citizens.

If it had not been for their elderly grandparents, Mary and especially Billie would not have functioned normally.

Jack Frost, in his book, EXPERIENCING FATHER'S EMBRACE, cautions us that "At an early age, ungodly beliefs begin to influence their (young children's) personalities. They begin to believe that adults are uncaring, abusive, and unreliable. Because they have been neglected, they lose the ability to trust others. Because they have not been nursed or properly fed, normal development goes haywire. Because they have not been hugged by their parents, they find it difficult to give love, and seek to get their un-healed needs met.

In order to escape the pain of rejection, these children may become self-destructive. They also develop uncontrollable anger, severe hyperactivity, learning disorders and compulsive tendencies.

Sadly, many of these young children are struggling with incredible psychological trauma because of the way they were abused or neglected as youngsters.

Reading a book by Melody Schreiber, WHAT WE DIDN'T EXPECT: PERSONAL STORIES ABOUT PREMATURE BIRTH, helped me realize how traumatized my sister, Phyllis and her husband must have been when they knew their baby was being born twenty-two weeks into her pregnancy. Being born early and at home compounded the situation. Her baby was placed in a neonatal intensive care unit where only the efficient nurses were allowed near the "preemies" for the first few hours of their lives.

"It is no secret that human beings need affection to thrive. Scientists have actually proven that humans are four to seven times more likely to succumb to sickness if they do not have a normal dose of nurturing love. Some studies have shown that people recover from illness quicker if they have a human being, or a pet, to supply that tenderness. Caring words, friendship, affectionate touch – all have healing qualities." (Frost, p. 38).

WHY? Because we all were created by God to receive and express love. If we do not receive it and learn to give it away, we may suffer emotionally and relationally and never reach our God-given potential. (para).

Finally, Mother had a great need to take better care of herself because she was getting sickly more often. She was giving her all to her grandchildren. Her own children were suffering from a lack of a mother's attention and were not going to elementary and high school regularly.

She wrote to Phyllis and told her to come and get her two children, which Phyllis and Willie, Sr. eventually did. Suddenly the accumulated weight became too much and Mother broke under the strain. She carried around all the worries, fears, anxieties and doubts she could carry for weeks on end.

Mother spread out her feelings before the Lord, prayerfully sorting things through and asking Him to dispose of the trash.

"Her mind needed to be renewed by the Holy Spirit," as John, the apostle declared.

"And we have come to know and have believed the love which God has for us. God is love. (1 JOHN 4: 16, NIV).

In doing so, "she discovered that she was exchanging her spirit of despair and struggles for a garment of praise."

I have trodden the winepress alone; from the nations, no one was with me. I trampled them in my anger and trod them down in my wrath; their blood spattered my garments, and I stained all my clothing. For the day of vengeance was in my heart, and the year of my redemption has come. I looked but there was no one to help, I was appalled that no one gave support, so my own arm worked salvation for me, and my own wrath sustained me. (ISAIAH 63: 3-5, NIV).

Mother was getting sicker and was sometimes not able to get out of bed. My younger siblings would take turns staying home from school to help take care of the Mary and Willie, Jr. and Mother. My younger siblings were worrying about how they were going to stay in school, working and sweating, and having enough money to help support the family and just survive. Daddy was often away on his job seventy-five miles away, working on the road in Wilmington, Delaware. I was still away in college.

When Phyllis came for her children, Mother was praising and praying for all of them:

Then came the love of the Father which is "uncommon Love" which is a gift of Christ. We all have been victims of common love – betrayed, burned, and broken by a form of love we thought was real but came with a price tag or a condition that we could not fulfill. Uncommon love is the Father's gift to us in Christ. He has dealt with our past and He owns our future. Today we must live in the present moment, filled and surrounded by uncommon love.

(Source: Graham Cooke, author and speaker).

"I will tell of the kindnesses of the Lord, the deeds for which He is to be praised; according to all the Lord has done for us, according to His compassion and many kindnesses."

God said, "Surely, they are my people, sons who will not be false to me; and so, He became their Savior. In all their distress, He too was distressed, and the angel of his presence saved them." (ISAIAH 63: 7-9, NIV).

After Phyllis took her children home with her to Florida, Mother was able to rest more and do the things she loved to do, play the piano for churches, go to the movies and other social Masonic events with Daddy and attend events that were held at her younger children's elementary and high schools.

She began to take back her life and her self-esteem. She realized that she did not have control of her life at that moment. It is important to communicate with people who matter to us, people who add value to our lives and who are essential to our lives. Mother loved her children and grandchildren dearly but it was not her responsibility to raise her children's children. These were her first grandchildren, small and needy.

But she wanted to return to using her talent of playing the piano and attending programs to use her voice in doing good things for others: inspiring, encouraging, educating and participating to spread the type of behavior that would make us strong and move us toward future opportunities.

Mother Lettie realized that she was a dream-maker, a change-maker and had to take back her own self-esteem and life. No one could do it for her. Someone said you cannot give to others until you first give to yourself and save your own life. She learned how to cope with her own life, again.

Mother enjoyed sponsoring musical programs on Saturday and Sunday evenings with singers like Sister Rosetta Thorp, and The Clara Ward Singers who participated readily with Mother.

Mother started her own group called the Heath Quartet, with her four oldest children when we were young. She continued with this group and added other church children and took us across Delaware and Pennsylvania schools and churches to participate in choir events.

Mark and Cheryl Chernoff, in their book, GETTING BACK TO HAPPY, stated, "Our journeys have been anything but easy and we have been forced to reinvent ourselves personally and professionally. We should be wholeheartedly grateful for the lessons we glean as we walk our way through it one day at a time." (p. xv, para).

How will we respond to the hand that we are dealt?

"We can either face what we are lacking and empower ourselves to play the game sensibly and resourcefully", or fall under the mast. (p. 212, para).

Then walk humbly with your God with prayer and supplication, knowing and believing that God loves us unconditionally. We were created in his image and He is love.

Everything happens for a reason; some say there is a reason for the season. I believe this is true. If God is for you and in your plans, who can be against you? People come into your life, especially children, for a reason, a season or a lifetime.

Mother took on a role that she did not ask for and made it her own. She said, "I may not remember what I ate this morning, but it helped me grow."

She knew that support and guidance would pay off. She made the task of raising her first grandchildren as her own, and we knew how faithful and loving she was to them. In this dynamic relationship with her grandchildren and God, we must lead with our effort and attitude. Then God leads through His divine providence. Some call it a miracle; others call it a coincidence.

Mother felt that if she could just give these grandchildren a good start, teach them to listen to their Creator because He was their dream - keeper, they would succeed.

Coach James Dru Joyce, II, (Lebron James' coach) wrote in his memoirs, BEYOND CHAMPIONSHIPS: A PLAYBOOK FOR WILLING IN LIFE, "Think of each day of your life as a beginning of a game, with the strongly held conviction that every time the ball gets thrown into the air, anything is possible. (Dru, p. 208).

Labran James wrote in his Forward to Coach Dru's book, "No matter what sort of obstacles we face, we can make our dreams a reality. We are no different from other kids in the world, as we all have dreams."

When Mary and Willie, Jr., the children went back to their parents, Phyllis Heath Pepper and Willie Pepper, and their other grandparents in Florida, we do not know if they were getting the nourishment of love and caring as when they were in the home of the Heath family. As we know, the game of life is always changing and many are involved in the changes.

Children have physical and mental challenges associated with growing up as well as adults have in growing old. Children have ill-health issues as well as aged persons.

Willie, Jr. had physical and mental problems from the beginning as he was a "preemie" infant. He was born at five and one-half months old.

The most compelling reason to trust God is His message of reconciliation and grace. This is the message for all times for all of us.

GOD GIVES US ALL HIS LOVE!

CHAPTER 25

REMEMBER WHO YOU ARE

A question that is personal as well as prophetic is "Who am I?" Life has some of the strangest ways of educating us. Our background, our genes, our heritage, our surroundings and our way of thinking will partially determine who we are or what we will be. Why does this matter?

All of us are unique, have different experiences even though we may grow up in the same house, in the same family. The truth is that everyone believes many things that cannot be tested or proven. Science nor religion is not capable of answering every question about ourselves or the universe. Every means of acquiring knowledge or understanding of self has many limits.

Dennis Kimbro said in his forward to Alene's book, DO RIGHT, DO GOOD, "Nothing is coincidental. I am convinced that many times in our lives, our Creator challenges us to do more and be more than what we think is possible. One may suggest that you accept that challenge by listening to the still small voice within you and taking the first step." (p. vii).

So many of us, like newly born turtles, are at risk at birth. We should all have a chance at life. God made each of us as unique individuals and unique animals. We all have a purpose to fulfill. How we react or fail to react toward our God gives purpose in life and determines the course of our future.

After high school, Willie, Jr. went to a program in Job Corp and completed this project. Attending additional schooling actually felt good. He stood more firmly inside himself and more conducive to his new life style and less of a magnetic pull for his high school life style.

He secured and held several jobs and occasionally sought other work. He was always on the go, seeking to improve himself. He wanted to pull himself in the best position to succeed in life.

For someone who had been at the mercy of others for so long, he was hungry and motivated to rise and be successful. Just thinking about his future made him have ambition and passion for continuing his education.

He was raised under a grandmother and aunts and uncles who were receiving college degrees. He wanted to move up the ladder, get a better job and take every opportunity the system had to offer.

Frederick Douglass, one of our Black Leaders of all time said, "It is easier to build strong children than to repair broken men."

Someone made this remark (an old Adage), "If you are not at the table, then you are on the menu."

Willie, Jr. did not know his family – his wife and children - because he lived so far away from them. There were times when Willie, Jr. came home to his family -his wife and children - and would sometimes abuse them as well as love them. But he would soon leave again. Yet, there was a strong love relationship between them. Willie, Jr. was a perfect example of what one can do in your life if you take advantage of the services, make the right decisions and move through the tough times. You can survive and meet your goals; and our people can create productive citizens and build themselves up.

REQUIREMENTS OF LOVE

Joyce Meyer, in her book, REDUCE ME TO LOVE, asked the question, "Are you willing and ready to become a student of the Love-Walk?

"If so, you need to know that it requires education and commitment. We must have our minds renewed to what love really is. It is not just a feeling we have; it is a decision we make – a decision to treat others the way Jesus would treat them."

"When we make a true commitment to walk in love, it usually causes a huge shift in our lifestyle. Many of our ways – our thoughts, our habits, our conversations – have to change." (p. 12).

For instance, we may be accustomed to spending all our extra money on ourselves only to discover that walking in love requires that we spend it on others, (para.)

"Love is tangible, it is not just an emotional feeling. It is a spiritual thing that cannot be seen or touched. But it is evident to everyone who comes in contact with it."

Eagerly pursue and seek to acquire love. Make it your aim, your great quest. (1 CORINTHIANS 14: 1, NIV).

Love does not come easy or without personal sacrifice; each time we choose to love someone, it will cost us something – great effort, commitment, time, money and energy. That is why we are told in the Book of Luke to count the cost before we make the commitment.

Jesus said to his disciples, "Anyone who does not carry his own cross and follow me cannot be my disciple." (LUKE 14: 27, NIV).

LOST FOREVER

Before Willie, Jr. died from a car accident in Florida, he sought to find his family who had moved to another town in Delaware. He wrote letters to his wife but she and her children had moved to another town. They never received his letters until after he died and his effects were brought home. The only family member he had a telephone number for was my sister, Nancy Heath Kellam, (his aunt).

While in the hospital in Florida from his car accident, he had someone call my sister who responded to his wife and children and informed them of his whereabouts. Willie, Jr. 's younger daughter,

Lentia, who was in college, flew to Florida to see him. By the time she arrived to see Willie, Jr., he died soon after and the daughter and my sister arranged to have his body sent to our home town in Delaware. He was buried near his mother, Phyllis Heath Pepper and his grandparents Lettie and George Heath.

WILLIE'S SUFFERING

We may never know the full extent of Willie, Jr's suffering and turmoil as life is full of challenges and successes. Infants and children suffer, too. We may not always understand their crying. This is their only way of communicating.

Scripturally, Paul's words to young Timothy were: "Do not let anyone look down on you because you are young." (1 TIMOTHY 4:12, NIV).

Paul encouraged Timothy to demonstrate his spiritual maturity by his actions, the way he spoke, lived his life, loved his parishioners, and exercised his faith in Christ. Young Timothy set an example for the world.

We may not catch a glimpse of the story of Willie, Jr.'s life, but we do know how his wife and children adored him and they suffered from the want of his love. Love begets love. When they were near each other, they showed their love for each other. However, there were times when Willie, Jr. was only privy to alcohol in his life.

I have heard it said that God has given all of us talents to achieve our goals. God gave Willie, Jr. talents, but he lacked the ability to show and achieve what was inside him.

GOOD THINGS COME TO THOSE WHO WAIT!

CHAPTER 26

SHE SACRIFICED HER FUTURE FOR "PUPPY" LOVE

By the time Terri was a young teenager she "fell" in love with Willie, Jr. In one of Joyce Meyer's books, REDUCE ME TO LOVE, it is pointed out that "one can desire to walk in love, but cannot do so because even though he or she has the urge to love unconditionally, they do not have the power to perform it. They may have elaborate plans, but always fail to carry them out." (p.17, para).

Terri Brown Pepper's unfulfilled desire was truly frustrating. She felt frustrated and wondered what was wrong with her. She was impatient with people, harsh, judgmental, sometimes selfish and unforgiving.

Without equivocation, a breakthrough in understanding came into her life when God began to show her that she could not love until she received His love for her. She mentally acknowledged through her Bible-teaching class as a youth that God loved her, but it was not a reality in her heart.

Terri was like a thirsty person with a glass of water sitting on the table in front of her who remained thirsty because she did not drink it.

LOVE HAS A BEGINNING AND A COMPLETION.

First God loves us and by faith we receive His love. Then we love ourselves in a balanced way, we give back to God and we learn to love others. "Love must follow this course or it is not complete."

The question is, "Are we lovable?"

That takes in a broad scope. We must think through this question before we can understand the true nature of God's love and his reason for loving us.

How can God love us, as imperfect as we are?

He can, because He wants to. It pleases Him. He foreordained us, and planned His love for us. He adopted us all as his children through Jesus Christ as it was His intent to do.

Ephesians 1 states "Grace and peace be unto you from God our Father and the Lord Jesus Christ. For He chose us in Him before the creation of the world to be holy and blameless in his sight. In love He predestined us to be adopted as His sons and daughters through Jesus Christ, in accordance with his pleasure and will. (EPHESIANS 1: 2-6, Para, NIV).

The positive or negative way we view God as our Father and provider will shape the way we live our lives as believers in the dark and dreary world.

An angel was awaiting me at the end of the tunnel of light; she had golden hair and an innocent stare, and I grasped for her hand in my plight.

All of us, to some extent, no matter how long or fervently we have walked with the Lord, have shades and colorations of misunderstandings about God.

Henry Ford once said, "Whether you believe you can or cannot is right."

Terri was going through a period of self-examination at a young age as she was making life-changing decisions and choices for herself and her family for many years.

Some time in our life, we will need a miracle from God. Many times, Terri has already found herself in positions that only her Creator could pull her out. She admittedly made mistakes and bad choices in her effort to find love and happiness. She had very little guidance when she moved away from home. She knew that others were criticizing her in the midst of her faults but she continued to lead her life as she saw fit.

As she read Scriptures, she found, "The Lord searches all hearts and understands all the intent of the thoughts." (1 CHRONICLES 28:9, para, NIV).

As she grew up, she learned how to fit in and acknowledge others as she connected with people. She projected decency and compassion.

Further, she learned about the power of Scriptures at an early age as they taught patience, self-control and supplied comfort. She learned how Jesus' words could change a life one verse at a time.

For whatever things were written before were written for our learning; that we through patience and comfort of the Scriptures, might have hope. (ROMANS 15: 4, NKJV).

When cares increase within me, your comfort gives me joy. (PSALM 94: 19, NIV).

As we go along in life, we find ourselves drawn to the passage of Scripture, that out of His glorious riches he may strengthen us with power through the Spirit in our inner being, so that Christ may dwell in our hearts through faith. (EPHESIANS 3: 16-19, para, NIV).

Terri frequently tells me, "God is a miracle worker."

He has spared her life many times. When she was lost, and needed a miracle, she needed more - a miracle that would change her heart and save her soul. She began to realize that if she began to look down upon the world and her activities as if she were outside them and she could not lever herself, her actions would ultimately lose their deeper meaning. This is the paradox; in her effort to find the ultimate truth and control over her existence as a human on earth, she risked ending up being a smaller person, not a larger person.

Thomas Hertog, quotes Aerndt in his book, ON THE ORIGIN OF TIME, "Earth is the very quintessence of the human condition. Whatever we find out about or do to the world are human discoveries and endeavors. No matter how abstract and imaginative our thoughts, or how far reaching their impact, our theories and our actions remain inextricably interwoven with our human earthly conditions."

TERRI TURNED TO HER CHURCH

Terri turned to her church.

Edward P. Wimberly states in his book, AFRICAN AMERICAN PASTORAL CARE, "In assisting the laity in its role within the caring ministry of the church, it is important to look at the total ministry of the church. Only when the total ministry is understood, is it possible to visualize the role of the laity in pastoral care within the ritual and worship context." (p.24).

Caring within a local black congregation is a response pattern to God's unfolding story in its midst. This unfolding story is one of liberation as well as healing, sustaining, guiding and reconciling. In response to God's story, the caring resources of the local black church are used to draw those within the church as well as those without the church into God's unfolding story. Caring is a ministry of the church and cannot be understood apart from the ecclesiological or theology of the church." (p. 25).

The purpose of God's rule is to draw all people and nations unto himself. His story is to defeat the powers of evil, oppression and suffering. His is a story of healing and wholeness whereby people live meaningful lives in their communities. This way God's resources can be made available to them and their growth and development.

I kept seeing a sign on the back of a truck, TEST IN PROGRESS, encouraging people to be understanding if they made mistakes, not just on the road but also in life. We need people to be more patient and accepting of our flaws and imperfections. These three words, TEST IN PROGRESS describe the whole human race. These tests are the daily reality for people we pass on the highway of life.

"From my minister," Terri said, "I heard these words," "All we like sheep have gone astray and the Lord hath laid on Him (Jesus) the iniquity of us all." (ISAIAH 53: 6, NKJV.)

Whosoever shall call upon the name of the Lord shall be saved. (ROMANS 10: 13, NIV.)
God will hear and honor our confession of his promises.

There is one body and one spirit, just as you are called to one hope when you are called; one Lord, one faith, one baptism, one God and Father of all, who is over all and through all and in all. (EPHESIANS 4:4-6, NIV).

God will give you a close-knit family of his own making.
Believe on the Lord Jesus Christ and thou shalt be saved. (ACTS 16: 31, NKJV).

WE SHARE A COMMON HOPE – THE HOPE OF HEAVEN.

CHAPTER 27

LOVE SHOWS DISCIPLINE

M y niece, Terri, expresses that God has given her talents – praying, caring for and loving others. She accepted motherhood and all that it entailed even though it was no easy task. She gave it her all as a young woman without much help and understanding from others. She sacrificed her youth for the love of her spouse who was also very young and immature. She realized that life was useless without love.

If I give all I possess to the poor; but have not love, I gain nothing. (1 CORINTHIANS 13:3, NIV).

Paul reminded his people that they were missing something, a very vital piece, one essential component. His believers possessed many spiritual gifts but lacked love. He used exaggerated language to emphasize his point.

Terri's famous words to me are, "Can't nobody 'do' me like Jesus; He's my friend." She realized that Jesus was 100% on her side. Although she was becoming more independent, she knew she needed someone on her side. That someone was the Holy Spirit.

In the past our Creator spoke to our ancestors through the prophets at many times and in various ways; in these last days He has spoken to us today through his son. He appointed Jesus as heir of all things, through whom He made the universe. (HEBREW 1:1-2, KJV).

The epistle of the HEBREWS states:

God, who at sundry times and in divers manners spoke in the time past unto the fathers by the prophets, hath in these last days spoken to us by the son, by whom also He made the worlds. He has spoken and he still speaks. According to the writer of Hebrews, He speaks to us today in the same way he spoke to Simeon through Jesus hundreds of years ago.

Over the years, many persons have focused on their God-given talents and made them their own. There is a rich folkloric tendency with persons, especially African Americans, whose lives have impacted others greatly; but their actions have gone unnoticed. So many have been overlooked for their talents and gifts.

Terri's independence allowed her to bare what others bury. She gave eye-opening self-protecting answers to her own questions. She had many health issues but sought to protect herself and became a health expert for herself. She is one of our unsung heroes, learning to think for herself.

Terri Brown Pepper was five -years younger than Willie Alex "Billie" Pepper, Jr., but she realized that she did not have to prove herself. She just needed to accept what God willed for her. God knows why he put her on earth, even though she was marginalized by others, especially her mother-in-law, Phyllis Pepper and was not recognized for her worth. She learned to be quiet and observe more; this act helped her to see things differently and she felt safer. She was relating to the Holy Spirit. She became more dedicated, compassionate and responsible. She became more hopeful for herself and her family. There were still unexpected situations and conditions that needed to be answered.

We have proven over and over again that our human knowledge will never be enough to rescue us from evil. (PROVERBS 4:14-16, para, NIV).

Though we have amassed immense knowledge and present remarkable insights, we still cannot stop the pain and heartache that we feel and sometimes inflict on others. We cannot halt the way of the wicked or stop the foolish, repetitive path that leads to hate and mistrust which causes us to stumble. (v. 19, para).

In Him we have redemption through His blood, the forgiveness of sin, in accordance with the riches of God's grace that he lavished on us with all wisdom and understanding. God's love is the power that forgives our sins, heals our emotional wounds and mends our broken hearts. (PSALM 147: 3, para, NIV).

Great is our Lord and mighty in power; His understanding has no limit. The Lord sustains the humble but casts the wicked to the ground. (v. 5-6).

Terri realized that she often feared the opinion of others; as she felt that she would not measure up. She was smart and wise but had placed her hope, not in God's unconditional love, but those who criticized and marginalized her. She could not control her weight and her emotions; and her internal battle intensified. She was miserable.

She is a Christian; even as a young person she desires to serve God. She is enslaved to her body and her emotions. Night after night, she cried into her pillow, pleading that God would heal her and make her normal. The life of prayer is essential for the believer. There is no wrong way to pray; there is nothing wrong with asking God for help. It is both human and natural. Prayer can change your life.

She and her family had a spiritual life. For millions of people, prayer and seeking God is a regular part of life, as natural as breathing. Oftentimes, people feel that they are not spiritual or religious enough to pray.

There is a reluctance based on a degree of humility, a degree of embarrassment, that shows an obstacle to prayer and the belief that the relationship with God depends on us or how good or significant we are. But God's love does not depend or rely on us and what we do. His love does not keep score. He has already sent us a savior to cure us from sin.

William A. Barry, in his book, A FRIENDSHIP LIKE NO OTHER, said, "God's offer of friendship does not depend on our significance but solely on God's desire for us." (p. 4).

Terri tells me, "He answered my prayers slowly and gently. First, He showed me my sins and forgave me, He gave me caring friends to talk to and reassurance from His word. Now I desire only to fear God and put my hope in His love and through his strength, I will delight in Him."

(Words paraphrased from Terri Brown Pepper and written with permission).

Instead of telling her to prove herself by showing her credentials, Terri's pastor and other parishioners in her congregation are encouraging her to demonstrate spiritual maturity through her actions now as in the earlier time in her life. No one can discredit her as a teacher and example to others, if she shows herself approved by a good example before God.

She is now called "Mama Terri" or "Mom Brown"

She is serving in a food distribution program at her church and community which ups her self-esteem and helps her to give encouragement and moral support to others less fortunate than she is. A great part of credit goes to her for the day to day good that she accomplishes. Even in her illnesses and suffering, she practices kindness and love. The hope and happiness that she receives comes from others such as her grandchildren and great-grandchildren. She daily loves them and wants what is best for them.

If Terri listens carefully, she will discover that the fears revealed in her questions will be presented in the Bible. The Bible is bluntly honest and has recorded the moral and spiritual truths and failures of those stories it tells. Jesus endorses the Bible and makes it clear that he believed the Old Testament was more that just history or national religious fables. (MATTHEW 4: 1-11, 5: 17-19, para, NIV).

He believed that the Scriptures were about him; they told the story of God's love and promise of a coming Messiah. (JOHN 5: 39-40, para, NIV).

JESUS LOVES THE LITTLE CHILDREN!

CHAPTER 28

ONE GREAT TRAGEDY IN LIFE

One tragic day, Terri and Willie, Jr.'s first-born son was struck by a bullet meant for someone else – his younger brother. Arshawon Brown Pepper was born on January 29, 1977 to Terri Lynn Brown Pepper and Willie Alex "Billie" Pepper, Jr. in Greenwood, Delaware and died on November 22, 2020 in Dover, Delaware. One moment of tragedy in his life rendered a God-given gift to all who knew him.

He was loved and adored by his family, especially his two younger sisters, Tikia and Lentia. He also had two younger brothers – Willie Alex, III and Jermaine. This event greatly changed his as well as his whole family's lives.

That fateful moment when Arshawon walked outside an establishment where he was playing a friendly game of cards in the Winter of 1999, he saw a man pointing a gun at his younger brother's head. He pushed his brother aside and took the bullet in his neck. The bullet was never removed from his neck. The removal of the bullet from Arshawon's neck would have caused instant death.

As he lay on the ground, he, as a twenty- one -year- old man, prayed, "Lord, help me live. I do not want to die. I want to live so I can show others the way."

Mary Smart said in her book, MY STORY, "I had been told that when someone dies, the first thing you forget is the sound of his voice." Terri heard her son's voice and she was terrified.

LOVE, FOR THE DAY IS NEAR!

What an incredible blessing for both brothers. They both lived. This was a contest between good and evil. Satan meant it for evil, but God triumphed over evil and saved both boys until such time as He would come again. Terri and Arshowan looked back on those dark days, and determination was the only thing that gave them hope. Living one more day at a time, as Tikia always says to me, "I'm living one day at a time," they realized that they were not alone. Arshowan lived over twenty more years in a wheel chair because he felt others beside him, holding his hand; helping him to live. He needed them and they needed him.

Putting on a new life requires an adjustment! Over time we grow into it, it suits us better. We may see things we did not see before.

Arshowan was blessed in his asking and receiving help from God.

The younger brother does not understand the world that he is living in but he is encouraged to be clothed with Jesus and become more like him in his thoughts and deeds. He will not reflect the kind, gentle, faithful ways of Jesus overnight. It is a long process of choosing to put on "the armor of light" every day because it is uncomfortable. Suffice it to say, God can change him for the better.

Mary Smart's Sunday school teacher said, "If you will pray to do what God wants you to do, he will change your life. If you will lose your life in the service of God, He will direct you. He will help you.

So, I challenge you to do that. Commit to the Heavenly Father, and He will guide your way.

PUTTING ON THE ARMOR OF LIGHT!

The apostle Paul instructed the Romans- Christ- followers -to "put on the armor of light" and practice right living. (ROMANS 13: 12, NIV).

And do this, understand the present time. The hour has come for you to wake up from your slumber, because our salvation is nearer now than when we first believed. The night is nearly over, the day is almost here. So, let us put aside the deeds of darkness and put on the armor of light. Clothe yourselves with the Lord Jesus Christ, and do not think about how to gratify the desires of the sinful nature. (ROMANS 13: 14, NIV).

HOW HE LIVED

Arshowan lived over twenty more years, sitting in a wheelchair as a reminder of God's grace and love. He lived and died to give his brother a life.

He found his own way and began his ministry of love in the dust. He learned to care for and nurture his mother, his sisters and brothers and others who surrounded him. He helped God's people care for others. As others, such as his little sister, Tikia, helped him, he helped those around him. He became a star in the community. He established a caring, loving relationship with whomever he met. Unknowingly, Arshowon became a shining light and a caring counselor to many. He was a shining example to all those in his path.

His condition and station in life was not for nought. God knew what he was doing! He took a crucial situation and added his glory to it. His aim was to enable others to draw insights which the naked eye could not see and put His therapeutic function on it.

That is why we must get wisdom and understanding. True wisdom that we so desperately need comes from God. Even though our knowledge falls short, God's wisdom proves to be what we need. His wisdom instructs Terri as well as all of us in a better truer life. As members, we come in many shapes and colors, widths and lengths, uneven edges and all. Some of us glitter from prominent places for the Kingdom. Others serve faithfully in smaller and accent positions.

As we grope in darkness, what do we want or need most? (THE LIGHT).

The last two lines of T. S. Eliot's poem. "The Rock" reads,

And we thank Thee that the darkness reminds us of light.
O Light Invisible, we give Thee thanks for Thy great glory.

We want direction and illumination. Darkness reminds us of our oppressive, burdensome self. It feels so heavy even though it is intangible. Only light, which is also intangible, pushes that feeling away.

LIGHT PROVIDES RELIEF.

Now it is time for the younger brother to ask for forgiveness and receive it. There is no time limit for asking for forgiveness. God the Creator is in charge of the laws of nature and has the prerogative and power to work outside of them. It is possible that God has established laws we know nothing about to govern and make miracles possible.

The truth is that everyone believes in something. How was it possible for one brother to love so much and live to tell it, to show it. This event proved that modern science does not always make things possible.

But God is an "All time, on time God," says Terri. He kept Arshawon alive as he saved his brother; then God allowed Arshawon to die.

Someday all believers will gather in one place and worship Jesus together. Walls are decorated with sapphire, amethyst and emerald stones and streets are pure gold and transparent like glass; there will be gates of pearls. The final touch: dominate colors of bright yellow and hot pink, glossy accent shades of blue, turquoise and red, varying widths and lengths across uneven random, overlapping shapes will be seen.

It was penned:

"It matters not how straight the gate or how charged with punishment the scroll; he is the master of his fate; he is the captain of his soul." (Invictus, para)

> JESUS DIED AND ROSE AGAIN TO SAVE US ALL! HE LIVES SO THAT WE MIGHT HAVE LIFE MORE ABUNDENTLY.

CHAPTER 29

NO AGE LIMIT

ove is powerful, no matter what the age. One must wonder, what kind of value does one place on love and unity with others? Why is it vital for us to lovingly consider others despite agreements or disagreements with one another? Because God "searches every heart and understands every thought." (1 CHRONICLES 28:9).

Regardless of her age, Terri has impacted her family life, the community, the nation. She is doing it by setting Christ - like examples for others as God provides whatever she needs. He is shaping her life with the gospel. So, whether she was one- year- old, or seventeen-years old or sixty-years old as she started out in life, what notion of belonging might have been possible as she is growing in spiritual maturity and devotion to Christ. She does not feel worthy of all she receives. She praises God without ceasing and increases her faith in Him daily.

Terri has become a legend over the years within her family, her community and her world during those impressionable days. She is wise beyond her years and others are reaping the benefits of her knowledge, thoughts and understanding. She is loving, compassionate, dedicated and responsible for her children and grandchildren. She is working towards a goal; her aspirations are meaningful and her commitment is steadfast. She tries not to let temporary setbacks and negative issues throw her off course. She declares new mercies each day for herself and feels that God is always near her. She realizes that if you do not leave your past behind you, you cannot have a future.

It is amazing how much one learns, remembers and experiences as a child. It is even more amazing how much one remembers when old age creeps up on you.

Many of our people have not been recognized for their achievements and accomplishments; let alone have their names put in a book. Therefore, little is known about them. Oftentimes, we may perform well, but it does not seem to matter. One achievement that Terri is noted for is raising five children, as she was only a teenager/ young adult herself. Come what may, she had help only from God and the elderly adults in her life. She had many challenges to overcome along the way. She says, "I do not do what I use to do."

She accepted her tasks humbly and graciously. God's love triumphs and He is merciful. She does not look like what she has been through.

I say, "Do not worry about your life, what you will eat or drink or what you will wear. Your heavenly Father knows that you need them. So, seek first His kingdom and his righteousness, and all these things will be added. Do not worry about tomorrow." (MATTHEW 6: 28-34, para, NIV).

If you are still living on earth, no matter what circumstances or challenges you are facing, there is "No such thing as impossible;" says Jairo Alvarez Botero.

"If you believe and are willing to pay the price to live your dreams, anything is possible," says Julio Melara, entrepreneur, publisher, author.

Joyce Meyer said, in her book, REDUCE ME TO LOVE, "If you want to know about love, try to find someone who operates in love and study that individual. Watch how he or she handles people and difficult or tense situations. All of us must not only learn about love but also seek, pursue and acquire it, because God's word boldly tells us that without it, we are absolutely nothing." (p. 13).

LOVE YOUR ENEMY

Matthew 5 denotes: "You must have love for your enemies."

You have heard it said, "Love your neighbor, and hate your enemy. But I tell you ' Love your enemy and pray for those who persecute you, that you may be sons of your Father in heaven. He causes His sun to rise on the evil and the good, and sends rain on the righteous and the unrighteous. If you love those who love you, what reward will you get? Are not even the tax collectors doing that? And if you greet only your brothers (and sisters) what are you doing more than others? Do not even pagans do that? Be perfect, therefore, as your heavenly Father is perfect." (MATTHEW 5: 43-48, para, NIV).

GIVE TO THE NEEDY

Be careful not to do your 'acts of righteousness' before men, to be seen by them. If you do, you will have no reward from your Father in heaven.

So, when you give to the needy, do not announce it with trumpets, as the hypocrites do in the synagogues and on the streets, to be honored by men. I tell you the truth, they have received their reward in full. But when you give to the needy, do not let your left hand know what your right hand is doing, so that your giving may be in secret. Then your Father, who sees what is done in secret, will reward you. (MATTHEW 1: 4, para, NIV).

REMEMBER, THE SCRIPTURE DENOTES, THE GREATEST OF THESE IS LOVE.

If I speak in the tongues of men and angles, but have not love, I am only a resounding gong or a clanging cymbal.

And if I have the gift of prophecy and can fathom all mysteries and all knowledge, and if I have faith so that I can move mountains, but have not love, I gain nothing. If I give all I possess to the poor and surrender my body to the flames, but have not love, I gain nothing.

Love is patient, love is kind. It does not envy, it does not boast, it is not proud. It is not rude, it is not self-seeking, it is not easily angered, it keeps no record of wrongs. Love does not delight in evil but rejoices in the truth.

Love and service to others always protects, always trusts, always hopes, always perseveres. (1 CORINTHIANS 13: 1-7, para, NIV).

And now these three remain, faith, hope and love. But the greatest of these is love. (v. 13).

The great artists keep us from smugness, from thinking that the truth is in us, rather than in God. They help us know that we are often closer to God in our doubts than in our certainties, that it is all right to be the small child who asks: Why? Why? Why?

If a man will begin with certainties, he shall end in doubt; but if he will be content to begin with doubts, he shall end on certainties. (Francis Bacon).

In his book, THE GREATEST THING IN THE WORLD, Henry Drummond says that "to love abundantly is to live abundantly and to love forever is to "live forever."

Life's journey is not easy. To love abundantly and love forever, you must learn to walk in love toward everyone. But to do that, you must first receive God's love for you because it is impossible to give to others something you do not have yourself.

> LEARN TO WALK IN LOVE FOR ALL PEOPLE.

CHAPTER 30

THE MELODY OF OUR LIVES

As the melody of our lives unfolds daily and over the years, the high points lie in the fact that God is never going to make a mistake with his plans and motif that He specially designed for us; whatever He does will endure forever. Whenever I tried to start and complete a task, I was determined to succeed. I did not always ask for help; I just tried to make it happen.

Luci Swindoll, in the WOMEN'S DEVOTIONAL BIBLE, states, "God brings out the beauty of harmony and richness as He directs every facet of our lives. This fact guarantees that all crises already have been met and overcome in Him." (para).

As we live and bear our burdens, it is easy to feel burdened by difficult circumstances and think, "Why should I give to others while I am still lacking?"

Do you remember the story of Joseph, the younger brother, who was sold into slavery to Egyptians by his older brothers only for Joseph to be able to help the brothers and their father when they were in need of food and water later. While Joseph was put into prison, God was showing him how to help others when they were in need. He could not have helped his older brothers or others had the God-given talent had risen from his own station in life to help others in need.

Normally, humans look at outward appearances but God looks at the heart. He excels at making outsiders insiders by choosing the meek and lowly to accomplish His purpose.

We must be assured that the melody of our lives is controlled by the Eternal God of the Universe who knows us from beginning to end; He gives us the strength and the ability to do His will. Let there be no mistake or question of what our song is about. Love! Love does not keep score.

JESUS ATE WITH SINNERS.

Jesus was invited to a great banquet. When he came into the Pharisee's home in the rich suburbs of Jerusalem, he noticed the wealthy people grabbing the best seats around the table near the front. Can you imagine what happened next?

When he sat down, Jesus probably put the napkin in his lap and quietly picked up an hors d'oeuvre. Dead silence hung over the room as the wealthy people looked nervously at one another. Jesus had put a damper on the party spirit!

He said,

"When you give a banquet, invite the poor, the crippled, the lame, the blind and you will be blessed. Although they cannot repay you, you will be repaid at the resurrection of the righteous." (LUKE 14: 13-14, NIV).

Jesus spoke the language of love. He understood us. You could hear love talking. He always said the right thing the right way. It is important how you talk to people. Jesus used the language of love; so must we if we would follow in his footsteps and if we are to see anything accomplished.

Paul says that love has good manners. So, let us try a few good manners and see how many people will respond positively. This is the language of love.

Love and faithfulness meet together; righteousness and peace kiss each other. Faithfulness springs forth from the earth, and righteousness looks down from heaven.

The Lord will indeed give that which is good, and our land will yield good harvest; righteousness goes before him and prepares the way. (PSALM 85: 10-15, NIV).

GOD SAYS THANK YOU

You must not sit and spin your wheels. If you have cast in all you possibly can of your money, time, energy and service, God understands. He affirms you and says thank you. Jesus always notices individuals who throw everything they have into the Lord's work. Once you finally achieve your dreams, the suffering and challenges you overcome along the way will make fulfillment and attainment even more rewarding. The path to success is challenging, yet God is in the plan and the reward is worth it.

Jesus was sitting near the treasury at the temple. He drew his disciples' attention to a poor widow. She was unaware that Jesus was watching. Her two small copper coins would have bought her a morsel of bread or five sparrows to eat. She decided to go hungry and give her money to God instead. (LUKE 12: 6-7, NIV).

Two small coins was not much! These coins were not noticed by others. They were not appreciated by others until Jesus came along and saw what she did and made sure the twelve disciples saw it.

Jesus made sure that Luke and Mark recorded this act and that the whole world would know about it!

Solomon's temple would stand without the help of the widow's coins, but Jesus knew that this sort of giving was the stuff of what the kingdom was made.

FROM STRUGGLES TO SUCCESS.

Jairo Alvarez Botero wrote in his memoir, NO SUCH THING AS IMPOSSIBLE: FROM ADVERSITY TO TRIUMPH, the story of his difficult and struggling life in Colombia before he came to Baton Rouge, Louisiana as an immigrant. As a brave, caring man he provided a good character while sharing his fortune with those less privileged. He improved himself through education as he graduated with honors from a business school in New York, from the eventual move of his young family from a fairly prosperous but dangerous life in Columbia to a new beginning in Baton Rouge; from the professional trials that eventually led him from marginal success to his proud accomplishments as a builder that made him a millionaire.

He drew his great faith and his father's profound wisdom to always do the right thing when lesser men would have run quickly and run far from the many difficult challenges that crossed his path. (p. v-vi, para).

Jesus always noticed the small things, the small offerings. Even if the widow herself did not think her offering was worth his notice, Jesus affirmed her in her service.

> He said, "I tell you the truth, this poor widow has put in more than all the others. All these people gave their gifts out of their wealth, but she gave out of her poverty and put in all she had to live on. (LUKE 21: 1: 4, para, NIV).

RICH IN SPIRIT

Terri Brown Pepper, my niece, (my nephew, Willie Alex "Billie" Pepper, Jr.'s widow), raised five children on her own and is now helping to raise grandchildren and great-grandchildren. They are so beautiful and precious to her and she loves them all. Her gifts from God are to love, to give, to be a servant to others.

The Scriptures tells us that Solomon "spoke three thousand proverbs." (1 KINGS 4: 32, NIV).

These wise sayings describe patterns that operate in our everyday life. They offer advice on how to conduct ourselves in various situations. Solomon's fundamental instructions is to fear and trust our Lord.

Remember, God has something to say about every aspect of our lives. Each person must lead his or her life to help others. Therefore, seek His wisdom in the decisions we make each day. Terri does just that!

Let the wise listen and add to their learning. The fear of the Lord is the beginning of knowledge. (PROVERBS 1: 5-7, NIV).

Terri gives service to those in her community, and in her neighborhood. On special days -holidays – she donates her time and talent to many people and warms the hearts of others. She donates herself to amplify the voices of the subjugated and silenced persons. She helps to safeguard rights and secure a safer, more equitable future for her family and others in need. She is compassionate, kind and generous.

Terri is committed to God's Word which is a key step toward a safer, more just world for all of us, no matter how we identify ourselves or whom we love.

In talking to her, I sense that Terri has unfulfilled desires and is often frustrated. Sometimes she expresses that she wonders what is wrong with her, there is so much frustration.

Karen Burton Mains said "Being a servant is one of the most important lessons for Christians to learn; but unfortunately, we often have to work through gross misconceptions. We have fears about entrusting ourselves to any boss; but we must learn in our spiritual journey that this Master, God, is unlike any other. He will not abuse us or misuse us."

A breakthrough in understanding came when God began to show Terri that she could love others as she received God's love for herself.

She desired to walk in love, but sometimes it seemed impossible. She had the urge, but no power to perform it.

Romans 7: 18-19 expresses to all of us, "I know that nothing good lives in me, that is, in my sinful nature. For I have the desire to do what is good, but I cannot carry it out. For what I do is not the good I want to do." (NIV).

You showed favor to your land, O Lord; you restored the fortunes of Jacob. You forgave the iniquity of your people and covered all their sins.

You set aside all your wrath and turned from your fierce anger. (PSALM 85: 1-3, NIV).

AN HONEST ADMISSION

A wise woman once said, "The person I have the most trouble with is the person I see in the mirror every day. This wise woman was Whitney Houston. She also said, "Surely this is an honest admission for all of us."

When one of us has grieved over our own spiritual shortcomings; "over doing those things I ought not to have done and leaving undone things which I ought to have done," no follower of Christ was ever more acutely conscious of this very trait and tendency than the apostle Paul. We can take comfort in this thought, but to not allow ourselves to be trapped in Satan's snare – wallowing in despair – is to disparage the limitless, liberating grace of God."

TALK TO GOD

Restore us again, O God our Savior, and put away your displeasure toward us. Will you be angry with us forever? Will you prolong your anger through all generations? Will you not revive us again, that your people may rejoice in you?

Show us your unfailing love, O Lord, and grant us your salvation.

I will listen to what God, the Lord will say. He promises peace to his people, his saints, but let them not return to folly.

Surely His salvation is near those who fear him that his glory may dwell in our land. (PSALM 85: 4-9, NIV).

Hear us, O Lord and answer us. We are poor and needy. Guard our lives for we are devoted to you. You are our God; save your servants who trust in you. (PSALM 86: 1-2, NIV).

He has our greatest interest at heart. He encourages us through our servanthood to be all that we can be and then gives us His own Holy Spirit to empower us to become good servants. He is a Master unlike any other. He is to be feared; He is worthy of our service. When we serve the Master, He makes us full, complete human beings filled with His own image. While teaching us to be more like Him, we become more of whom He created us to be.

Jesus said, "For who is greater, the one who is at the table or the one who serves? But I am with you as one who serves. You are those who stood by me in my trials. And I confer on you a kingdom just as my Father conferred one on me, so that you may eat and drink at my table in my kingdom and sit on thrones judging the twelve tribes of Israel." (LUKE 22: 27-29, NIV).

Down from Jesus' cross poured redemptive love in quantity enough for the whole human race – enough for you; enough for me. Far from decreasing love because of our behavior against him, it seems rather to increase. The same situation still exists today and will exist as long as life lasts and the earth stands. As the God-Man hung above them, praying for them, he loved them with the kind of love that could have healed them on the spot!

"Father, forgive them, for they know not what they do." (LUKE 23: 34, NIV).

There is nothing in God's word that is contrary to God's will. 2 Peter tells us the Lord is not willing that anyone should perish. We should pray for those outside the body of Christ, but we must remember that the person for whom we are praying has a free will, just as you and I have.

Christenson stated, "God never superimposes His will upon anyone, but the timing and sovereignty are his. It is God's will that we pray that everyone be saved, but we are to leave the results with Him. God's word tells us we believers have two Intercessors – Christ at the right hand and the Holy Spirit dwelling in us. The Holy Spirit takes our prayers when we do not know what we should pray for and brings them to the Father "according to the will of God. (ROMANS 8: 26-27, para, NIV).

THE ASCENSION

When he had led them out to the vicinity of Bethany, he lifted up His hands and blessed them. While he was blessing them, he left them and was taken up into heaven. Then they worshiped him and returned to Jerusalem with great joy. And they stayed continually at the temple, praising Him. (LUKE 24: 50: -53, NIV).

HALLELUJAH, YOU'RE WORTHY TO BE PRAISED!

CHAPTER 31

INVISIBLE SCARS

nvisible scars are those deep hurts and wounds that others cannot see or understand. But they are real pain and suffering scars. How we respond to hurt and danger says a lot about us. David is the youngest child in the family of several children. Why would a mother send her youngest child out to pasture to tend the sheep herd. How could she trust him to do a good job? Why, O why, Lord?

In Psalm 6, David wrote of his deep struggling:

O Lord, heal me for my bones are in agony.
My soul is in anguish; how long, Lord, how long?
Turn, O Lord, and deliver me;
Save me because of your unfailing love. (PSALM 6: 2- 4, NIV).
I am worn out from groaning;
All night long I flood my bed with weeping,
And drench my couch with tears.
My eyes grow weak with sorrow;
They fail because of all my foes.

Away from me, all you who are evil.
For the Lord has heard my weeping.
The Lord has heard my cry for mercy;
The Lord accepts my prayer.
All my enemies will be ashamed and dismayed.
They will turn back in sudden disgrace. (PSALM 6: 6-10,NIV).

David's mother did not make a mistake. She sent a young child out to be a shepherd boy! He came back a king! God knew what He was doing and he helped David's mother to understand his will for David.

GOD NEVER MAKES A MISTAKE

Evelyn Christenson, in her book, WHAT HAPPENS WHEN WOMEN PRAY, states, "In order to pray effectively in God's will, you may need a new view of God – as One who never makes a mistake." (p. 76).

Is your God "an all-wise" Father, and an "on-time God" who knows the end from the beginning. (Terri oftentimes speaks those words).

We may want something badly and pray in earnest for it. We may pray for something that seems very good to us, but God knows the "what ifs" in our lives. He knows the calamities that might occur if he answered our prayer in the way we think best. He also knows about all our difficult situations and wants to turn them into something tremendously good. This view of God as an omniscient Father comes into focus very clearly as the years pass." (p. 77, para).

One of the advantages of growing older is that we can look back and see God has not made a single mistake in our lives. Maybe we will get to heaven before we understand some things, but it is exciting to recognize as years come and go that God has worked everything for good if we have really loved Him. As we review our past history of what has happened to us, we realize that the difficult things were there for a reason, and God has made no mistakes.

The prophet Micah confessed this even while enduring a heart rending "Winter" as the Israelites turned away from God. As Micah assessed the bleak situation, he lamented that not one upright person seemed to remain.

What misery is mine! The godly have been swept from the land; not one upright man remains. (MICAH 7: 1-2, NIV).

So then, those who suffer according to God's will should commit themselves to their Creator and continue to do good. (1 PETER 4: 19, NIV).

Another very interesting point Christenson made was that we must make prayer requests, not prayer answers. The difference is that when we pray answers, we are demanding that God do something and we are telling Him we want it done now – just the way we want it, Lord.

When we are bringing our request to Him, we are saying, "Lord, here is the need – the circumstance, the person, or whatever it may be; then we ask Him to answer according to His omniscient will." (p 78.)

ISRAEL WILL RISE

Do not gloat over me, my enemy! Though I have fallen, I will rise. Though I sit in darkness, the Lord will be my light. Because I have sinned against him, I will bear the Lord's wrath, until he pleads my case and established my right. He will bring me out into the light and I will see his righteousness. (MICAH 7: 8-10, NIV).

Shepherd your people with your staff; the flock of your inheritance.… Nations will see and be ashamed, deprived of all their power. As in the days when you came out of Egypt, I will show them my wonders. (v. 14,16).

> # HOPE IS THE CRACK OF LIGHT
> # THAT HIT THE DOOR!

CHAPTER 32

STANDING IN THE NEED OF PRAYER

t's Me, It's me, it's me, Oh Lord. Standing in the need of prayer.

If you or someone is suffering or having a rough time, check in with Jesus. Turn to God in prayer; fill your mind with the power of the Holy Spirit. Let Him touch you with the power of His word. Then, focus on His restorative strength to heal you and lift you up as one of those who needs a blessing.

> *Hundreds of years after David composed his Shepherd Song, the Twenty-Third Psalm, Jesus said, "I am the Good Shepherd." (HEBREW 13:30, NIV).*

Our Lord has a shepherd's heart, faithfulness, strength and tenderness. With David's thoughts in mind, we must acknowledge the many persons that have made great contributions directly and indirectly to the development, unfolding and expansion of our people's achievements and accomplishments.

Prayer changes things. Dear God, be with those who are struggling with hardships. Help them to feel your comfort and love. Heal them accordingly and let thy will be done.

Paul wrote to Timothy, "I thank God, whom I serve, as my forefathers did, with a clear conscience, as night and day, I constantly remember you in my prayers. Recalling your tears, I long to see you, so that I may be filled with joy. I have been reminded of your sincere faith, which first lived in your grandmother Lois and your mother Eunice and, I am persuaded, now lives in you, also."

"For this reason, I remind you to fan into flame the gift of God, which is in you through the laying on of hands. For God did not give us a spirit of timidity, but a spirit of power, of love and of self-discipline." (2 TIMOTHY 1: 3-7, NIV).

MY SPECIAL TEACHER

My special elderly schoolteacher, Miss Mary Daniels, taught children in the public schools for forty years; she retired from teaching, then volunteered in a mission school.

This is why I wanted to go into the missionary field. I was too young after college to become a member of this field in Africa. But later, after I retired from being in Social Work in New Orleans and the Psychological Counseling field in a college setting for thirty- six years, I received an opportunity to go into the missionary field in two countries in Africa – Kenya, Africa and Senegal, West Africa and one area in China -Canton.

Miss Daniels was asked, "How do you go on day after day with your work?"

She replied, "I do not stop and think about it."

She felt that God wanted her in the mission field and she had accepted this fact. She was happy to do her work and she enjoyed seeing children learn. Her work was exhilarating and quite adequate and satisfying. She did not have great wealth and possessions, but with daily prayer, she was grateful for her life. When I was in elementary school as one of her pupils, my mother would let me go home with her to help wash her dishes and help around the house. She would send me to her strawberry field to pick a few for us to eat that night. I loved working in her big beautiful home.

In the late 1960's I came back home from Louisiana to Delaware to find my special teacher on her death-bed.

I was offered the opportunity to say good – bye to her before she died. God gave her all those years to work with children; she never had children of her own and her husband died at a young age from a rare disease. Yet her need for children gave her the spirit to work with other people's children – both in this country and abroad.

God wanted her to do good and gave her the patience to work with little children for seventy years.

> *In the same way, let your light shine before others, so that they may see your good works and give glory to your Father who is in heaven. (MATTHEW 5: 16, ESV).*

God wants us to use our time and energy to bless and heal someone and interact as an opportunity to make someone's day brighter. God will show you where you are needed and give you the grace to make a positive impact on someone else's heart.

JESUS BEGINS TO PREACH

> *When Jesus heard that John had been put into prison, he returned to Galilee …. to fulfill what was said through the prophet Isaiah.*

> *"The people living in darkness have seen a great light; on those living in the land of the shadow of death, a light has dawned."*

From that time on, Jesus began to preach, "Repent, for the kingdom of heaven is near." (MATTHEW 4: 12-14, 16-17, NIV).

WE ARE ALL STANDING IN THE NEED
OF PRAYER AND GOD'S LOVE.

PART FOUR

NEW GENERATIONS

CHAPTER 33

PREPARATIONS FOR THE NEW GENERATIONS

Today's children and youth are the future of tomorrow. This phase is often heard today. Yet they have much to say in our live time today. Therefore, they must be taught to include a competitive spirit, self-disciplined stance, and confidence to their commitments and goals.

"More than half a century ago, before the discovery of DNA, the Austrian Physicist and philosopher Erwin Schrodinger inspired a generation of scientists by rephrasing for them the timeless philosophical question: WHAT IS LIFE? He wrote his book bearing that name in 1944 which like a crystal repeats its structure as it grows. But life is far more fascinating and unpredictable than any crystallizing mineral.

The difference in structure is of the same kind as that between an ordinary wallpaper in which the same pattern is repeated again and again in regular periodicity and a masterpiece of embroidery which shows no dull repetition, but an elaborate, coherent meaningful design by the great Master." (Schrodinger, MY VIEW OF THE WORLD, p. 5)

He addresses life's fullness without sacrificing any science, and reproduces not only Schrodinger's title, but his spirit.

Our ancestors found spirits and gods everywhere animating all of nature. Life maintains by making more of itself. The world as a vast machine fails to account for our self-awareness and self-determination, and did not come into existence on its own.

After centuries of humans meddling with steamy concoctions in a Faustian quest to be godlike, a secret discovery in 1953 seemed to reveal the vast secret of life. Life was chemical and the material basis of heredity was DNA whose helical and stair-case-like structure made clear how molecules copied themselves.

"Replication was no longer beholden to a mysterious vital principle; it was the straightforward result of interacting molecules. The description of how DNA fabricated a copy of itself out of ordinary carbon, nitrogen and phosphorus atoms was the most spectacular of all mechanism's successes. Paradoxically, this success born of self-directed minds seemed to portray life as the result of atoms involuntarily interacting according to changeless and inviolable chemical law." (Schrodinger, p.7).

DNA's AFFECT ON LIFE

The world as a vast machine fails to account for our own self-awareness and self-determination because the mechanical world-view denies choice. Mechanisms do not act; they react and do not come into existence on their own. Like an uncoiling spring pushing the soft gears of life, DNA copies itself as it directs the making of proteins that together form living bodies in general. Understanding how DNA works may be the greatest scientific breakthrough in history. Nonetheless, neither DNA nor any other kind of molecule can, by itself, explain life. (p. 8, para).

I often heard my mother say that her first baby, Phyllis Heath, was born early, therefore bearing the name of "preemie." She weighed less than three pounds at birth; maybe the type of birth is in the DNA because I learned much later that my mother was born early, less than three pounds- that's generations of infants born much before their due date.

Phyllis Heath Pepper's second child, Willie Alex "Billie," Pepper, Jr. weighed less than three pounds at birth. Before birth, both mother, Lettie Harper Heath and Phyllis Heath Pepper had another trimester to check off; but the time was here. Your water broke. Both mother and daughter were about to become a parent earlier than they expected. They were mothers now. Their first lesson was about separation. They were connected to things other than themselves. They lived.

Phyllis and her husband Willie, Sr. stayed at home with our mother and father in Delaware after giving birth to their son, Willie, Jr. He stayed in the hospital, placed in his minuscule hospital bed to be wheeled off to the Intensive Care Unit. The parents and grandparents left the hospital.

Only the mother, Phyllis could return daily to see Willie, Jr. for two weeks, and then the father and mother were allowed to see Willie, Jr. The infant was progressing very slowly and the parents became wary and disheartened and felt that the baby would not survive.

They left the Milford Memorial hospital in Delaware after three weeks of visiting the infant and returned to Florida and their jobs. Willie, Jr.'s grandparents, Lettie and George Heath returned nightly to see the baby until such time that he was released from the hospital in a stable condition and taken to the grandparents' home. Finally, after over nine weeks, the baby was sent home with grueling care to be administer by the grandmother, Lettie and two young teenage aunts, Nancy and Hattie to care for him.

They were very diligent and supportive and Willie, Jr. began to grow into a happy baby, although everyone else in the household had sleep deprivation, falling asleep only to wake what seemed like every few minutes.

Mother wrote regularly to keep Phyllis aware of the progress of her baby. After ten months Phyllis and Willie came and took the child home with them, only to bring him back in a few months. They were weary from caring from such a small, needy infant. They realized it was a round the clock task to keep him alive. This went on for years, changing parents and grandparents and schools.

NEW GENERATIONS

We have named the young leaders of the world millennials and Gen Z; we must prepare our new generations for real freedom. Some of the mysteries of life can be the most rewarding experiences ever.

"There is an urgent need for collective healing that invites Black and Brown women to tell their stories from the crown down. While narrative therapy as a practice is credited to New Zealand based family therapist Michael White and David Epston, in their book, TRAUMA, TRESSES AND TRUTH, retelling important incidents and stories has served as a healing modality for millennia. White and Epston recognized within a therapeutic context that we all carry internalized and evolving self-narratives that influence how we feel, think, and behave. Some stories are healing while others are problematic.

Narrative therapy invites people to reauthor problematic stories. Narrative differs from other therapies in that the storyteller is regarded as an expert." (Source: FOREWORD, Afiya M. Mbililishaka, Clinical Psychologist and Hairstylist).

BRIGHTEN THEIR FUTURE

Educating children and teens is the best way to brighten their future and we must take responsibility for it. It could be a teacher, mentor, tutor, family member or a friend – we all remember someone in our childhood who encouraged us to follow our dreams and helped us see our potential. Even if one such person dripped into our lives fleetingly, it is those moments that can make or break an individual. This is why some professionals and entrepreneurs are reaching a hand down to the next generation of "changemakers" to lift them up and give them the tools to succeed.

Jesus pursues us in love. We as adults must use our backgrounds and skills to meet youngsters where they are and help them get where God wants them to be. We must encourage all leaders to invest in the youth and to do different things; if we work together just like one body, with unity, we can help our young people grow and thrive.

I remember an elderly old black lady who started coming to our church one day when I was about nine-years-old. She was a part of a group of migrant workers who came from Florida to Delaware to work in the fields and apple orchards. Her family and other members of her group returned to Florida or Pennsylvania or New York to meet other crop seasons.

But Miss Burton stayed in Greenwood, Delaware along with three of her young grandchildren. She made her home there and accepted our church as her home church.

Each Sunday morning, she would sing the same song; "I Will Trust In The Lord 'Till I Die," and end her testimony with: "I came here to serve the Lord; If I can't do you no good, I "ain't gonna" do you no harm."

The children, along with some of the adults "cracked up laughing," but I bet they remembered that old "saying" from that old lady.

JUST FIX EDUCATION

If we could just fix education, we could fix so many other things. Education is a mindset in how we raise our children as a community. What better way than to pour into our communities and our world a better place than what we found. It is our responsibility to move forward and leave things better than we found it.

Wes Moore ruminated, "Kids need to care that you care before they care what you think." (Source: Wes Moore, THE OTHER WES MOORE: ONE NAME: TWO FATES).

Nelson Mandela, leader in South Africa and the world, said," Any country, any society which does not care for its children is no nation at all. Mandela implicitly understood that we are all tied to one another – inevitably and irrevocably – whether we want to accept it or not. (Source: Chris Niles. UNICEF. "Nelson Mandela: "Any Society Which Does Not Care for its Children is No Nation at All." July 17, 2013.)

Continuing education is so important in any industry. It is said that community can be any place, any person and the more we are able to expand our definition of what it means to be in community with people, the better stewards we can be of one another; and the better stewards we can be in the place where we live. If the situation or the context where you make decisions do not change, then second changes do not matter much.

Young people want to be somewhere that is vibrant. There is one problem with this; people become comfortable in what works for them, not recognizing that it does not work for everyone.

David Brooks wrote in his book, ROAD TO CHARACTER, about a group of people who faced a "moral crisis." Brooks is a well-known conservative speaker, but that does not mean he does not extend great generosity of spirit to all those trying to make it.

He said: "When they had quieted themselves, they had opened up space for grace to flood in. They found themselves helped by people they did not expect would help them. They found themselves understood and cared for by others in ways they did not imagine beforehand. They found a vocation or calling; They committed themselves to some long obedience and dedicated themselves to some desperate lark that gives life purpose."

We must not tolerate mediocrity but instead put forth more energy sometimes requiring us to do things differently. The millennials and Gen Z must keep their minds open and focused on progress and equity.

"Diversity of thought and diversity of experiences provide a breeding ground for opportunities and change," said Norisha Kirks Glover, of NRK Construction Industry.

We must join her with the privileges of sharing the good news and good works with others. Sometimes when we love someone, we feel we just cannot do enough for him or her. We may even go without things we need ourselves. Many parents feel that way about their children. Love makes us generous. But generosity is more than giving.

Jesus could have showered gifts on us; but he did not. He provided only for his disciple's and other's basic needs. He saw to it that they had enough to eat and shelter. He watched them counting coins but he could have filled their laps with riches.

He taught them: "Freely you have received, freely give. Do not take along any gold or silver or copper in your belt; take no bag for the journey, or extra tunic, or sandals or a staff; for the worker is worth his keep."

Whatever town or village you enter, search for some worthy person there and stay at his house until you leave. As you enter the home, give it your greeting and your blessing. (MATTHEW 10: 9-12, NIV).

This is what God has called us to do. We do not need to be concerned whether we can do a perfect job. He will help us walk with Him and learn more of him. God is love and love does not keep score.

Then Jesus came to them and said, "All authority in heaven and on earth has been given to me. Therefore, go and make disciples of all nations, baptizing them in the name of the Father and of the Son and of the Holy Spirit, and teaching them to obey everything I have commanded you. And surely, I am with you always, to the very end of the age."

Jesus said, "So, do not worry, what you shall eat or what you shall drink. For the pagans run after all these things, and your heavenly Father knows."

AMERICA'S PLIGHT

For centuries, there have been those who have led the struggles for a different kind of America, one that is just and caring for all Americans, especially children. Social historians concur that adults increasingly view children as vulnerable, innocent and dependent human beings whose parents and other adults need to prepare them for life. We must help our new generations make a clear path for the future to make the future a reality. Resolving conflict and misery is one of the first steps toward improving our society. We must support each other and direct our attention to the productivity of others.

Suffice it to say, we must create a time in which our current struggles and defeats are nothing more than a distant memory as we bring nations to proven methods that uphold human rights and rise out of poverty, advancing peace and preventing human suffering. Your broken heart does not have to get the final word. Pursue the way of justice and sooth your broken heart and damaged ego. Choose the way of surrender, faith and love.

These issues are still the major concerns today. Not everyone is going to love you; but you must learn to value yourself, love yourself. You will discover how to significantly make a difference by finding many ways you can get involved with others. Therefore, you must discover your purpose in life and help children find their purpose. Feel comfortable in creating your own path, encouraging others along the way.

God intentionally sculpted each person in the world, giving purpose to every day of our lives before we drew our first breathe. We must save our children and help them bring their dreams to fruition, they will be our salvation or our ruination. God has something just for you and me each day. Everyone needs a blessing. We must pray and receive our blessings.

As it is written, The Benevolent Person scatters abroad; He gives to the poor; His deeds of justice and goodness and kindness and benevolence will go on and endure forever. (2 CORINTHAINS 9:9, para, NIV).

Benjamin Watson said in his book, UNDER OUR SKIN: GETTING FREE FROM THE FEARS AND FRUSTATIONS THAT DIVIDE US, "I pray that we will move away from the fear and frustrations that divide us."

Watson, who is a football player and was with the Saints in New Orleans, Louisiana at one time, continues, "The key to the word 'intentional' starts with the racial problem of "Us versus Them." What if there were just an "Us." What if we made it personal by erasing the racial and hateful divides in our lives? What if we sought intentional relationships with people of another color, not of our race?" (p. 198-199, para).

America is still significantly separated along racial lines, therefore natural opportunities are not available to make friends with someone of another race or culture. It will require both races and cultures to make a concerted intentional effort to find opportunities at school, work, church and volunteer groups to work side by side to interact positively with one another.

Let us as young people especially, examine our own lives and remove negative thoughts and behavior toward others. We need to separate ourselves from relationships in which negativity is perpetuated.

> *"Now go, lead the people to the place I spoke of, and my angel will go with you." (EXODUS 32: 43, NIV).*

> *I believe that His mercies are new every morning. Does the sun rise in the East and set in the West each day? Is the sky blue?*

> *God said, "Let the water teem with living creatures." (GENESIS 1: 20, NIV).*

> *For You created all things; my innermost being. You knit me together in my mother's womb. I praise Yor because I am fearfully and wonderfully made. Your works are wonderful, I know that full well. My frame was not hidden from You when I was made in the secret place.*

> *When I was woven in the depts of the earth, your eyes saw my unformed body. All the days ordained for me were written in Your book before one of them came to be. (PSALM 139: 13-16, para, NIV).*

Love takes creativity, wisdom, work, caring, strength and the purpose of God's ministry on earth through Jesus.

Luke's story of the shepherds encounter in an angelic stench gives us information like no other that precede and surround Jesus's birth. As the church's first historian, his book is based on investigation, documents and eye witness accounts. He does not state what he saw with his own eyes; as Matthew and John did.

Rather, Luke investigates everything from the beginning. He interviews eye witnesses: one of whom was likely Mary the mother of Jesus and tells of her angelic encounter and poetic response known as the Magnificat. (LUKE 1: 46-55). Luke alone did his research and records events that would have been known to a select few. The shepherds probably did not tell their own story because several decades after the happenings of the birth of Jesus, Luke would have found the shepherds and heard their story. It is more plausible that Luke heard the story about the night of Jesus' birth from Mary as she would have treasured these events in her heart. (LUKE 2: 19).

Luke's account of this story is so strange: yet in His Sovereignty, God chose to have the Savior of the world born in a scandalous situation: a group of smelly shepherds, outsiders-strangers who showed up after the birth of the child. "These strangers were living on the edge of society and clinging to the rung on the bottom of the social hierarchy of that day but were the ones who announced the King's arrival."

(Source: Dennis Moles, UNEXPECTED HOPE, p. 28).

God does not need the high and mighty, nor does he desire only the gifted and brilliant individuals to share his messages of peace and love to the world.

We are to be encouraged and have faith for God helps those who need it, not those who feel empowered. He chooses the meek and lowly to accomplish His purpose. He needs the persons who are willing to serve.

We must teach our children to be good stewards of our environment; share what we have with others. We should start slowly and with well intentions.

Willie F. Wooten wrote in his book, BREAKING THE CURSE OF BLACK AMERICA, "In this end-time, it is imperative that all men walk in the liberty wherein Christ has made us free. To be entangled in bondage because of generational errors does not have to exist and must be addressed. The goal of the enemy is to steal, kill and destroy, but God's purpose is that we have life and that more abundantly."

Many times, it is hard to bring forth topics such as ethnicity and racism because of the controversy that could possibly unfold.

"However," Wooten says, "my desire is not to offend but to exhort those who are open to receive the truth." (p. 12).

AN EXAMPLE DURING OUR LIFETIME

A great example of this person is Kamala Harris, first woman and Black person as vice president of the United States of America. Dan Morian ruminates in his book, KAMALA'S WAY, "There is little that is conventional about Kamala Harris, yet her personal story also represents the best of America. From her modest beginning in Oakland through her activist days at Howard University, Harris grew up as a child with a single no-nonsense cancer-research mother from India, born in the Fall of 1964 and a father, an accomplished Jamaican-born Economic Professor. They split-up when she was five-years old.

From both her parents she inherited a sense of social justice. From her mother, she also inherited a great work ethic, an attention to detail, and most of all, a talent for getting around closed doors. "(p. 1, para).

Anyone who belongs to Christ and wants to live right will have trouble from others. Paul indicates to Timothy, one of his understudy's, "If we have a trouble – free existence, then either we do not belong to Christ or we have no desire to live right." (2 TIMOTHY 3: 12, NIV).

Our Creator is setting things in order so that Black America will not allow another generation to walk in ignorance or be deceived. He is giving us a new mind-set so that we will not walk in darkness of the unrighteous. There are many Christians who have no knowledge of the years of suffering and hindrances that have kept us from advancing; but now we must rise, shine, for thy light has now come.

"We cannot leave well enough alone, because well enough has not given us a breakthrough," said Wooten. He is looking "to bring about enlightenment to Black America and to expose the misconception concerning those who highly influenced our ethnicity." (p. 13).

WHAT LEGACY ARE WE LEAVING?

I related to my eight grandchildren the other day that they will steer the culture of tomorrow. We have a limited number of years to teach them right from wrong. Children absorb our every comment, look and action. They are the legacy that we leave to the world. When the subject is education, our children will model themselves after us. When it comes to race, they will see our reactions to racial incidents on television and other places and can predict our opinions and reactions. When it comes to sexual behavior, our children will take us as models. When it is about social and religious life, our children will learn to pattern themselves after us.

"Only when we share time together and make it personal will we lay aside the prejudice of our minds and experience the true meaning and understanding of our hearts.

BLACK LIVES MATTER!
OUR CHILDREN'S LIVES MATTER!
ALL LIVES MATTER!
AND THAT IS WHAT BEING PRO-LIFE REALLY MEANS!

(Source: Watson, p. 119, para).

Sometimes we may think that we have next to nothing to give; but Jesus multiplied the offerings of a small boy's barley loaves and fish. His mother, who was not named in our Bible saw to it that her child had enough to eat on his journey and enough to share with the multitude of hungry people. It is what God is teaching us and what we must teach our young people to open the doors to share in what God has given us. It is never too late to get ready. Narrow is the way which leads to life and life abundantly.

There may be days of darkness and distress,
When sin has power to tempt, and care to press.
Yet in the darkest day I will not fear,
For midst the shadows, you will still be near.
Thank you, Lord Jesus.

(Source: Carrie Ten Boom)

I urge, then, that requests, prayers, intercessions and thanksgiving be made for everyone. (1 TIMOTHY 2:1, NIV).

Scripture tells us, "Often hospitality is connected to our blessings and to God. In many of the stories told in the Bible, strangers turn out to be angels, blessings are brought by angels, tales of good news are brought in by a neighbor and promises of God are brought in. As advice for the younger generations who will pick up the torch in all works, I encourage others to keep your mind focused and "stayed on Jesus."

My heart overflows to share the hope and joy I have found in Jesus. What could be better than to praise and serve him. We should think of ways of scheduling an opportunity to love others. The norms of our society and our frantic lives militate against Jesus's command to love our neighbors. (MARK 12: 31, para, NIV).

Actually, the possibilities are endless to live to meet the needs and make others happy; you will find "joy unspeakable" in the process. (1 PETER 1: 8, KJV).

We must recognize the fact that our thoughts affect others. We make a mistake when we have the opinion that our thoughts do not affect other people. So, we must choose our thoughts carefully because they affect us and consequently the people around us. We should always find new thoughts to avoid thinking negatively; teaching our young people to renew their thoughts and attitudes daily. Teach others to love on purpose.

And be constantly renewed in the spirit of your mind; having a fresh mental and spiritual attitude. (EPHESIANS 4: 23, para, NIV).

OUR THOUGHTS AND PRAYERS AFFECT OTHERS!

CHAPTER 34

HELP WITH THE SMALL THINGS

Does God always say yes to our small requests? We all know the answer is no, but He hears us. He listens. Many people feel that they should not bother God with small things. That is a mentality we need to get over because He cares about us, all of us. When love takes charge of us, we learn to love others and think good thoughts about people on purpose. We look for the good in everyone and find the good in ourselves as well.

If God loves us so, we ought to love one another. (1 JOHN 4: 11, para, NIV).

Sometimes our faith may feel more wobbly than other times. We may be struggling just to hang on. We may be grappling with a loss right now or struggling with a hard lesson. A song is given:

THE GIFT OF LOVE

Though I may speak with bravest fire,
And have the gift to all inspire,

And have not love, my words are vain,
As sounding brass and hopeless gain.

Though I may give all I possess,
And striving so, my love profess;
But not be given by love within,
The profit soon turns strangely thin.

(Source: Words: Hal Hopson, 1972, I CORINTHIANS 13: 1-3, NIV).

But Jesus, through the Holy Spirit, is constantly telling us that everything will be alright and that we do not need to worry about our financial obligations, our children's behavior, our relationships with spouses and neighbors. He will help us understand our situation and learn to accept it. We can draw on the strength of our forebears, whose capacity for hope and faith overcame the injustice and cruelty of their oppressors.

In the Old Testament, David spoke and said, "The Lord is my light, whom shall I fear," first as a little shepherd boy then as a king. He is my shepherd, my guide, my provider, my Lord, no matter what else is going on in the world.

I will keep you from all hurt, harm and danger. When we need strength, God will strengthen us. He will bring you from a shepherd boy to a great king. By praying to him, He will take you higher. God will take you higher. When we feel lost spiritually, we know how to find our way, because God is our GPS. We have His support.

Sometimes, small things we pray for help us understand what the larger and harder things are all about. He meets our needs everyday as we help others. God is generous and refills our pouch when we are generous. He directs us to love deeply and unconditionally. He offers grace to help us fill the tough assignments, when we do not have the where-with-all to do so.

Come, Spirit, come, our hearts control,
Our spirits long to be made whole.
Let inward love guide every deed,

By this we worship and are freed.
(Music: Traditional English Melody adopted- Hal Hopson).

We can go to God in the most interment times and He will put everything aside and lift us up. He will send help.

In Ecclesiastes, we learn that:

Two are better than one, because they have a good return for their work. If one falls down, his friend can help him up! But pity the man who falls and has no one to help him up. Also, if two lie down together, they will keep warm. But how can one keep warm alone?

Though one may be overpowered, two can defend themselves. A chord of three strands is not quickly broken. (ECCLESIASTES 4: 9-12,NIV).

When an individual accepts Jesus Christ as Savior, he is born again. Further, his spirit is made new.

Further, we denote in 2 Corinthians that when anyone is in Christ, he is a new creature, old things pass away; and all things are new. (2 CORINTHIANS 5: 17, NIV).

This is a process that requires breaking old habits and forming new ones. Out of the renewed spirit, every other area of our lives can experience newness of life. It is time for everyone to get started. As we think good thoughts about people and our attitude starts to change toward them, our relationship starts to change for the better.

> ## WHEN WE NEED STRENGTH, GOD WILL STRENGTHEN US!

CHAPTER 35

LIVE IN THE MOMENT

Oftentimes it may feel as if you are rushing through life, missing out on the joy of the moment. Slow down and experience what God has for you and will show you. Do not measure your journey in miles. God never intended for you to strain and stress all your life. You are here because you have faith in your God and His life for you.

My husband, Bertrand, says constantly, I have made it thus far, almost ninety-years of age, because He is not through with me yet. He is still walking, talking, driving every day, eating on his own every day' and I thank God.

Therefore, we should measure everything through the purpose your Creator has for your life.

Joel Osteen says in his book, YOUR GREATER IS COMING, "We all face setbacks in life, things we do not understand. We may have lost a loved one, had a friend walk out on our relationship, or are dealing with an illness. When we go through loss and bad breaks, it is easy to think that is the way it is always going to be. But our God is a God of restoration.

He does not stop every difficulty, and He does not keep us from every challenge. (p.1, para).

David said in Psalm 71, "Though You have made me see troubles, many and bitter, allowed me to suffer much hardship, but You will restore me to even greater honor; You will restore my life again, from the depths of the earth; you will again bring me up. You will increase my honor and comfort me once again" (PSALM 71: 20-21, para, NIV).

Life is full of challenges, yet you must realize that the most important moment is right now. You have the talents build inside you; resist the urge to rush through life just to get to the good stuff.

When I retired from working at Southern University in Baton Rouge, Louisiana after helping students for thirty-six years as a Psychological Counselor and administrator, one of my close friends who knew I loved to read, gave me several of Daniele Steele's books and Leo Tolstoy's WAR AND PEACE book of several hundred pages. She said, "You will have time to read to your hearts content now."

No matter what stage of life we find ourselves in, we are never able to do all the things we desire to do. Doing productive and creative work and making wise decisions on how to spend our time is fulfilling in God's sight. This may bring us into deeper relationship with our Creator and less time to focus on frustrations and restlessness.

We must find time enough for leisure and rest and refresh our body and soul. Also, time spent with God each day is a priority for our spiritual health. We should find inward peace as well as outward control. It is the submission of our viewpoint, schedules, dreams and God's purpose that teach us to live in the moment with patience and love.

It is easy to become *too* focused on the here and now by not finding time for the things most important to us.

But Ecclesiastes says that God has "set eternity" in our heart; reminding us to make a priority of things that are eternal. This can bring us face to face with something of the greatest importance; God's eternal perspective! (ECCLESIASTES 3: 13, para, NIV).

The Bible says, "All of you together are Christ's body, and each of you is a part of it." (1 CORINTHIANS 12: 27, NLT).

Madeleine L'Engle once said, "The great artists keep us from frozenness, from smugness, from thinking that the truth is in us, rather than in God, in Christ our Lord."

They help us to know that we are often closer to God in our doubts than in our certainties, that it is all right to be like the small child who constantly asks, why, why, why.

David continues in Psalm 71: "I will praise You with the harp for your faithfulness, O my God; I will sing praise to you with the lyre, O Holy One of Israel. My lips will shout for joy when I sing praise to you; I, whom you redeemed." (PSALM 1: 22-23, NIV).

WHAT'S LOVE?

God is love. Love never fails. Where there are prophecies, they will cease; where there are tongues, they will be stilled; where there is knowledge, it will pass away. For we know in part and we prophesy in part, but when the perfection comes, the imperfect disappears. When I was a child, I talked like a child, I thought like a child, I reasoned like a child. When I became a man (woman), I put childish ways behind me. Now we see but a poor reflection as in a mirror; then we shall see face to face. Now I know in part, then I shall know fully, even as I am fully known. Scripturally, this is sound teaching from God.

We are not really living the life of the spirit until we allow the Holy Spirit to control every area of our lives. Teach our children to be led by the Spirit as this is central to a victorious Christian life.

Each of us has a purpose on the earth. If God has no purpose for us, He would take us out of this world as soon as we accept His son, Jesus Christ so we could begin right away enjoying heaven and living in His presence.

Suffice it to say, God has a purpose for each of us and we should learn what it is and cooperate with it. It does no good to talk to people about Christ unless we are living a Christian life style to back up our words.

And now these three remain: faith, hope and love. But the greatest of these is love. (1 CORINTHIANS 13: 8-13, NIV).

THE MOST IMPORTANT MOMENT IS RIGHT NOW!

CHAPTER 36

GENERATIONS TOGETHER, GENERATIONS APART

Looking to the future and teaching futuristic issues, we much step into the past; the history of our ancestors.

For my life, our records and documents show the genealogy of the De La Fountaine, Fountain-Smith, Fountain-Collins, Fountain-Harper, Harper-Heath, Heath-Pepper, Heath-Griffin, Heath-Kellam, Heath-Purnell Family. I enjoy searching and processing family history and explaining it to my grandchildren what it all means. However, I have found very little in history books about my family history and achievements.

Nicholas De La Fountain, Sr., born in Normandy, France in 1691, was the father of Nicholas, Jr, and grandfather of Nicholas, III. The senior member of the family brought his group from France to America and started afresh after being persecuted under French laws and religion.

Nicholas De La Fountaine, III and wife, Lea Buria were the father and mother of Nicholas Alexander and Pierre De La Fountaine. (Ancestry.com.)

Nicholas Alexander De La Fountaine (next generation) was the father of Nicholas and William Charles Fountain, (the family name was changed to Fountain when they moved to America and the next generation was born. The two grandsons were born in Maryland, married and raised their families in Maryland. (Ancestry. Com.)

There were several generations of William Fountains. It is possible that the great-grandson named William, III or his son William Charles Fountain was the one called Captain Fountain or maybe it was his son.

William Fountain, III, was born in Maryland around 1725 and died in 1792 in Maryland. He married Sarah Turpin who was born in Ethiopia, Africa in 1723 and died in 1793. They had children; among them was John Turpin Fountain. Sarah Turpin Fountain was the great aunt of Thomas Jefferson.

William Turpin Fountain, I and his family, among them, his son, John Turpin Fountain, resided in England for a short period and then sailed to America. William Turpin Fountain, III had many slaves, around sixty at a time.

John Turpin Fountain was born in 1791. He was the great-nephew of Sarah Turpin. He married Henrietta Elizabeth Ballard. They had two sons, John Elzey Fountain, born in 1819 and died in1874. The second son was named Willian Charles Fountain, Jr. after one of his uncles. He was born in 1822 and died around 1874. The Turpins and Fountains were apparently related to each other with the men having the same names: John, Charles and William. (This made the research of these family members very difficult to determine which generation was being dealt with. This whole family was white.)

Moreover, there was another White man, William Charles Fountain, III, born of English descent who married a black woman after he set her free. He had forty or fifty slaves but chose the one he loved and in a "common Law" marriage lived with her.

William Turpin Fountain, another ancestor, also gave his slave woman, Mary, her freedom and married her in Canada which was very unusual. He did not have a white wife as many southern planters and plantation owners of that day. This White man brought his slave woman "fresh off the boat" in Baton Rouge, Louisiana and changed her name from Sarah to Mary. Much later, he married her in Canada.

He brought her back to his place in Goochland, Virginia and lived with her in his home.

After four children were born to this couple, they journeyed from Goochland, Virginia to Canada, and a marriage took place. When they returned home from Canada, the neighbors learned of the marriage and burned their house down. William Charles (Turpin) Fountain reconstructed the home almost immediately. (Source: Judith Rollins, ALL IS NEVER SAID, p. 21).

Often there was a White wife with a Black mistress. Usually, the slave mistress was maintained in a separate dwelling. Not so in this case. William Charles (Turpin) Fountain was determined to live with his Black wife and their children.

It was accepted that any slave could sit in church with the master's children, but the slave who was alone could only sit in the balcony or the gallery. But a mammy or nanny could bring her master's children and sit with them in the white section of the church. This family all sat together in church with Mary being beautifully dressed in clothes from Paris.

John Turpin Fountain (either William Turpin Fountain's brother or cousin) also had a daughter by his slave woman and gave her freedom from slavery. They named the daughter, Mary Elizabeth Fountain. She was born around 1829 and died 1867 in Maryland or Delaware. Mary Elizabeth was also given her freedom and she was the spitting image of her White father, John Turpin Fountain. He and his father gave all the slaves born to them their freedom and papers of freedom.

John gave his daughter his last name, Fountain, and gave her acres of land to live on with her young family. This property was located in Middleford, Delaware. Mary Elizabeth Fountain was allowed to marry Charles Smith, a slave and he was given his freedom. They had three sons – John Henry Fountain, Chad Fountain and John Charles Fountain. They were given their freedom. (Noted here is that the three sons of Mary Elizabeth Fountain and Charles Smith were given the last name of Mary Elizabeth Fountain, not the father, Charles Smith. Smith was the last person in the family to be given his freedom.)

John Henry Fountain, the oldest of the three sons born to Mary Elizabeth Fountain and Charles Smith, was loaned to a White farmer in Trinity, Delaware as a child. He became blind due to an accident and was returned to his family in Middleford.

Suffice it to say, many whites and mulattos owned slaves, but as an example the slave masters were more sympathetic toward their own children, giving them their papers of freedom and helping them get established and have a better live. They were no longer chattel.

Therefore, there were many descendants and offspring of slave masters who were children of White men. Many slave women were proud to acknowledge that their children had white blood in their veins.

Several accounts reveal that this is true as with Sally Heming's story. According to Annette Gordon-Reed's book, THOMAS JEFFERSON AND SALLY HEMINGS: AN AMERICAN CONTROVERY, not only did Sally Heming's children go free, they were all freed in what was considered as prime time of their lives, as children and young adults with long futures ahead. This is noted because many slaves were set free and given papers of freedom in their waning years. (p. 3).

This became a part of the Underground Railroad as some slave masters attempted to recapture former slaves and put them back under their rule as chattel.

Oral history reveals that the Underground Railroad was considered a "Praying Center."

As in the midst of wicked people, Noah was an example of one who could live a godly life in an evil world, a life pleasing to God in every way in his every day environment. Noah found favor with the Lord through no merit of his own but through his personal faith in God. As with Noah, God could see that the slaves in the Underground Railroad Movement were blameless and upright in the midst of wickedness. They were not perfect in character but in their lives were revealing a genuineness of faith in God. They were able to keep a close relationship with God. Noah walked with God; God is love. (GENESIS 6: 9, NIV).

It is not the environment but the heart that determines one's walk with the Lord. Did these down-trodden people find favor with God? We must question ourselves: "Do I find favor with God?"

Remembering our weaknesses and failures, we realize that we have no merit by which God can accept us. However, God knows all about us and has provided a way in which we can be accepted by him. Our Creator gives us grace to live victoriously. He gives us more grace. (JAMES 4:6, NIV).

TIMES WERE CRITICAL

Times were critical. Times are still critical. When Jesus told us it was the Father's good pleasure to give us his Kingdom, to lead us into freedom and fulfillment, he was saying, it is the divine nature of the Universe to flow in and through you, fulfilling all your needs. (Source: THE CREATIVE LIFE, p. 24, para).

The Old Testament stresses that God can be understood through God's visible works - that is the natural world. In Christian Theology, this is made more explicit: God is known as a person. As Jesus says in the Gospel of John,

"WHOEVER HAS SEEN ME, HAS SEEN THE FATHER."

We can seek God through things that are known to us. There is a CENTER that is a place of meeting of the human person: a place of meeting of the human spirit and divine Spirit. We are able to meet the whole of reality, divine and human, time and space, nature and history, evil and good, and persons and things.

Centering is a move toward your own center, where you encounter God. It is not about God and you alone, for any encounter with God will inevitably lead you outward, to the rest of creation. (Source: Pennington, FINDING GRACE AT THE CENTER, para, 277).

> NO MATTER WHAT DOCUMENTS AND HISTORY SAY, GOD MUST BE THE LOVE OF OUR LIVES!

CHAPTER 37

CONNECT THE DOTS

Our ancestors, De La Fountaine from France – renamed themselves Fountains in America, and were a part of the Underground Railroad according to oral history from my grandmother, Sadie Mae Fountain Harper. When I learned this at an early age, around eight years old, it haunted me.

I came across a book about Harriet Tubman in our "Bookmobile" and asked my mother about it. I have always desired to learn more about the Underground Railroad and Harriet Tubman. I often heard stories about Harriet Tubman and revered her so much for her bravery.

She walked with the love of God before her. She was fierce and courageous and my mother wanted us to grow up with a spirit of helping others as she did. She worked to save her family and other human beings from misery and shame. No one connected the dots for me but apparently there was a connection between the Fountains and Harriet Tubman because their actions and skills were the same. The vast difference between the two was: Harriet moved around; the Fountains stayed put in their own habitat.

I wanted to know more about my ancestor's involvement in the Underground Railroad Movement. They worked to free slaves with the help of other slaves, freed slaves and whites.

It is not uncommon for Tubman to have been helped by Captain Fountain, one of our ancestors.

Mother had a book about Harriet Tubman which she treasured and kept in her cider chest. I would get this book and read a little at a time. According to this book by William Still, UNDERGROUND RAILROAD RECORDS, in 1872, Harriet Tubman was described as a "woman of no pretentions, a most ordinary specimen of humanity." (p. 296).

She was born a slave around 1820, originally named Araminta Ross by her slave master on the Brodas Plantation in Bucktown, Dorchester County, Maryland. She later changed her name to Harriet, which was her mother's name, and married John Tubman.

William Still was a freed slave himself and was well aware of Tubman's character. She was described as a dark- complexioned woman, of median height and a woman of great mental fortitude.

Many books were written about Tubman and through my reading and oral tradition, I learned that Tubman helped to free over seven hundred slaves, including her mother and father, her sisters and brothers and her husband. This woman who was a spy for the Union soldiers, a nurse and a leader called Moses, no doubt had help from captains of ships such as Captains William Fountain and John Fountain.

Tubman traveled from North and South Carolina to Virginia, Delaware, Maryland, Pennsylvania, New York and into Canada. This was one of the Underground Railroad routes as it was also Captain William's ship route. Other slaves were brought to safety through Ohio and other mid-western states.

I have talked to my grandchildren, especially the boys, Christian-Paris Bertrand Griffin, III and Michael Griffin, II. They were Boy Scouts and had taken trips along these routes. Some of the things that happened during slavery; they have seen evidence of it. They had no idea that life in the olden days was like this for blacks.

I have heard that there is a statue of Harriet Tubman in a small town in New York and I would like to see it.

It occurred to me that my great-great-grandmother, Mary Elizabeth Fountain and Harriet Tubman were around the same age. No doubt, there may have been a connection with them. Therefore, half brothers and sisters were on Captain Fountain's ships, and were placed under the bales of hay in the horse barns such as was on the Fountain Homestead in Middleford, Delaware.

This family, the Fountains helped to hide their own family members and other slaves in Delaware and Maryland until they could get to a safe place in New York and Canada.

In 2006 my husband, Bertrand and my sister Nancy and her husband, Albert Kellam went to Canada-Nova Scotia and other parts of Canada looking for grave marking, churches and books about the movement of slaves into Canada, documented through oral history of both our grandmothers. We found all three, grave markings, churches with maps and pictures of slaves and books in libraries about slaves and freed slaves. What was so interesting was a book about the De La Fountain and Cannon families from the mid-Atlantic states which was a part of our family names. They had apparently been taken or escaped to this part of the world for safety and remained there.

There were other slave owners from North Carolina and Virginia who were constantly seeking their run-away slaves and were suspicious of such persons as Captain Fountain. Other slave masters knew our ancestors had slaves on their ships and farms in Delaware, Virginia and Maryland. These slave owners knew that the captains of these ships carried slaves beyond the Mason-Dixon line, according to Charles Blocksom from Seaford, Delaware in his book, UNDERGROUND RAILROAD. Mr. Blocksom's grandchildren attended Jason High School and Delaware State University with me. Finding all these documents later in a library in Baton Rouge, Louisiana made me realize that these were my relatives. I realize also that I must not dwell on the past but actualize it to move on to the future.

We need to tune out the mean-spirited voices that try to keep us down. Because of Jesus, our past and our ancestor's trials and tribulations do not define our future.

My ancestors are on both sides of the coin. I must listen to my Maker and see myself the way He sees me. Although I have stumbled and fallen down; we as humans all have fallen down. We must move on and fully develop and mature.

My grandmother Sadie told me that her slave-ancestors could not read or write; therefore, they could not record or document the places where they had traveled or who had helped them. They had only oral history to rely on.

Moreover, my other ancestors (White members), taught their freed slaves many things and the teachings were mutual.

A MOTHER BORN INTO SLAVERY

A mother born into slavery had her children take the same name as the slave owner. Mary Elizabeth was born into slavery; therefore, her last name was Fountain and all her children were Fountains. This is also an example of a child taking the last name of a freed mother. There was much love there!

The Fountain children were taught by their mother, Mary Elizabeth Fountain, to stick together, to learn from each other, to own property and build upon it. They were taught to set good examples for their own children.

As John Henry Fountain was Mary Elizabeth's first child, he was loaned to other White farmers, such as Mr. and Mrs. Henry Jacobs in Trinty, Delaware and other farmers to pick crops, feed the animals and be an all-around-"yard-boy" until he became blind due to an unknown illness and an accident.

He was not sold, only loaned to Mr. Jacobs and other farmers until he could not work any longer due to blindness.

There is a famous story in the Bible: As Jesus and his disciples were leaving the city of Jericho, a blind man. Bartimaeus was sitting by the roadside begging. When he heard that it was Jesus of Nazareth passing, he began to shout, "Jesus, Son of David, have mercy on me."

Many rebuked him and told him to be quiet. But he shouted louder; "Son of David, have mercy on me!"

Jesus stopped and said, "Call him."

So, they called to the blind man. "Cheer up. On your feet! Jesus is calling you."

Throwing his cloak aside, Bartimaeus jumped up and came to Jesus.

"What do you want me to do for you?" Jesus asked him.

The blind man said, "Rabbi, I want to see."

"Go" Jesus said. "Your faith has healed you."

Immediately, he received his sight and followed Jesus along the road. (MARK 10: 46-52, NIV).

In recent years, some people who are blind have challenged traditional interpretation of this story, questioning whether it helps to consider blindness something that always needs healing. Likewise, man takes issue with the Gospels frequent passages.

When John Henry Fountain returned to his family, he was allowed to get married as a late teenager to Amanda, born around 1858, who was from another slave family household. Amanda's father's name was unknown but we later found that her mother's name was Martha Collins. (Source: Amanda Fountain's Delaware State Certificate of Death).

According to my grandmother, Sadie Mae Fountain who was the oldest daughter of Amanda, her mother was fair-skinned, with light-brown eyes and long wavy hair that she could sit on. Amanda Fountain was very beautiful. She was about five-feet, six inches tall which was tall for a woman in those days. From all appearance, Amanda's father was apparently a White man.

Amanda Collins Fountain worked for a white family in Seaford, Delaware. She got along well with the family she worked for. They may have been her relatives. She cooked and cleaned and delivered babies for them and other families. She became an excellent Mid-wife and worked throughout the Sussex County delivering babies. That became her specialty, according to Grandmom Sadie as she told her mother's story to me when I was seven and eight years old.

I was told my grandmother and her mother looked very much alike, same coloring and stature. Grandmom Sadie was an inch or two taller than her mother, Amanda.

JOHN HENRY FOUNTAIN AND AMANDA COLLINS FOUNTAIN

After John Henry and Amanda Fountain were married, they had seven children to live and several to die in childbirth. Their children were Charles Wesley, Sadie Mae, Lettie, (my mother was named for her aunt, Lettie), Clarence, (our uncle Clarence was named for his Uncle Clarence), Martin (called Marty), Louis, and Sylvester – all Fountains according to the 1900 United States Census Bureau Report. These were the children listed in the household along with two adults, their parents. The number of "still-born" children is not known.

The 1910 United States Census Bureau Report revealed that only Sylvester Fountain was listed in the household with his parents. All the other children had left the Fountain Homestead in Middleford, Delaware.

Around the mid-eighteenth century, the Fountain name had gone as far as Maryland, Pennsylvania, New York and into Halifax, Nova Scotia, Digby County, Birchtown County, Shelbourne County, Liverpool, Queens County and Yarmouth County, Canada.

Some of the Fountains may have gone as far as Sierre Leon, Africa, which was their aim.

SADIE MAE FOUNTAIN AND HERBERT SIDNEY HARPER

Sadie Mae and her older brother, Charles Wesley Fountain left home to seek their fortunes. They did not want to live on the family farm in Sussex County, Delaware. They lived in a boarding house first in Wilmington, Delaware, then in Philadelphia, Pennsylvania. This brother and sister married their sweethearts; Sadie Mae Fountain married Herbert Sidney Harper on August 6, 1904, in Philadelphia, Pennsylvania, (documented by their marriage certificate by a magistrate.) Sadie Mae was only sixteen or seventeen and Herbert was over twenty-two. They met in Delaware and Herbert followed Sadie to Philadelphia.

Charles Wesley Fountain married a young woman from New Jersey. The brother and sister remained close in contact to each other.

Sadie Mae and Herbert Harper had two children: Lettie Sidney Harper, born on December 8, 1908 in Philadelphia, Pennsylvania. Clarence Burton Harper, the second child born to Sadie and Herbert was born on February 2, 1919. They lived in Philadelphia until their house was burned down. The Harper family moved back to Middleford, Delaware, the birth place of Sadie Mae.

By this time, Sadie's mother, Amanda Fountain was very ill and Sadie's father who was blind had moved back home from the Camp for the Blind. Sadie took over management of the Fountain Homestead in Middleford, Delaware.

There is Someone who cares about each of us, who watches closely over each individual. GOD! Through Him we can find rest and peace in spite of the catastrophes that harass us. God offers us a place to stand and hope in a lost world. He does not keep score and offers a new beginning to those who return to him.

Isaiah 40 denotes:

Do you not know? Have you not heard?

The Lord is the everlasting God, the Creator of the ends of the earth. He will not grow tired or weary, and His understanding no one can fathom.

He gives strength to the weary, and increases the power of the weak. Those who hope in the Lord will renew their strength.

They will soar on wings like eagles; they will run and not grow weary; they will walk and not faint. (ISAIAH 40: 28-31, NIV).

SADIE'S DAUGHTER

Sadie's daughter, Lettie grew up and was given the best of schooling, first the elementary school in Philadelphia, the Neal Elementary

School in Middleford, the Harper Boarding School in North Carolina (high School), then Cheyney State College (University) in Cheyney, Pennsylvania in music, and Delaware State College (University) in Elementary Education in Dover, Delaware.

Lettie completed high school and received her diploma, and two college degrees. She was a brilliant pianist and played for Marian Anderson, a contralto soloist, for two years until Anderson went further, developing her career in foreign countries.

Marian Anderson and Lettie Harper were both born in Philadelphia, Pennsylvania and were very close friends as children. They later met up again in Cheyney State College and hung out together as musicians. Anderson moved on with her career, soaring to higher heights. She sang in many foreign countries.

I was later named for Marian Anderson in 1939, the year she sang at the foot of the Lincoln Monument in Washington, D.C.

Lettie stayed closer to home and played for churches, bars and taught children how to play the piano. She earned money to help her family along the way. She lived a few miles away from her family and was very independent and content with life.

After Lettie was married, she had several children. I was one of them and was named for Marian Anderson in August of 1939. Mother (Lettie went to hear Marian Anderson sing at the foot of the Lincoln Monument to over seventy-five thousand persons after being refused to sing at the Convention Hall by the Daughters of the American Revolution members who were all White. Anderson was Black.

Eleanor Roosevelt, the wife of President Theodore Roosevelt, arranged for Anderson to sing at the Lincoln Monument, which was heard on the radio by thousands of other people.

God was in the plan and He is love.

CLARENCE HARPER

Clarence was Lettie's younger brother and completed the Neal Middle School in Middleford, Delaware. When he was old enough, seventeen, he entered the United States Army.

LETTIE HARPER HEATH AND
GEORGE WESLEY HEATH, SR.

In the meanwhile, Lettie Harper married the "love of her life", George Wesley Heath in the Methodist church in Seaford, Delaware on April 9, 1934. Their reception was held outside her parent's home in the decorated yard - The Fountain Homestead. Lettie and George were happy in their marriage.

The Harper parents, reflecting on their own earlier selves, undoubtedly identified with the young married couple as they were "fraught with uncertainty, anxiety, disorientation, confusion, and even a sense of loss."

(Source: Hibbs and Rostain, YOU'RE NOT DONE YET: PARENTING YOUNG ADULTS IN AN AGE OF UNCERTAINTY, pp. 44-45, para).

They remembered their own unsettling times, and stayed on the Fountain Homestead.

However, Lettie had two college degrees and wanted to pursue her career in teaching. Lettie and George Heath (Mother and Daddy) immediately began planning to build their home and start a family. They wanted to be independent and raise their children in their own home. Lettie's parents offered them space and land at the Fountain Homestead. But they built their own home and accepted only furniture instead.

GOD WAS IN THE PLAN.

CHAPTER 38

PROUD OF HIS NAME

D addy had the Heath name and if he was any thing like his name, he was like a tree planted by the water and was steady as a rock.

Three of his children, Phyllis, George, Jr. and Marian (me) were born in a small cabin owned by Mr. Snoot, the owner of a large farm with crops of vegetables and livestock. The Heath family lived in a small cabin on Mr. Snoot's property; they were happy and love flowed though out the little cabin. They had several children back-to-back which rendered our mother, Lettie sickly until these children were born.

One day, Daddy asked my Grandpop Herbert for two beds that were not being used upstairs in the Fountain Homestead. Family and neighbors were suspicious of Daddy's movements because they could hear him in his old truck at night moving around. Daddy took the beds away on his old Model T-Ford truck. This is how Grandpop knew Daddy was moving off Mr. Snoot's farm and into our new home. In his building, Daddy had built an outside privy for our obvious needs and a smoke house to cure and preserve meat for family and neighbors.

After my parents moved to their new home in Greenwood built by George Heath, Sr. himself, they had four more children – Daniel,

Joseph, Nancy and Hattie Elvira. All seven of us were born before, during or after World War II. Later I learned that Mother and Daddy had fourteen children, but seven of them died in childbirth. (See Griffin, CULTURAL GUMBO: OUR ROOTS, OUR STORIES).

Grandmom Sadie and Mother Lettie were close and confided in each other daily. When Mother and Daddy began to move from the Seaford area, Daddy promised his mother-in-law and father-in-law that he would bring Lettie and their children to see them every evening. Daddy knew that he had to keep his promise and visit our grandparents every evening as he drove away from our little cabin (shack) where his first three children were born and from the Fountain Homestead where we had spent so many good times. We moved to our new home in Greenwood, Delaware among the trees.

He began praying, "Lord, keep us safe, keep my family safe."

He was frightened for all that he was doing with his family, yet he gained confidence from past experiences and sacrifices. Daddy knew that he could come to the "throne of Grace" with confidence in Jesus Christ because his work must continue. He loved what he was doing for his family and his small church, which he had moved next to.

Daddy was a "God fearing man" and was able to attend church much more after he moved his family off the white man, Mr. Snoot's farm. His mother, Hattie Heath had taught Daddy to pray without ceasing. He was going through a period of self-examination. He was making life-changing decisions for himself and his entire family.

The Lord searches all hearts and understands all the intent of the thoughts". (1 CHRONICLES 28: 9, para, NIV).

So now I charge you in the sight of Israel and of the assembly of the Lord, and in the hearing of our God: Be careful to follow all the commands of the Lord your God, that you may possess this good land and pass it on as an inheritance to your descendants forever. (1 CHRONICLES 28: 8, NIV.)

And you, my son Solomon, acknowledge the God of your father, and serve him with wholehearted devotion and with a willing mind, for the Lord searches every heart and understands every motive behind the thoughts. If you seek Him, he will be found by you, but if you forsake Him, He will reject you forever. Consider now, for the Lord has chosen you to build a temple as a sanctuary. Be strong and do the work. (1 CHRONICLES 2: 9-10, NIV).

Oswald Chambers said in his PRAYING WITH CONFIDENCE pamphlet "When we pray and read Scriptures, we are able to see what is really going on inside. The Bible shows us our deep-seated feelings and true motives. It takes us into the nooks and crannies where we hide old grudges and secrets, hatreds and bitter resentments. Through honest prayer, we can bring these things to the surface, see them for what they are and ask God to help us deal with them. (p.16).

Daddy knew he was carrying a lot of baggage with him to his new house. He had left his parents' home in the state of Virginia with bitter feelings toward his father as his father was very hateful towards him. His mother tried to protect Daddy but there seemed to be no "love lost" between father and son.

Daddy wanted to get rid of this scorn and hatred so he could live an effective and successful family life.

Mother was happy to move into our new home. She trusted Daddy. We moved into the home by lamp light because Daddy had not completed the wiring of the new home for electricity. So, we lived by candles and lamp light for a while. Our home consisted of two bedrooms, a kitchen and a living room. Daddy had brought the green table and two green chairs he had made when we lived in Mr. Snoot's cabin. He made an additional two chairs to fit around the table. He had made a bassinette for Phyllis when she was born. Mother placed me in the bassinette with pillows around so I could sit up. We had an old wood stove which heated the whole house day and night. One of the bedrooms was for the children and the other one was for the mother and father.

Our world was in crisis. My parents and grandparents had lived through World War 1 and were in the middle of World War 11. There was Globalization beginning before our very eyes. The countries were moving away toward the new international phenomenon between nations such as distance, culture, modern travel, invention of radio, television and telephone technology, and continued with the computer and cyberspace much later.

Daddy was very industrious and a force to be reckoned with in the Black and White communities. Ours was a small gregarious community in Sussex County, Delaware. Our town folks were supportive of each other, almost no crime, a two-room elementary school with two teachers, Miss Mary Daniels and Mother Lettie (a substitute-teacher) and a principal, Mr. Thomas Jolley.

Our Heath family attended the Graham African Methodist Episcopal Church that was one-door from our house. Daddy was the Sunday School superintendent as long as I can remember. He studied the Bible as a child and was expected to become a minister, according to his mother, (my grandmother), Hattie Drucilla Wise (Weiss, another spelling) Heath.

Daddy desired to become a doctor but his family in Virginia did not have the funds to sent him away to school. So, he walked away from them and found work in various and sundry places.

In our small town of Greenwood, there were three White churches; a White Methodist Episcopal Church and two Baptist Churches were "up-town." Our small AME church was "across town."

Olivia Griffin, our little eight-year-old grandchild, asked a potent question. "Grandma, when you saw Black and White communities, did they live in the same town?

"Yes", I answered, "but they had different facilities, like different schools and different churches and different sections of the town. We had the same United States Post Office and some of the same stores. Mother and Daddy had a restaurant and store which both Blacks and Whites frequently came to buy special dishes that my parents cooked and fresh vegetables from Mother's garden and fresh grapes, cherries and apples from our fruit trees.

Daddy frequently went on the boat at night with the fishermen and brought back plenty of fish, crabs and shrimp and cooked them for ourselves and our restaurant. He had built a small grocery store for the needs of the Black community. Early on, when he saw Whites entering his small store, he decided to build the restaurant which helped the whole community.

GEORGE WESLEY HEATH, Sr. AND WORLD WAR II

World War, II began in the United States when the Japanese Air Force bombed Pearl Harbor on December 7, 1941 and the United States retaliated by declaring war on Japan. This conflict was already brewing in Europe. The cold war became a global war after Germany, which had already hit Poland in September 1939, declared war on the United States on December 11, 1941.

Mother and Daddy were having children fast, which made Mother concerned about Daddy going into the armed services. So, Daddy joined the CCC (Civilian Conservation Corps), which was a military - style training program, mainly for Black soldiers. Army officers (All White) commanded units of Black civilian troops. Blacks entered these units and performed public service tasks including supporting Black Army troops.

George Heath, Sr. maintained his job working on the roads and highways for a private company in Delaware through the week and gave service to the CCC Camp on the week-ends, which brought in a little extra money for the family. The only thing he regretted was to not have entered the foreign war and fought beside U. S. soldiers as his younger brothers and his brother-in-law did.

He told me one time, "I have never been anywhere outside my back door, and my brothers traveled all over the world."

He helped tear down old buildings and haul the debris and lumber off the land in Dover, Delaware and helped build the DOVER AIR FORCE BASE. He got permission to bring the lumber from the old torn down buildings to his own little stretch of land on his old Model T Ford truck.

Daddy reconstructed the buildings, making four small huts on our property from the old lumber and the framed windows.

The Black male soldiers working at the Civilian Conservation Corp were clearing the wooded areas, tearing down and moving old buildings and constructing Dover Air Force Base. Daddy helped build these structures as well as the roads inside the Base.

After a lifetime of hard work, of labor, and a mind - set of getting ahead, Daddy did not choose a career, his life's work was thrust upon him. He overcame crisis after crisis.

Myles Munroe, in his book, OVERCOMING CRISIS, states "Living on earth requires that we must expect the unexpected and prepare for the unseen. It is the nature of life."

Each one of us will face some type of crisis in life. We will all encounter situations over which we have no control or cannot prevent.

LOOK TO THE LORD; HE'S GOT YOUR BACK!

CHAPTER 39

WOMEN IN PERIL

Women dealing with issues such as disrespect for themselves and their children and other people is a concern and situation many mothers face. Suffice it to say, without a father in the home, issues such as bullying, fighting, snitching, disrespect for authority, predators, weapons, stealing, and other bad habits face the family lifestyle.

Malcolm X said, "The most disrespected person in America is the Black woman. The most unprotected person in America is the Black woman. The most neglected person in America is the Black woman.

As they struggle through their own fears and disappointments, Psalm 42 is a good example that reflects their own hearts. With a thirsty, downcast soul, the author(s) cried out and expressed the honest emotions of their hearts until they discovered truths they had forgotten. They could only express words of how empty they felt.

LIFE OUT OF CONTROL

Often women that are generations apart are single mothers due to no fault of their own. They love hard. Many husbands have health issues, serious concerns and weaknesses and live apart from their families.

In the United States Declaration of Independence, our founding fathers wrote: "We hold these truths to be self-evident, that all men are created equal, that they are endowed by their Creator with certain unalienable rights, that among these are Life, Liberty and the Pursuit of Happiness."

It appears that women were not included in the Declaration of Independence creed just yet. But somehow, they were made to believe that anything is possible; that is, "No such thing is impossible."

They did not let the lack of freedom and the "pursuit of happiness" get the best of them. One day everything will change in my life and many things did change.

> JUST HOLD ON: GOD GIVES
> OPPORTUNITY TO EVERYONE!

CHAPTER 40

EVERYONE HAS A PLACE TO FILL

On an impactful scale, we can take the empty, unfilled areas of our lives and fill them with space that needs filling. Our lives have felt empty some days, from loss or conflict or unhealed parts of our hearts; a memory flashed when there was nothing and every space needed filling.

If life feels empty, we can ask God to recreate, rebuild, restore and renew our lives. Not just our lives to be filled and refilled, but refilled to overflowing so that we can offer the overflow of love to others who need their empty places filled.

One such couple who was the love of my mother's life were her grandparents- John Henry and Amanda Collins Fountain. John was born in the eighteenth century around 1853. He went blind at an early age. As a young child, around five, he ran into a hanging tree limb which caught him in the left eye. By the time he was six years old he was totally blind. He stumbled and fell many times. Life was very tedious for him.

He was no longer useful as a slave to his master to do menial jobs. The plantation owner sent him home to his mother, Mary Elizabeth Fountain and father, Charles Smith. They lived around six miles from old man Langley's farm in Trinity, Delaware where John Henry had lived all his life.

John Henry was very despondent and dejected in his youth and early adulthood. He could not see; he could not read or learn. He felt useless, depressed and discouraged to his family.

Yet he knew that everything has a place. However, he was very unique in many ways. He was loving and kind to those around him. But he often felt sad and lonely. His mother, Mary Elizabeth often found John Henry outside in the field with the animals, on his knees praying. She would bring him food to eat as she brought the animals food to eat.

John Henry had a beautiful heart, and good things are always beautiful. He learned to walk among the animals in the fields.

He met Amanda in the fields. They fell in love. When he married in his late teens, he had a loving, caring wife who worshipped him and had more than seven children by him. Because he was blind and could not work, his wife, Amanda was the bread winner in the family. She learned to be a Mid-wife and taught, Sadie her same career. They lived on the Fountain Homestead all their lives.

The family eventually learned of the Camp for the Blind in Philadelphia, Pennsylvania and sent him there when he became an older adult. There he lived for many years.

John Henry was able to be brought home to Middleford, Delaware in Sussex County occasionally to visit his wife and seven children. However, he felt useless to them. The older children left home to make their own way in the world and to be closer to their father in Philadelphia.

John Henry learned and taught his children "It is not important to hold all the good cards in life. However, it is important how well you play with the cards you hold."

His children enjoyed their father when he was home and when they visited him at the Camp for the Blind.

Later, Amanda Collins Fountain began getting ill and became more and more dependent on her children. The two older children,

Sadie Fountain and Charles Wesley Fountain had left the Homestead years ago.

Sadie Mae Fountain lived in Philadelphia and married Herbert Sidney Harper where she lived with her husband and two children for several years. They built a home and store; Sadie managed the store. There was a fire in their home and store which left them homeless. Sadie and Herbert moved back to Seaford, Delaware with their two children, Lettie and Clarence.

Charles Wesley Fountain, Sadie's older brother moved to New Jersey and remained there to raise his family.

Sadie took over the management of the household and the farm for her mother, Amanda Fountain as she was becoming more ill and worn. When he got older, John Henry moved back to Middleford with his wife and children.

John Henry Fountain lived a long life and died around 1937 in Middleford where he was born. He was able to "see" his first two great grandchildren and touch them -Phyllis and George Heath.

In his waning years, he was sent home to sit out on his back porch and "watch" his old grey blind mule. They were pals, and John Henry shucked corn each day and fed his old mule who walked around and around the black walnut tree.

John Henry looked to his heart for what he truly wanted and what brought him closest to following God. He was a member of his church for over seventy years and was taken to John Wesley Methodist Church regularly as he was a sincere Christian. He asked for daily strength and enduring peace.

He knew that one of the basic differences between God and human beings is: God gives, gives, gives and then forgives. Man gets, gets, gets and then forgets.

John Henry prayed, "I know that someday I will stand before you, O Lord. But I long to hear from You now. What do you want me to do? What do You want from me?"

"I believe that one day the time is coming when You will again let me experience Your kindness. I believe that You will once again give me songs to sing in the night." His two great grand children were dear to him and he felt it his place to sing and pray with them each day.

He talked to his dear babies and walked around in the yard, which was a great fulfillment for the children and their great grandfather. Some people glitter for the kingdom in prominent places, while others yearn to serve faithfully in accent positions.

John Henry mourned, "My loving wife is gone, died in my arms with my children and grandchildren around us.

Peace is not the absence of problems or disappointments. It is the presence of God's wholeness and daily gifts to us. Often when we lose all hope and think this is the end, God smiles above and says, "Relax dear, it's a bend, not the end. So, be thankful for your life."

John Henry realized that each day was a love gift from God and a fresh start as well as an opportunity to grow closer to his Maker.

His children, grandchildren, and great grandchildren in his later life were growing up around him and with the Holy Spirit dwelling inside him, his life became more precious every day.

And the peace of God, which transcends all understanding, will guard your heart and your mind in Christ Jesus. (PHILIPPIANS 4: 7, NIV).

John Henry met Amanda outside his church long ago as she walked along in a nearby field. She was a beautiful fair complexioned young teen-age girl with very long beautiful median brown hair and median brown eyes. Of course, John Henry could not see Amanda's beauty, he could only sense it in his spirit. He was possibly a year or two older than she was and he nor anyone else knew her last name. (Through research, I found Amanda's mother's name, which was Martha Collins.)

Amanda's Delaware State Death Certificate verified that her mother's name was Martha Collins. Her father's name was unknown, (possibly someone in the slave master's family as Amanda was very fair complexioned. She was born on March 12, 1861, (her birth place was not recorded) and died on November 26, 1920 in Middleford, Delaware. The cause of her death was listed as toxemia and collapse of the uterus. That means a baby apparently died with her, which was not recorded.

(Source: Ancestry.com and Delaware State Death Certificate).

Amanda Collins Fountain's Death Certificate had two different spellings of Amanda's last name – Founting and Fountian. It was signed on November 28, 1920 by M. C. Watson, State of Delaware Bureau of Vital Statistics.

Love sparked between this young couple early on and they were allowed to marry right away. They began their family soon after their marriage. They had seven children to live to adulthood and several others to die in child birth or an early age.

The living children were Charles Wesley Fountain, Sadie Mae Fountain, Lettie Fountain, Clarence Fountain, Martin (called Marty) Fountain, Louis Fountain and Sylvester Fountain according to oral history and 1900 and 1910 United States Federal Census Bureau Records

The Fountain family was considered as middle- class Negroes. African Americans of pale skin or mulatto coloring had an advantage according to all that was taught in that day. Because their ancestors were white, and they had mixed blood, the superior race gave these persons the concept of the intelligence and refining qualities of the superior race.

According to Annette Provine Woodard in her book, INTEGRATING DELAWARE, "Light skinned African Americans were perceived as being more refined and intelligent than dark skinned ones."

"Prejudice is a powerful force and allowances were made for and opportunities given to persons who were not so dark or foreign looking. These bright-skinned Negroes must know their place around Whites and avoid confrontation with any White person, however." said Woodard. (p. 16).

"White relatives helped their Black kin, especially if they were lighter skinned. Because of my great-grandmother, Amanda Collins Fountain and great-grandfather, John Henry Fountain and grandmother, Sadie Mae Fountain having partly Caucasian coloring, this fact improved the family's economic and educational opportunities and rendered them in the nineteenth and twentieth centuries to be called aristocracy, mulatto elite, black bourgeoisie or even middle class." (Woodard, p. 15, para).

Acres of land were given to John Henry Fountain and Amanda Collins Fountain and their children by Nicholas De La Fountaine, and two or three generations of Fountain Family members were freed.

Moreover, I learned through my grandmother's oral history that the De La Fountaine family from France and the next generations of the same family born on ships and in the Mid-Atlantic states, including the Black members were a part of the Underground Railroad Movement as well as the White members of the family.

Even until this day, this family would not have revealed this knowledge to the world. It was too dangerous in the eighteenth and nineteenth centuries to disclose this secret because it is one of those mysteries that involved our ancestors and we do not know how involved our folk were.

We could not tell the story of slavery and freedom of slaves. God was in the plan. He put the De La Fountaine/Fountains, both Black and White members in the midst of a dichotomy that was owning slaves to save slaves. If Captain William Charles had not owned slaves, he could not have picked up run-away slaves and taken them into the Underground Railroad Movement.

> ## THE STORY OF SLAVERY IS A MYSTERY!

CHAPTER 41

HOW MUCH MORE, LORD?

Willie Alex "Billie" Pepper, Jr was born on May 31, 1957. He was born as a premature infant, "a preemie" and weighted little more than two pounds. He was taken immediately to Milford Memorial Hospital in Milford, Delaware where he stayed for more than six weeks. It seems as if this infant became an experiment to see how long a premature infant could live. He was not expected to live.

By all appearances, he was a white child with blonde hair and green eyes. He was a misnomer (an error in naming a person, or a name wrongly applied.)

His mother, Phyllis Heath Pepper and father, Willie Alex Pepper, Sr. expected the doctors to throw Billie away, so they went back to Florida where Willie, Sr. was from.

Billie's grandparents, Lettie and George Heath, went to see him every evening and prayed over him. He was their first grandson and they "willed" him to live. After about six weeks, the doctor felt Billie was strong enough to go home so his grandparents took him home with them. He had an older sister, Mary, living with them, so he fit right in.

The brother and sister were as different as day and night. Mary was dark complexioned with beautiful curly hair. Bille was very fair complexioned with green eyes and blonde long straight hair. They were very close, always holding hands. Mary was strong, smart and happy at her Heath grandparent's home.

Billie was very dependent on everyone around him. My mother, Lettie Heath, was his primary care-giver. He required much help which was a strain on her. Lettie held him constantly, fed him, nurtured him, prayed over him. He grew up as a beautiful baby boy.

I came home from college, my freshman year and found Billie and Mary with my parents. Mary had been born in Painter, Virginia the year before Billie, with my Grandmother Hattie Wise Heath, as Phyllis' Mid-wife.

I had not seen either child but knew about Mary. They were both my older sister's children but my mother and father gave them their first start. They were provided for by their grandparents and a loving great-grandmother who served as the Mid-wife for Mary's birth.

They may have been little in the world, and even to their parents, Phyllis and Willie, but their grandparents' eyes were not big enough to see them, their ears were not large enough to hear them.

Jesus' words in Matthew 10: 37-42 are not cryptic or hidden. They do not have an ambiguous meaning. They are astoundingly clear. Devotion and love are evidenced by actions, not words.

A main action is focusing on giving to God's little ones. Christ is not just focusing on chronological age. He is calling us to give to anyone who is of "little account" in the eyes of this world. This includes the poor, the sick, refugees, all who are disadvantaged in anyway.

Without the tending of God and our people, our souls grow barren and dry. Meditating on His word day and night, however, and delighting in His law, is like a tree planted by the water. Our leaves will not wither and whatever we do will prosper. Pruned and planted in Him, we are evergreen – reviving and thriving. (PSALM 1: 2-3, para, NIV).

This is what Mary and Billie's grandparents wanted for them. They also wanted the parents to raise their children. So, Lettie Heath, the grandmother sent for Mary and Billie's mother, Phyllis Heath Pepper. Mother sent a letter with prayers. There are no lost letters in heaven.

BEGINNIG STEPS

For starters, my parents, Lettie and George, were raising their children and by the time they had two grandchildren to raise, they began slowly and with good intentions. They were trying to overcome their reservations and feelings of awkwardness. This was not about them, but they knew to call in reinforcements: persons who were more highly skilled. They called on their own parents, the children's great grandmothers – Hattie Heath and Sadie Harper who could give them pep talks and skills in raising small children.

This certainly helped the generations of Fountains, Harpers, Heaths and Peppers to come closer. My mother, Lettie often visited in her mother and father, Sadie Fountain Harper and Herbert Harper's home. By the time the two great grandchildren were born, Sadie was ill and finally passed away but great grandfather, Herbert was very much alive.

These two children were given the benefit of love and caring from generations of kin folks which helped them grow properly. They ate together, played together, prayed together, attended church together and learned their ABC's together. The generations loved to cook, bake and eat together. And there was always room for one or two more persons.

When I came home from college before the Christmas break, my first semester, I came home to a loving, caring generational family. I was welcomed back into the fold, with these two additional little ones. I felt, "I need to get together with my family more often."

My mother was getting weaker and needed more help. She was still doing her work at the church, playing for two choirs, trying to keep up her house, managing her store and restaurant and caring for two grandchildren who were nursery and kindergarten age.

My two younger sisters were the only two Heath children left home to help out and they were in school all day. Another time when I came home, I realized that my mother was worn out, and decided to drop out of college to help my mother. She had two ramboncious grandchildren to care for without much help. I wanted to adopt my niece and nephew as they were a "hand full" for my mother. On more than one occasion, I tried to figure out how I could help.

It was my senior year in college and my mother was still caring for her grandchildren. Phyllis and her husband visited in our home occasionally but her two grandchildren still lived in Greenwood.

Mother became ill and was sick in the hospital for two months. Phyllis had taken her two children to live with her at the time.

MOTHER DIED

Things were smoothing out. My mother was once again able to move around and become self-sufficient. By this time the two youngest sisters were in high school. As a believer in God, Mother ran this race with perseverance. One of the ways to ensure we can keep going is to be free of the weight of unforgiveness, pettiness and other issues that will hinder us. Mother ran this race and ran it well. She did not loss hope until the very end.

My two younger sisters came home from school on December 6, 1960, which was my Mother's fifty-second birthday, to find that Mother was on the floor unconscious and was being taken to the hospital by ambulance. Our neighbor, Helen Trader, had not seen Mother all day which was unusual and went to see about her. She found her on the kitchen floor with a broken plate in her hand and called for help. We do not know how long Mother laid on the floor that day. When she got to the hospital, the doctors gave her a few days to live. She lived two months in the hospital.

Mother had damaged her right leg apparently with the broken plate. I have often wondered about that whole episode, as mother had seemed despondent around the Thanksgiving holiday, like she felt less needed by her family since her two youngest children, Nancy and Hattie Elviria were near their graduations from high school and would not need her any more. Moreover, her two young grandchildren Mary and Billie were taken to live with their parents.

LOVE REQUIRES MUCH

Love requires time, sacrifice, energy and prayer. Our chances to love one another seldom comes at an opportune time. We must intentionally schedule time to love and care for our family and neighbors.

We lived near many "mothers only" households. Some families seemed richer than ours and others seemed poorer. Those young people who lived in poverty, had problems with "skipping school," plus, physical, mental and behavioral problems.

Our home was a welcoming place for our friends, young and old. Friends and family were always coming and going. We lived next to the church, so children and adults alike were always dropping in. Many of Mother's family and friends were growing up, moving away, going in the service, to other schools and other towns. Mother was feeling the loss of her family and friends and becoming despondent.

GOD DOES NOT JUDGE THE WAY WE DO THINGS.

1 Samuel tells us, "People judge by outward appearance, but the Lord looks at the heart." (1 SAMUEL 16: 7, para, NIV).

It is time to act; ask God to help you to make a decision, to push through those roadblocks; overcome those hindrances and begin praying as you would like to for meaningful action.

If you are discouraged, do not let that stop you. Keep praying; you will soon pray with renewed confidence. Ask God to save you from the deserved penalty of your own sins. He does not keep score.

THE LAST TIME

That Thanksgiving, 1960, was the last time our family was all together, alive. Phyllis seemed to be searching for her own identity and was going through a phase in her own life which was neither linear nor smooth. Her search for self was fraught with uncertainty, anxiety, disorientation, confusion and a doubting sense of her own worth. She and her husband had come to pick up her children. They constantly were in an awful mood together; they seemed uncomfortable in this family setting. We were facing challenges and they seemed immature with a lack of personality development.

Our three brothers, George, Daniel and Joseph were leaving the United States to go to Morocco, North Africa. They were in the Navy. While they were home, they managed to be with their friends and socialize regularly. They did not involve themselves in family conflicts.

As I was leaving to complete my last year in college, my mother told me, "Trust Him to rescue you. This will be the most important request or prayer you will ever make. It is this prayer for salvation that provides an unshakable foundation for all the other prayers you will offer up to God."

Mother and I talked everyday and she encouraged me and her other children as I tried to encourage her.

It is powerful to see the degree to which Jesus is willing to go to impact our broken lives.

A generous and hospitable spirit is what really matters. Our presence is what really matters. When we invite our family and friends into our space, eat a meal with them, and include the poor, sick, disabled, the lame, blind and others who are different from us, that is obeying Jesus by loving each other. (LUKE 14: 13-14, para, NIV).

MOTHER WAS BLESSED BY BLESSING OTHERS!

CHAPTER 42

LET LOVE ABIDE

n the beginning of time, God made us and gave Himself to us. All of humanity, every living creature that has breath needs love. We are given all that we need by our Creator to live our lives with pride and dignity. We will always need the love of God and He will always need our love and praise. We still need His help as we reach out to Him with the urgency and all the maturity to live with joy and sincerity. Today we are working to produce even more persons who are geared to meet the needs of new generations.

I have learned that you do not have to go to another country to be a missionary or an ambassador.

2 Corinthians 5: 20 teaches "So we are Christ's ambassadors.

We can be a big part of helping change and transform lives daily. One of the great joys of serving God is to serve others. We are given the resources by God to grow and help others to grow through scriptures and prayer. Nothing in life is overwhelming unless we allow it to be. Make each moment count and "Live one day at a time," as my niece Tikia tells me each time I speak to her.

Each day is a blessing, for tomorrow is a mystery and is not promised to us. Do not dwell on the past, but enjoy life to its fullest.

Our people can continue to grow more resourceful; when life gives us a tumble, remember there is an answer for everything. No matter how treacherous life may seem, the clouds will clear. Look forward to the future and embrace it as a gift from heaven.

What an awesome reality; it is that we were created, male and female, in His own image. There we are, in the first book of the Bible, distinguished from lower animals, literally created in the image of God. Surely, humankind was no afterthought with God and it was His creation that God offered his fullest self-revelation.

Why should we care about where we belong on the Tree of Life? Because not only does it tell us where we came from; it tells us who we are.

George Wells Parker, in his book, THE CHILDREN OF THE SUN, states our beginnings in this manner:

"In the beginning of the world, when the fingers of love swept aside the curtains of Time, our Dusty Mother, ETHIOPIA, held the stage.

It was She who wooed civilization and gave birth to the nations.

EGYPT was Her first born and with a tour of the Chaldees, she sent her sons and daughters who scattered empires from Africa to Asis as the wonton winds of Autumn scatter the seeds of flowers.

Beside the beautiful Mediterranean, she built Phoenicia, and in ships with purple sails, she sent her children to the blue Aegan, there to find Greece, the marvel of men and the queen of history.

Troy was hers, and from the burning city fled swarthy Aeneas, set the ferment for Rome, the Eternal City.

On the Isles of all the oceans, and from where the Southern Cross bends low to kiss the restless waves to where the Artic holds its frozen world, her hand has touched.

Literature, art, religion, science, and civilizations are hers, and eternity but lives in the warmth of her radiant glow."

Much accounts of our beginnings of civilization and all its riches are interwoven into the fabric of our culture as we have written poems, songs-spirituals, ballads, hymns, classical and jazz music and presented the past and present generations with health and educational opportunities and the onset of living a good life.

In today's Scripture, Jesus tells us to not only like him but love him – love him with all our hearts, minds and souls. (MATTHEW 22: 37, NIV).

Further, the Bible instructs us to tell everyone about the amazing things Jesus does. (PSALM 96: 3, NIV).

When it come to your faith life, following Christ is more than just a few clicks on a smartphone or an electric keypad. We must pray for strength and courage to fight the evil prey. As temptation tries to lead us to the place that we fear most, we know that You are there to save us from ourselves and our sins.

It is all about building a relationship with Jesus and others. Your precious loving arms have caught and held me time and time again.

My spirit seeks You as my nearest friend. In my secret place I dwell as in Your shadow I abide; the Lord, You are my Shepherd. You are always by my side. (PSALM 91, para, NIV).

It is about reading His Holy word and talking with him daily.

I am reminded that during my teenage years we studied books of the Bible months at a time. One such book was ESTHER, the seventeenth book in the Bible. Esther was a young Jewish woman who became queen of Persia. Her position as queen led her to be used by God to help deliver her people from a sinister plot to destroy them.

One of her relatives, Mordecia challenged her to use her position to do the right thing or God would find someone else to fill her role. At the risk of her own life, Esther stepped up and did the right thing. As a result, the evil plot was exposed, the perpetrators were punished and Esther's people as well as her own life was saved. What's more, God's plan was to bring Esther into the palace for such a time as this.

The main theme of Esther's story is to show that God is in charge; He often uses us for good circumstances and to help others.

It is about gathering with others and praising and worshipping Him. The next time you hear someone ask you how to share, and follow a wise teacher, tell them to "CHECK IN WITH JESUS."

When you share Jesus with others, they may be offended, but you can prayerfully consider the words and tone you use in your message.

"The more gentleness, kindness, and love sprinkled into your conversation, the more others will be willing to taste the delicious truth of Jesus and devour His Good News." (Source: Ericka Loyes, MORNINGS WITH JESUS, September/October, 2023).

Suffice it to say, we must help our generations make a clear path for the future and make the future a reality. We must create a time in which our current struggles are nothing more than a distant memory. It is ours to do – support each other and direct our attention on the productivity and success of our generations.

He is by our side every step of the way; that still holds true today. Here is a phrase we can all live by; "God First, others Second, me Third."

(Source: Evelyn Seamons, Salesian Inspirational Book, p. 7, para).

Barack Obama said at the 2004 Democratic National Convention, "When I see a child in Chicago (or elsewhere) who cannot read, that disturbs me. When I see an elderly person in a drug store who cannot pay for his or her medicine, that upsets me. We are all God's children."

"We are all one people and should help one another," said Obama. (para).

Other person's experiences become a lot easier when we hurt for one another. God provides us with the strength to help each other. Not everyone is going to love you or love God. But God loves you in- spite of yourself and He does not keep score.

If you have put up security for your neighbor, if you have struck hands in pledge for another, you have been trapped by what you said, ensnared by the words of your mouth, then, do this my son, to free yourself, since you have fallen into your neighbor's hand; go and humble yourself, press your plea with your neighbor! Allow no sleep to your eyes, no slumber to your eyelids. (PROVERBS 6: 1-4, NIV).

Keep your father's commands and do not forsake your mother's teachings. (v.20)

SATAN'S STRATEGY

Satan is very clever. His strategy is always to confuse reality to make evil seem good. Most of the time, our needs are being met as was Eve's. How can you get at someone who is contented with good?

Working on Eve's mind, with his own mind on evil, Satan approaches Eve with a theological discussion about God.

Satan speaks through a serpent: Did God really say, "You must not eat from any tree in the garden?"

The serpent makes an overstatement that he allows Eve to correct, but in doing so, he makes her aware of a restriction. He indicates, "God is keeping something from Eve."

The woman corrects the serpent. "No, God is not like that. Eve makes her own overstatement of what God said:

Instead of declaring that the garden is lavish in its provisions for her needs, and that one tree does not make all that much difference, the woman lets the serpent trick her. He focuses her attention on the one tree, suggesting that God is keeping something from her. He casts doubt upon God's character.

Eve's attention is riveted to the tree – not the garden full of goodness, not God's fellowship and provision. She is thinking: Just the tree! It pleases the eye! It looks good!

It always looks good when Satan gets us to concentrate on the temptation instead of on God.

This temptation has been replayed over and over again in the history of humankind; probably in each of our lives. "The history of human life is the history of breaking," said Dr. M. R DeHann, founder of OUR DAILY BREAD MINISTRIES. "Such brokenness extends beyond childhood toys and the family automobile. It touches everything in our world. Nowhere do we feel the pain of brokenness more profoundly than in our relationships."

The specifics are different, but the strategy is often the same. How many times has a serpent tempted us to think: "A good God would not keep me from this, would He?

Thus, the serpent won the encounter with Eve. She took the fruit and gave some to her husband. (GENESIS 3: 1-6, para, NIV)

The next move for God was to provide His own body and blood as a ransom for their sins. These things happened to them as examples and were written down as warnings for us, on whom the fulfillment of the ages has come. So, if you think you are standing firm, be careful that you do not fall! No temptation has seized you except what is common to man. And God is faithful; He will not let you be tempted beyond what you can bear. But when you are tempted, He will provide a way out so that you can stand up under it. (1 CORINTHIANS 10: 11-13, para, NIV).

PAUL'S CHARGE TO TIMOTHY

In 1 Timothy 6: 6-11, Paul wrote, "But you, man of God, flee from all these worldly things. The sins of some, on the other hand, pursue righteousness. Fight the good fight of the faithful. Godliness with contentment is great gain."

"Command others to do good, to be rich in good deeds, and be generous and willing to share, pursue righteousness full of faith, love, endurance and gentleness. Take hold of the eternal life to which you were called when you made your good confession in the presence of many witnesses.

In the sight of God, who gives life to everything, and of Jesus Christ, who while testifying before Pontius Pilate, made the good confession. I charge you to keep this command without spot or blame until the appearing of our Lord Jesus Christ, which God will bring about in His own time: God the blessed and only Ruler, the King of Kings, who alone is immortal and who lives in unapproachable light, whom no one has seen or can see. To Him be honor and might forever." (1 TIMOTHY 6: 11-16, NIV).

LET LOVE ABIDE!

ACKNOWLEDGEMENTS

Neither time nor space allows me to acknowledge and thank all the wonderful persons for the countless acts of support and encouragement I received from individuals who walked with me during the writing of this narrative. The actions, thoughts, observations, and feelings of these grand-spirited people cannot be overstated. I am thankful for the solidarity, the lessons and thoughts of my ancestors.

As the generations go by, there are many lessons learned through our parents and grandparents who encouraged us to choose hope and faith instead of fear and dismay. My grandparents helped me by sharing experiences, and many situations – good and bad.

Let me thank my young cousin, Janet Nock Moreno for the documentations of our relatives and ancestors' history.

Secondly my husband, Bertrand Griffin had cousins, Frances and Saundra Gillespie and Rose Kelly who developed genealogy charts and oral history which I inserted in my books.

The staff of the Scotlandville library has given me tremendous assistance in writing my books. Several of them did not want their names mentioned so I deleted mentioning any of them. Suffice it to say, my job was made easier because of their help.

The Louisiana Archives Association is another source which was helpful in assistance and encouragement throughout my life.

What is good and wholesome and successful in my life, I owe to God, my parents and grandparents, husband, family, teachers and friends.

> *The Lord God is in your midst,*
> *A warrior who gives victory.*
> *He will rejoice over you with gladness,*
> *He will renew His love,*
> *He will exalt over you with loud singing.*
> *(ZEPHANIAH 3: 17, NRV).*

CONCLUSION

Each and every story begins inside a story that was already begun by another person. Infants are born and are tiny gifts from God. We are all sweet miracles of goodness and love. Long before we take our first breath, we did not choose our life, but it was chosen for us. We were all sent to teach valuable lessons such as patience, cooperation, dedication, understanding, and love.

It is said that man is born with an insatiable curiosity about who he is, who is the source of his being. This is something that religious leaders struggled to understand as they worked long and hard to maintain a distance between themselves and sinners.

By contrast, Jesus seemed to welcome the opportunity to associate and eat with the "impure" people the religious establishment seemed to shun or avoid.

> *The answer: While Jesus was having dinner at Matthew's house, many tax collectors and sinners came and ate with him and his disciples. When the Pharisees saw this, they asked his disciples, "Why does your teacher eat with tax collectors and sinners?"*

On hearing this, Jesus said, "But go and learn what this means: I desire mercy, not sacrifice. For I have not come to call the righteous, but sinners. (MATTHEW 9: 10-13, NIV).

Jesus' interactions with sinful people were characterized by compassion instead of condemnation. He touched them instead of retreating from them. Jesus was beyond being tainted by the sinfulness of the many people he encountered. He was all about deeply touching their lives and pulling them out of their sinfulness and into a commitment to a life that is dedicated to God.

What you do, what you say and what you know becomes what you believe. "Actions speak louder than words," it is often said.

What you do for others will help you as well. Many lives and communities need revitalizing. The key to success is working with quality, value and consistency.

"Where do I fit in," you might ask?" What does this mean to me?

There is an answer. There is hope! You have a God who gave his son to show you who He is and how much He loves you. God offers you the gift of His forgiveness and love-a gift which can only be accepted by faith. So, we must make the most of whatever is given to us.

There are many types of love, many expressions of love. Sometimes we do not know how to love or to what extent we can love another or love God.

At Christmas time we hear the song called "The Little Drummer Boy." The lyrics of the song explain that the little drummer boy could not buy a gift or do something brave for the Christ child. He did not think he had anything to offer. But then he realized that he could love the infant; he could play a song for him.

So quit thinking about what you cannot do and start concentrating on what we can do.

Lorraine Hansberry, a very young woman with an overpowering vision, in her stage play, A RAISIN IN THE SUN, said, "You have got the talent, you have got the depth, the inner artistry to give something free and fresh and important to the world. All that you need now is a little more self-confidence; a little more self-honesty and self-criticism;

and finally, a little less of the feeling that you alone can think all things through by yourself." (p. 173, para).

We can celebrate and praise God and offer those gifts that we do have. He will honor even seemingly small actions; He will show us how to love and forgive others. The Little Drummer Boy did the best he could, and that was enough. There is no such thing as "impossible with God's love."

LOVE DOES NOT KEEP SCORE!

BIBLIOGRAPHY

Ackerman, Diane. A NATURAL HISTORY OF LOVE. New York: Random House, 1994.

Adams, Yolanda. POINTS OF POWER. New York: Hachette Book Group, 2010.

Ali, Ayaan Hirsi. NOMAD: FROM ISLAM TO AMERICA. New York: Simon & Schuster Company, 2010.

Allen, Richard. THE CONCEPT OF SELF: A STUDY OF BLACK IDENTITY AND SELF-ESTEEM. Michigan: Wayne State University Press, 2001.

Altmann, Tanya Remer, ed. THE WONDER YEARS. New York: Bantom Books, 2006.

Anderson, Elijah. STREETWISE: RACE, CLASS AND CHANGE IN AN URBAN COMMUNITY. Chicago: University of Chicago, 1990.

Amadi, Peace. WHY DO I FEEL THIS WAY? Illinois: InterVarsity Press, 2021.

Angelou, Maya. LETTERS TO MY DAUGHTER. New York: Random House, 2008.

_____. MOM & ME & MOM. New York: Random House, 2013.

_____. SINGING AND SWINGING AND GETTING MERRY LIKE CHRISTMAS. New York: Bantom Books, 1976.

_____. ALL GOD'S CHILDREN GOT TRAVELING SHOES. New York: Random House.

_____. A SONG FLUNG UP TO HEAVEN. NEW YORK: Random House.

_____. RAINBOW IN THE CLOUD. NEW YORK: Random House, 2014.

_____. THE HEART OF A WOMAN. New York: Random House.

Archard, David. CHILDREN, RIGHTS, AND CHILDHOOD. London: Routledge, 1993.

Aries, Philippe. CENTURIES OF CHILDHOOD: A SOCIAL HISTORY OF FAMILY LIFE. New York: Vintage Books, 1962.

Armour, Vernice. ZERO TO BREAKTHROUGH. New York: Durham Publishing Company, 2011.

Argyle, M. THE PSYCHOLOGY OF HAPPINESS. England: Routledge, 2001.

Arnett, J. J. EMERGING ADULTHOOD: THE WINDING ROAD FROM THE LATE TEENS THROUGH THE TWENTIES. New York: Oxford University Press, 2014.

Austin, Linda, M.D. WHAT'S HOLDING YOU BACK? New York: Persue Books Group, 2000.

Barry, William A., SJ. GOD AND YOU: PRAYER AS A PERSONAL RELATIONSHIP. New Jersey: Paulist, 1987.

Baumeister, Roy and John Tierney. WILLPOWER: REDISCOVERING THE GREATEST HUMAN STRENGTH. New York: Penguin Press, 2011.

Beamer, Lisa. LET'S ROLL! ORDINARY PEOPLE, EXTRAORDINARY COURAGE. Illinois: Tyndale House Publishers, Inc. 2002.

Benedict, Ruth. PATTERNS OF CULTURE. Mentor, Maryland, 1989.

Bertinelli, Valerie. LOSING IT. New York: Free Press, 2008.

Black, Barry C. THE BLESSING OF ADVERSITY. New York: Tyndale House Publishing, 2011.

Blake, Charles. FREE TO DREAM.

Blanco, Richard. FOR ALL OF US, ONE TODAY. Boston: Beacon Press, 2013.

Blanton, Smiley. LOVE OR PERISH. New York: Crest, Fawcett World Library.

Blocksom, Charles. THE UNDERGROUND RAILROAD. Delaware: University of Delaware.

Bly, Nellie. UP CLOSE AND DOWN HOME. New York: Zebra Books, 1993.

Bennett, William J., ed. THE BOOK OF VIRTUES. New York: Simon and Schuster Publishing Company, 1993.

Beilecki, Tessa. HOLY DARING. New York: Element, Inc. 1994.

Bloomer, George. THROW OFF WHAT HOLDS YOU BACK. Florida: Chrisma House, 2003.

Boers, Arthur Paul. THE WAY IS MADE BY WALKING. Illinois: Inner Varsity Press, 2007.

Boatsman, Rachel. WHO CAN YOU TRUST? New York: Hachette Book Group, 2017.

Botero, Jairo Alvarez. NO SUCH THING AS IMPOSSIBLE: FROM ADVERSITY TO TRIUMPH. Indiana: *AuthorHouse, 2008.*

Boyd, Gregory A. GOD OF THE POSSIBLE. Michigan: Baker Book House, 2000.

Brock, Jared A. THE ROAD TO DAWN. New York: Hachette Book Group, 2018.

Brown, H. THE CHALLENGE OF MAN'S FUTURE. New York: Viking Press, 1954.

Brown, James. ROLE OF A LIFE TIME. New York: Hachette Book Group, 2009.

Buttworth, Eric. THE CREATIVE LIFE. New York: Penguin Putman, Inc., 2001.

Carlson, Richard, Ph.D. and Kristine Carlson. DON'T SWEAT THE SMALL STUFF IN LOVE.

Carnegie, Dale. HOW TO WIN FRIENDS AND INFLUENCE PEOPLE. New York: Simon and Schuster Publishing Company, 1984.

Cash, June Carter. FROM THE HEART. New York: St. Martin Press.

Center on the Developing Child. "EXCESSIVE STRESS DISRUPTS THE ARCHITECTURE OF THE DEVELOPING BRAIN. Mass: Harvard University, 2014.

Chakrabarty, Prosanta. EXPLAINING LIFE THROUGH EVOLUTION. Massachusetts: 2023.

Christenson, Evelyn. WHAT HAPPENS WHEN WOMEN PRAY? Colorado: Chariot Victor, 1991

Chambers, Robert. VESTAGES OF THE NATURAL HISTORY OF CREATION. London: John Churchill, 1844.

Coady, Roxanne J. & Joy Johannessen. THE BOOK THAT CHANGED MY LIFE. New York: Penguin Group, Inc., 2006.

Coates, Ta-Nehisi. BETWEEN THE WORLD AND ME. New York: Spiegel and Grau, 2015.

_____. THE BEAUTIFUL STRUGGLE. New York: Spiegel and Grau, 2009.

Collins, Randall. SOCIOLOGY OF MARRIAGE and Family. Chicago: Nelson-Hall Company, 1940.

Comer, James P. & Alvin F. Poussaint. RAISING BLACK CHILDREN. New York: Penguin Group, 1992.

COMMON. AND THEN I RISE: A GUIDE TO LOVING AND TAKING CARE OF SELF. New York: HarperCollins Publishing Company, 2024.

Copage, Eric V. BLACK PEARLS: BOOK OF LOVE. New York: William Morrow & Company 1996.

Cosby, Bill. TIME FLIES. New York: Doubleday Publishing Company, 1987.

Cuddy, Amy. PRESENCE. New York: Little, Brown and Company, 2014.

Cunningham, Lawrnce S. & Keith J. Egan. CHRISTIAN SPIRITUALITY: THEMES FROM THE TRADITION. New Jersey: Paulist, 1996.

Darwin, Charles Robert. ON THE ORIGIN OF SPECIES. 1959.

——————— THE DESCENT OF MAN. 1859.

——————— THE DESCENT OF MAN AND SELECTION IN RELATION TO SEX. New York: D. Appleton, 1896.

Davis, Sampson, George Jenkins, and Rameck Hunt. THE PACT: THREE YOUNG MEN MAKE A PROMISE AND FULFILL A DREAM. New York: Riverhead Books, 2003.

Deng, Rebecca. WHAT THEY MEANT FOR EVIL. New York: Hachette Book Group, 2019.

Dew, James K, Jr. LET THIS MIND BE IN YOU. Tennessee: B & H Publishing Group, 2023.

Dewall, Frances. THE AGE OF EMPATHY. New York: Crown Group, 2009.

Dias, Hannah Carmona. BEAUTIFUL, WONDERFUL, STRONG LITTLE ME. New York: Eifrig Publishing Company, 2019. (Children's Book).

Diaz, Junot, ed. THE BEACON BEST OF 2001. Massachusetts: Beacon Press Books, 2001.

Doe, Marcus. CATCHING RICE BIRDS: A STORY OF LETTING VENGEANCE GO. Massachusetts: Hendrickson Publishing Company, 2016.

Descartes, BODY AND SPIRIT IN THE HIDDEN HISTORY OF THE WEST. New York: Simon and Schuster, 1989.

Dollar, Creflo A, Jr. THE COLOR OF LOVE: UNDERSTANDING GOD'S ANSWER TO RACISM: SEPARATION AND DIVISION. Tulsa: Harrison House, 1997.

Drummond, Henry. THE GREATEST THING IN THE WORLD. London: Hodder and Stoughton, 1980.

Felder, Cain Hope. STONY THE ROAD WE TROD. African American Biblical Interpretation Fortress Press, 1991.

Fitzgerald, Helen. THE MOURNING HANDBOOK. New York: Simon and Schuster Publishing Company.

Flutter, Walter and Latherne. A STRANGE FREEDOM. Boston: Boston Press, 1998.

Follmi, Danielle and Oliver. ORIGINS: AFRICAN WISDOM FOR EVERY DAY. Harvey N. Abrams Publishers, Inc.

Fredman, Edwin H. GENERATION TO GENERATION. New York: The Gulf Press, 1985.

Frost, Jack. EXPERIENCING FATHER'S EMBRACE. Pennsylvania: Destiny Image Publishers, Inc., 2002.

Garrison, N. A. GAEDALUS 147. GENETIC ANCESTRY TESTING WITH TRIBES: ETHICS, IDENTITY AND HEALTH IMPLICATIONS. 1918.

Gbowee, Leymah. MIGHTY BE OUR POWERS. New York: Perseus Book Group, 2011.

Gerbault, P. et al. "Evolution of Lactose Persistence: An Example of Human Niche Construction," BIOLOGICAL SCIENCES 366, no. 1566, 2011.

Glassner, Darry and Rosanna Hertz. OUR STUDIES, OURSELVES. New York.

Gottman, Julie Schwartz, Ph.D. and John Gottman, Ph.D. FIGHT RIGHT. New York: Penguin Random: 2024.

Gould. ROCKS OF AGES: SCIENCE AND RELIGION IN THE FULLNESS OF LIFE. New York: Ballantine Books, 2002.

Gratch, Alon, Ph. D. IF LOVE COULD THINK. New York: Harmony Books, 2014.

Haeckel. THE WORLD OF LIFE, A MANIFESTATION OF CREATIVE POWER, DIRECTIVE MIND AND ULTIMATE PURPOSE. London: Chapman and Hall, 1914.

Hill, Rob. I GOT YOU. Spirit Filled Creations, 2013.

Haffner, Debra W. BEYOND THE BIG TALK. New York: Newmarket Press, 2001.

Hamburg, David A. TODAY'S CHILDREN: CREATING A FUTURE FOR A GENERATION IN CRISIS. New York: Times Books, 1992.

Hertog, Thomas. ON THE ORIGIN OF TIME. New York: Bantam Books of Penguin Random House, LLC. 2023.

Hibbs, B. Janet, Ph.D. and Anthony Rostain, M. A. New York: St. Martin Publishing Group, 2024.

Holiday Ryan, THE OBSTACLE IS THE WAY. New York: Penguin Group, 2014.

Holmes, Marjorie. I'VE GOT TO TALK TO SOMEBODY, GOD. New York: Doubleday Publishing Company, 1969.

_____. HOW CAN I FIND YOU, GOD? New York: Doubleday and Company, 1975.

Holub, Ana. FORGIVE AND BE FREE. MINN: Llewellyn Publications, 2014.

Hug, L. and B. Baker. A NEW VIEW OF THE TREE OF LIFE. Nature Microbiology 1, 2016.

Hull, Gloria T. ed. GIVE US THIS DAY. New York: Wo Norton and Company, 1984.

Ilibagiza, Immaculee. THE BOY WHO MET JESUS: SEGATASHYA OF KIBEHO. New York: Hay House, Inc., 2011.

Hughes, Gerald. GOD OF SURPRISES. Michigan: Eerdmans, 2008.

Hunter, Kristin. GOD BLESS THE CHILD. New York: Scribner Company, 1964.

Iduma, Emmanuel. I AM STILL WITH YOU: A RECKONING WITH SILENCE, INHERITANCE, AND HISTORY. North Carolina: Algonquin Books of Chapel Hill, 2023.

Ignatius of Loyola. A PILGRIM'S TESTAMENT: THE MEMOIRS OF SAINT IGNATIUS OF LOYOLA. St. Louis, MO.: Institute of Jesuit Sources, 1995.

_____. THE SPIRITUAL EXERCISES OF SAINT IGNATIUS. Illinois: Loyola, 1992.

James, William & Quinton Dixie. THIS FAR BY FAITH. New York: HarperCollins Publishing Company, 2003.

Jeffrey, Mars. SEASON OF LIFE. New York: Simon and Schuster, Inc., 2003.

Johnson, Walter. SOUL BY SOUL. Cambridge: Harvard University Press, 1999.

Josh, McPhee. CELEBRATE PEOPLE'S HISTORY. New York: The Feminist Press, 1910.

Joyce, Coach James Dru, II. BEYOND CHAMPIONSHIPS: A PLAYBOOK FOR WINNING AT LIFE. Michigan: Zondervon Books, 2014.

June, Lee. THE BLACK FAMILY. Michigan: Zondervon Publishing House, 1964.

Kalanithi, Paul. WHEN BREATH BECOMES AIR. New York: Random House, 2016.

Kea, Elizabeth, ed. AMAZED BY GRACE. Tennessee: W. Publishing Group, Thomas Nelson, Inc., 2003.

Kornfield, Jack. A PATH WITH HEART. Shambhala Publication, 1994.

Kromus, Sidney. THE BLACK MIDDLE CLASS. Ohio: Charles E. Merrill Company, 1972.

Lee, Sally, editor. THE BEST ADVICE I EVER GOT. New York: St. Martin Press, 2001.

Leiba, Elizabeth. PROTECTING MY PEACE: EMBRACING INNER BEAUTY & ANCESTRAL POWER. Florida: Mango Publishing Group, 2024.

Leon, Kenny. TAKE YOU WHEREVER YOU GO. New York: Grand Central Publishing Company, 2018.

Lesser, Elizabeth. BROKEN OPEN: HOW DIFFICULT TIMES CAN HELP US GROW. New York: Villard Books, 2004.

Lewis, Anthony. PORTRAIT OF A DECADE. New York: Random House, 1964.

Lewis, C. S. MERE CHRISTIANITY. New York: HarperCollins, 1952.

_____ THE FOUR LOVES. New York: Harcourt Brace Jovanovich, Inc. 1960.

_____ SURPRISED BY JOY: THE SHAPE OF MY EARLY LIFE. California: HarperCollins, 2017.

_____ APOSTLE TO THE SKEPTICS. Oregon: Wipf & Stock, 2008.

Lovatt, -Smith, Lisa. WHO KNOWS TOMORROW? New York: Weinstein Books, 2014.

Lucado, Max. STORIES FOR YOUR SOUL: ORDINARY PEOPLE, EXTRAORDINARY GOD. New York: HarperCollins, 2024.

Margulis, Lynn and Dorion Sagan. WHAT IS LIFE? California: University of California, 2000.

Martin, James, S. J. LEARNING TO PRAY: A GUIDE FOR EVERYONE. New York: HarperCollins, 1993.

Martin, Roland S. LISTENING TO THE SPIRIT WITHIN. ROMAR Media Group.

Mays, Benjamin. WALKING INTEGRITY. Georgia: Meres University Press, 1995.

Mbugua, Judy. OUR TIME HAS COME. London: The Guernsey Press, 1974.

McGready, Mary Rose. SOMETIMES GOD HAS A KID'S FACE. New York: Covenant House, 2010.

Meredith, James and William Doyle. A MISSION FOR GOD. Atria Book Press, 2012.

Merton, Thomas. LOVE AND LIKING. Commonwealth Publishing Company, 1997.

Meyers, Joyce. REDUCE ME TO LOVE. Missouri: Life in the World, Inc., 2000.

_____. YOU CAN BEGIN AGAIN. New York: Hachette Book Group, 2014.

_____. LIVING BEYOND YOUR FEELINGS. New York: Hachette Book Group, 2011.

Moore, Wes. THE OTHER WES MOORE: ONE NAME, TWO FATES. New York: Spiegel and Grau, 2011.

Morrison, Toni. THE ORIGIN OF OTHERS. 2017.

Munroe, Myles. SEASONS OF CHANGE. Maryland: Pneuma Life Publishing Company, 1998.

_____. OVERCOMING CRISIS: THE SECRETS TO THIVING IN CHALLENGING TIMES. Pennsylvania: Destiny Image Publishers, 2009.

Nelt, N. & A. D. Levine. WHERE WOMEN STAND. New York: Random House, 1997.

Niles, Chris. NELSON MANDELA: ANY SOCIETY WHICH DOES NOT CARE FOR ITS CHILDREN IS NO NATION AT ALL. UNICEF, July 17, 2013.

Nouwen, Henri. THE INNER VOICE OF LOVE. New York: Doubleday Publishing Company, 1996.

Obama, Barack. A PROMASED LAND. New York: Crown Publishers Group, 2020.

_____ THE AUDACITY OF HOPE, New York: Crown Publishers GROUP, 1995.

_____ DREAMS OF MY FATHER: A STORY OF RACE AND INHERITANCE. Edinburgh: Conongate Books, 2007.

Oparin, A. I. THE ORIGIN OF LIFE. New York: Macmillan, 1938.

Osteen, Joel. YOUR GREATER IS COMING. New York: Hachette Book Group, 2022.

Palmer, Parker. THE ACTIVE LIFE. New York: HarperCollins Publishing Company, 1990.

Pasteur, Alfred B & Ivory Toldson. ROOTS OF SOUL. New York: Doubleday Press, 1982.

Paul, D. B. "The Selection of the Survival of the fittest." JOURNAL OF THE HISTORY OF BIOLOGY. Cambridge: University of Cambridge, 2003.

Peck, M. Scott. THE ROAD LESS TRAVELED. New York: Simon and Schuster Publishing Company, 1978.

Parker, George Wells. THE CHILDREN OF THE SUN.

Peterson, J.B. 12 RULES FOR LIFE: AN ANTODOTE TO CHAOS. New York: Penguin Random House, 2018.

Pipher, May. THE MIDDLE OF EVERYWHERE. Nebraska: Harcourt Publishing Company, Inc., 2002.

Pope -Hennessy, James. SINS OF THE FATHER. London: Phoenix Press, 1967.

Rahner, Karl. THE MYSTICAL WAY IN EVERYDAY LIFE. New York: Orbis Books, 2010.

Ramming, Cyndy. ALL MOTHERS WORK. New York: Avon Books, 1996.

Rebey, Lois Mayday. WOMEN OF A GENEROUS SPIRIT. Colorado: Water-brooks Press, 1998.

Reynolds Edward. STAND THE STORM. Chicago: Ivan R. Dee, Inc., 1985.

Rieger, Shay. OUR FAMILY. New York: Lathroe, Lee and Sheard Company, 1972.

Roberts, Sarah Jakes. DON'T SETTLE FOR SAFE. Tennessee: W. Publishing Group, Thomas Nelson, 2017.

_____ WOMEN EVOLVE. Tennessee: W. Publishing Group. 2017.

Robertson, Gil L. FAMILY AFFAIR. Canada: Agate Publishing Company, 2009.

Roosevelt, Eleanor. IT SEEMS TO ME. New York: Norton Publishing Company,1954.

Sasse, Ben. THEM: WHY WE HATE EACH OTHER AND HOW TO HEAL. New York: St. Martin Press, 2018.

Schreiber, Melody. WHAT WE DIDN"T EXPECT. New York: Melville Publishing House, 2020.

Schrodinger, Erwin. MY VIEW OF THE WORLD. Cambridge: Cambridge University press, 1907.

Salzberg, Sharon. A HEART AS WIDE AS THE WORLD. Shambhala Publishing Company, 1977.

Sheen, Fulton J. LIFE IS WORTH LIVING. California: Ignatius Press, 1953.

Shipp, Josh. THE GROWN-UP GUIDE TO TEENAGE HUMANS. New York: HarperCollins Publishing Company, 2017.

Shields, Charles J. LORRAINE HANSBERRY: THE LIFE BEHIND A RAISIN IN THE SUN. New York: Henry Holt and Company, 2022.

Shotwell, Alexis. KNOWING OTHERWISE: RACE, GENDER, AND IMPLICIT UNDERSTANDING. Pennsylvania: Pennsylvania State University, 2011.

Siegal, Judith P. WHAT CHILDREN LEARN FROM THEIR PARENTS. New York: HarperCollins Publishing Company, 2000.

Siegal, Daniel J. THE POWER AND PURPOSE OF THE TEENAGE BRAIN. New York: Jeremy P. Thatcher Publishing Company, 2013.

Simonton, D. K. GREATNESS: WHO MAKES HISTORY AND WHY? New York: Guilford Press, 1994.

Smart, Elizabeth and Chris Stewart. MY STORY. New York: St Martin Press, 2013.

Smith, Emily Esfahani. THE POWER OF MEANING: THE CRAFTING OF A LIFE THAT MATTERS. New York: Crown Group, 2017.

Sowell, Thomas. THE VISION OF THE ANOINTED. New York: HarperCollins Publishing Company, 1995.

Spurgeon, Charles H. ACCORDING TO PROMISE. South Carolina: The Gospel Hour.

ST. Germain with Jon Sternfeld. A STONE OF HOPE. New York: HarperCollins Publishing Company, 2017.

Stamphill, Ira. I KNOW WHO HOLDS TOMORROW. New York: New Spring Publishing House, 1950.

Starr, Anthony. SOLITUDE: A RETURN TO THE SELF. New York: Free Press, 1988.

Steele, Danielle. AGAINST ALL ODDS. New York: Random House, 2017.

Stevenson, Bryan. JUST MERCY: A STORY OF JUSTICE AND REDEMPTION. New York: Spiegel and Grau, 2015.

Steward, Jeffrey C. THE NEW NEGRO: THE LIFE OF ALAIN LOCKE. New York: Oxford University, 2018.

Still, William. UNDERGROUND RAILROAD RECORDS. Philadelphia: William Still Book, 1872.

Tannen, Deborah. YOU JUST DON'T UNDERSTAND. New York: Ballentine Publishing Company, 1990.

Terr, L. BEYOND LOVE AND WORK. New York: Scribner Publishing Company 1990.

Turkle, Sherry. ALONE TOGETHER: WHY WE EXPECT MORE FROM TECHNOLOGY AND LESS FROM EACH OTHER. New York: Basic Books, 2010.

Turner-Brown, Rev. Dr. Patricia A., D. Min. WHAT WILL GET US THROUGH? Indiana: Author House, 2021.

Tutu, Desmond. IN GOD'S HANDS. New York: Bloomsbury Publishing Company, 2014.

Vanzant, Lyanla. ONE DAY MY SOUL JUST OPENED UP. New York: Simon and Schuster Publishing Company, 1998.

Viorst, Judith. NECESSARY LOSSES. New York: Simon and Schuster Publishing Company, 1986.

Wanzer, Lyzette. TRAUMA, TRESSES AND TRUTH. Illinois: Lawrence Hill Books 2023.

Williamson, Marrianne. THE HEALING OF AMERICA. New York: Simon & Schuster Publishing Company, 1977.

Walker, Alice. SAVING THE LIVE THAT IS YOUR OWN: IN SEARCH OF OUR MOTHER'S GARDEN. San Diego: Harcourt Brace Jovanovich, 1983.

Watkins, Linda. GOD JUST SHOWED UP. U.S.A. Moody Bible Institute, 2001.

Watson, Benjamin. UNDER OUR SKIN: GETTING FREE FROM THE FEARS AND FRUSTRATIONS THAT DIVIDE US. New York: Tyndale House Publishers and Random House, 2015.

Welwood, John. LOVE AND AWAKENING. New York: HarperCollins Publishing Company, 1996.

Westover, Tara. EDUCATED. New York: Randon House.

White, Richard Antoine. I'M POSSIBLE: A STORY OF SURVIVAL, A TUBA AND THE MIRACLE OF A BIG DREAM. New York: Flatiron Books, 2021.

Williams Juanita. THIS FAR BY FAITH.

Williams, Mary. THE LOST DAUGHTER. New York: Penguin Group, 2013.

Woodson, J. BROWN GIRL DREAMING. New York: Penguin Random House, 2016.

Wooten, Willie F. BREAKING THE CURSE OF BLACK AMERICA. Illinois: Lumen U. S. Publications 2005.

WRITE BETTER, SPEAK BETTER. New York: Reader's Digest, The Reader's Digest Association, 1972.

Wright, Tom. PAUL FOR EVERYONE: THE PRISON LETTERS. Louisville: Society for Promoting Christian Knowledge, 2004.

Younge, Gary. WHO ARE WE? New York: Perseus Books Group, 2011.

Zaleski, Phillip. THE BEST SPIRITUAL WRITING 2001. New York: HarperCollins Publishing Company, 2001.

Zimmer, C. LIFE'S EDGE: THE SEARCH FOR WHAT IT MEANS TO BE ALIVE. London: Macmillan, 2021.

SELECTED READINGS

Crowder, Bill. WINDOWS ON CHRISTMAS. Michigan: Our Daily Bread Publishing Company, 2007.

_____ SURPRISED BY GRACE: HOW JESUS DEFIES OUR EXPECTATIONS. Michigan: OUR DAILY BREAD, 2022.

MORNINGS WITH JESUS. MARCH/APRIL, 2024.

Pittman, James. WHAT DO YOU DO WITH A BROKEN RELATIONSHIP? 2024 Our Daily Bread Ministries, Grand Rapids, Michigan

Statkoski, Kay. A GRANDMOTHER'S PRAYER.

REFERENCE BOOKS

AMERICAN DICTIONARY OF THE ENGLISH LANGUAGE, 10th edition, San Francisco Foundation for American Christian Education, 1998.

ENCLOPAEDIA JUDAICA. Volume 16, UR-Z, WOMAN. Legal Status and Religious Participation. Supplementary Entries, (Jerusalem, Israel: Keterpress Enterprises, 1978.)

Laird, Charlton. WEBSTER'S NEW ROGER'S A-Z THERAUSUS. Ohio: Wiley Publishing Company, 2003.

MATTHEW HENRY'S COMMENTARY ON THE WHOLE BIBLE. New Modern Edition, Copyright, Hendrickson Publishers, Inc., 1991.

RIVERSIDE WEBSTER'S 11 NEW COLLEGE DICTIONARY. New York: Houghton Mifflin Company, 1995.

THE HOLY BIBLE. New International Version, Michigan: Vondervon, 1973.

THE NEW ENCYCLOPEDIA BRITANNICA. Volume 1-24, New York: Encyclopedia Britannica, Inc. First Edition, 1768-1771, Fifteenth Edition, 1986.

WEBSTER'S II NEW COLLEGE DICTIONARY. New York: Houghton Mifflin Company, 1995.

WEBSTER'S NEW WORLD COLLEGE DICTIONARY. Fourth Edition, New York: Macmillan USA, 1999.

ABOUT THE AUTHOR

Marian Olivia Heath Griffin resides in Baton Rouge, Louisiana with her husband, Bertrand Griffin of sixty-one years. She is a Licensed Professional Counselor and College Administrator serving in this capacity for thirty-six years at Southern University, Baton Rouge, the last seven years as Director of International Student Services.

After retiring from Southern University in the Student Affairs Department, she began writing her family's stories and history.

Griffin has worked with children, youth and young adults her entire career in music and counseling. She graduated from Delaware State University in music, (establishing children and youth choirs in several churches), sociology and Psychology, a Master's Degree in Social Work from Atlanta University School of Social Work, a master's program at the Interdenominational Theological Center in Atlanta, and Christian Education Degree at New Orleans Baptist Theological Seminary in New Orleans. During her work period at Southern University, she received a Master's Degree in Mass Communication and Photography. She did further study at Louisiana State University, and Northwestern University in Evanston, Illinois.

Griffin has enjoyed traveling in all fifty states and six continents with her husband, Bertrand, sister, Nancy Kellam and her husband, Albert Kellam, and their three children: Rev. Bertrand Griffin, II (Rev. Kotosha Seals Griffin), Karen Griffin Phenix, (Keith Phenix), Dr. Michael G. Griffin (Tracie Haydel Griffin), and eight grandchildren: Nia, Kiara, Christian-Paris Bertrand, III, Michael II. Amelia-Grai, Victoria, Olivia and Sophia – all Griffins. She joined several travel groups.

PHOTO SECTION

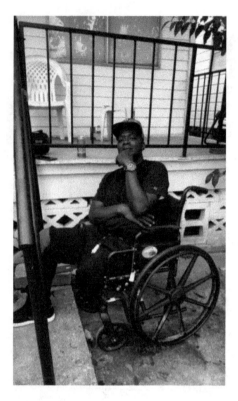

📖 Libraries *Change Lives*

Ever since she was a little girl, Marian Griffin loved to sit at the feet of older family members and listen to stories about her ancestors. By paying close attention, Marian was able to capture her ancestor's oral history and eventually write and publish dozens of books. Each one of her books covers either her family or her husband's family and their experiences. Marian shares, "The books aren't just about my family but family in general." Marian's first published book, *Cultural Gumbo: Our Roots, Our Stories*, goes back to the era before Africans were brought west as slaves. Her inspiration for writing is so that her children, grandchildren, and the world can learn, not just their family history, but also Black history.

When Marian began her writing journey, she went to the Library to find books on topics related to certain time periods and family members. The librarians in the Black Heritage Room at the Scotlandville Branch Library offered much assistance in her pursuits. When Marian wanted specific information about her mother-in-law for her book, a staff member pointed her in the direction of the Louisiana Archives where she was able

Marian Griffin stands with some of the books she has written

to find information that she used in her book, *Cultural Gumbo*. "Whatever topic I asked for, they would research it, and then I would go find the books." With many of her books highlighting family, much of her research included looking for her ancestors to fill in the gaps. "I also took a computer course at the Main Library, and I learned a plethora of information about how to research ancestors."

With all of the help Marian received, she was able to complete her books and decided to dedicate a couple of her books to the librarians that helped her so much along the way. Her dedication in *Cultural Gumbo: Our Roots, Our Stories* states: "I am grateful to the genealogy staff in the East Baton Rouge Parish Main Library on Goodwood Boulevard and the library staff, Carol, Chad, and Jennifer at the Scotlandville Branch Library on Scenic Highway, Baton Rouge, Louisiana, who are commended for their assistance in researching data." Marian encourages other authors to use the Library as a resource "because I feel that they're going to steer you in the right direction to get the information that you need."

Printed in the USA
CPSIA information can be obtained
at www.ICGtesting.com
CBHW050929051024
15373CB00049B/1459

9 798894 192567